THE
HISTORY OF THE BENGALI LANGUAGE

THE HISTORY OF THE BENGALI LANGUAGE

BY

BIJAYCHANDRA MAZUMDAR,
LECTURER IN THE DEPARTMENTS OF COMPARATIVE PHILOLOGY, ANTHROPOLOGY AND INDIAN VERNACULARS, CALCUTTA UNIVERSITY

GYAN

Published by

Gyan Publishing House
5, Ansari Road
Daryaganj, New Delhi-110002
Phone: 011-47034999, 9811692060
E-mail: books@gyanbooks.com

Distribution Network
gyanbooks.com
India, USA, Canada, UK, Australia, France

ISBN : 978-81-212-3535-8 (PB)
First Published, 1920

2nd Impression 2020

Printed at: Gyan Press, Delhi.

The
History of the Bengali Language
Author: Bijaychandra Mazumdar

THE HISTORY OF THE BENGALI LANGUAGE

BY

BIJAYCHANDRA MAZUMDAR,
Lecturer in the Departments of Comparative Philology,
Anthropology and Indian Vernaculars,
Calcutta University

PUBLISHED BY THE
UNIVERSITY OF CALCUTTA
1920

PREFACE

The following lectures on the History of the Bengali Language are intended to give a sketch, in broad outline, of the origins of that language and the various influences, linguistic, ethnic, social, that shaped and moulded its earlier history. One essential requirement of a scientific procedure in an investigation of this sort, I have steadily kept in view. The ethnic as well as the social history of a people or group of peoples must corroborate and light up the linguistic history, if the latter is to be rescued from the realm of prehistoric romance to which the story of philological origins, as so often told, must be however reluctantly assigned by the critical or scientific historian of to-day. One or two incidental results of my application of this anthropological test may be here mentioned. I have had no occasion to invent different Aryan belts for the imaginary migratory movements of some unknowable patois-speaking hordes, to account for the distinctive and peculiar phenomena of the provincial languages or dialects, *e.g.*, those of Bengal: they are fitly explained by the successive ethnic contacts and mixtures with neighbouring or surrounding indigenous peoples. Similarly I have had no hesitation in recognizing within proper limits, the principle of miscegenation in the growth of language, as of race, provided that the organic accretions from outside grow to the living radicle or nucleus which persists as an independent or individual entity. In this way I have sought to explain many of the phenomena, regarding the grafting of Dravidian structural and syntactical elements, on some languages or dialects of so-called Aryan stock (including those of Bengal). One interesting example of this is to be seen in the accent systems of the different Bengali dialects, which naturally show traces of that ethnic miscegenation to which the anthropological history of the people, bears an unmistakable testimony, the more so as tone and accent are among what may be called tertiary racial characters of speech, and in their deep working predispositions, and relative stability, supply fit material for experimental variations of this sort.

In the course of these lectures, I have dealt with the more important topics relating to the origins of the Bengali language, explaining my own views and conclusions, rather than combating the theories that hold the field, and I have used the illustrative material briefly and suggestively, rather than exhaustively.

A few words may be necessary to explain the occasion of the present publication. It was in 1909 that I first gave a definite shape to the results of my study of the Bengali language and its history, but certain eye troubles which began at about that time, interfered with the immediate completion of my plans. Three or four years later, after those troubles had ceased with the total loss of eye-sight, I turned to my materials again, and worked at them, till in 1917, not knowing what to do with these unpublished papers, I sent them at the instance of a friend, to the Hon'ble Sir Asutosh Mukerjee, President of the Council of Post-Graduate Teaching in Arts in the University of Calcutta to see if any use could be made of them in connection with that scientific study of the Vernacular, which had long been one of Sir Asutosh's cherished projects in his scheme of University reconstruction and extension. To my great surprise, not unmixed with thankfulness, I found myself called upon, months later, to deliver a course of lectures on the History of the Bengali Language, in the Post-Graduate Department in the University of Calcutta.

I took the advantage of the opportunity so generously afforded, to revise my original papers, in view of a number of facts, that had been since brought to light. I have to thankfully acknowledge, that when revising these papers, I was very much benefited by some highly valuable suggestions, which my friend, the eminent scholar Dr. Brojendranath Seal very generously offered.

Having had to use an amanuensis, and being without the means of inspecting either the manuscripts or the printed proofs, I am afraid, the following pages must contain numerous errors and misprints, for which the reader will, I know, excuse me. I am thankful to my young friend and colleague Babu Hemantakumar Sarkar, M.A., who has prepared the indexical contents and has brought several serious misprints to my notice.

I cannot end these prefatory words, without giving an expression, however feeble and halting, to the feeling of deep gratitude which overpowers me, when I think of the opportunity, which Sir Asutosh as the presiding genius of University education in Bengal, has opened to one circumstanced like me, an opportunity not only of that active self-expression, which has now become the staff of my life, but also of the fruition of my life's studies and constructive endeavours in one important direction.

B. C. MAZUMDAR

INDEXICAL CONTENTS

LECTURE I

Introduction

A. *Preliminary.*—How Philology is related to Ethnology—pp. 1-2; the unscientific methods of Philologists criticised by Karl Pearson, pp. 2, 3; Grierson's theory, about the origin of Indian Dialects, pp. 3, 4; Risley's explanation, p. 6; Grammar and not vocabulary which gives a dialect its character, p. 6. B. *Preparatory.*—Bengali-speaking tracts, pp. 7, 8; Bengali loosely called a sanskritic language, p. 8; Aryan vernacular, a better name, p. 8; the term Aryan has no ethnic significance, p. 8; structure and accent system are great factors in a language, p. 8; for derivation of words sound suggestions are misleading, p. 9; subjects necessary to discuss, as a preparatory measure :—(1) Geographical limits of Ancient Vanga or Bengal and the character of the Pre-Aryan tribes of Bengal, (2) The form of Aryan speech first introduced in Bengal, (3) The Aryan or Aryanized and the non-Aryan hordes which made inroads into Bengal from the earliest known time to the end of the 12th century A. D., p. 9; some important propositions stated :—

(1) Linguistic miscegenation—Keane's view—structure may be influenced to some extent by foreign influence —the mixture of vocabularies is not of much consequence—The example of Urdu—pp. 10-11.

(2) When a new structure is gradually built with new elements on a fresh basis, a new language is evolved; The natural and organised mode of thinking of a people can never be radically changed, p. 12.

LECTURE II

Ancient Bengal and its Peoples.

Section I. The antiquity of the names Vanga and Bāṅglā

pp. 25-26; The unholy Vanga, p. 26; sea voyage allowed in some northern countries of the Aryans, p. 26; Researches in Farther India by Phayre and Gerini—Early colonisation of Burma by the Dravidians and then by the Aryans, p. 27; Telegu supremacy in Arakan and Chittagong in 850 B.C.—Bengali colony in Annam not later than 7th century B.C., p. 27; the leader of the Bengali adventurer Luck-lom coming from the province of Bong-long, p. 28; belonged to Nāga Vaṁsa—Bong-long the original form of Bāṅglā—people of Bong-long known by the name Bong—Vanga as the name of a tribe in old Hindu Literature—Anga, Vanga, Kalinga regarded by the Aryans to have been of non-Aryan origin—Kins of Bong tribe replaced by Buddhist Kṣatriyas of Magadh in Annam in second decade of 3rd century B. C., p. 28; Dravidian tradition regarding many Nāga-worshipping tribes proceeding to south from Bengal and its neighbourhood—The Marans, Cheras and Pangala Tirayers, the most important, p. 29; The Pangalas, or people of তীরবঙ্গ founded kingdom at Kanchi, p. 30; The Vangas, a sea-faring people, p. 31. [pp. 18-31.

LECTURE III

Ancient Bengal and its Peoples (*contd.*)

Section II.—The Geography of Old Bāṅglā and of other related tracts

Home of the non-Aryan Vangas as we find in the Mahabharata and Purāṇas—A portion of Kālaka-vana, came to be designated as Jhāḍakhaṇḍa—A portion of Jhāḍakhaṇḍa got the name Rāḍha or Lāḍha, p. 32—Temple of Vaidyanath situated in Rāḍha—Anga corresponds to Bhagalpur, Suhma to portions of Midnapūr, with

---

LECTURE IV

Ancient Bengal and its Peoples (*concld.*)

Section III.—Gauḍa, Rāḍha and Banga

LECTURE V

The Influence of the Dravidian Speeches on Bengali

LECTURE VI

Bengali Phonology

LECTURE VII

SOME FACTORS RELATING TO PHONOLOGY AND ACCENT

LECTURE VIII

PHONOLOGY AND ACCENT (*contd.*)

LECTURE IX

PHONOLOGY AND ACCENT (*concld.*)

LECTURE X

HOW CHĀNDASA IS RELATED TO LATER ARYAN SPEECHES.

LECTURE XI

Pāli and other old Prākṛtas

LECTURE XII

The Literary Prākṛtas

ADDITIONS AND CORRECTIONS

P. 2, L. 33 *for* spaeks *read* speaks.

P. 32, L. 18 „ Avāranga *read* Ayaranga (Ācāranga)

P. 68, L. 25 „ ধীয় „ দীয়

„ „ 26 „ তদীয় „ ত্বদীয়

Addition.—Of words listed in pp. 71—74 the following have been traced by me to known origins:—(1) আলি (Dravidian), (2) কুড়ি (Mongolian—see Lecture XIII), (3) ঠেং (from জঙ্ঘা, see Lecture XIII), (4) ভিড়ান (from বেষ্টন), (5) ভুল (from বিহ্বল, see Lecture XIII), (6) মাগি (Dravidian, see Lecture XIII), and (7) হাট্ (from সংঘট্ট, see Lecture XIII).

P. 72, L. 26, the words *eel to* should go over to column 2 *before* words 'keep fish.'

P. 83, L. 14—also at other places—*for* metathysis *read* metathesis.

P. 131, last line, *for* বৃসা-কপি *read* বৃষাকপি.

P. 169, L. 7, *for* hiyeratic *read* hieratic and other places.

P. 175, L. 26, *for* time *read* tense.

P. 176, L. 20, *for* heterogenuous *read* heterogeneous.

P. 177, L. 10, *for* বভুব *read* বভূব.

P. 178, L. 9, *for* recent *read* accent.

P 179, L. 18, *for* mainteinance *read* maintenance.

For p. 343 *read* p. 243.

The History of the Bengali Language

LECTURE I

INTRODUCTION

A. Preliminary

I should state at the outset, that my inquiry regarding the origin and development of the Bengali Language will necessarily lead me to consider and discuss some facts relating to the ancient and modern inhabitants of Bengal; for, in my opinion, a discussion which is merely philological and does not take into account the people or peoples, whose language is the subject-matter of inquiry, is bound to prove abortive. The philologists, for example, may establish, by a comparative grammatical study of the modern vernaculars of Northern India, that the inhabitants of different provinces speak one form or another of some common ancient speech. So far so good. The linguistic taxonomists, again, may classify the modern vernaculars in different groups by looking into their essential structural peculiarities, and may also, with reference to the phonetic peculiarities of each speech, set down some rules to indicate what sound or peculiarity of one speech should be equated with what other sound or peculiarity of another. No one can belittle the usefulness of this work, but we cannot afford to forget that neither Vararuchi nor Grimm nor Verner, nor all of them taken together, can be wholly relied upon to explain all the deviations from the norm. How the ear of a man will be the recipient of a sound, or how he will imitate it in speech, will depend upon his culture; what the "apabhramśa" will be in one stage of culture, will not be so in another. Consequently, the generalised rules of equation applicable to some words of one speech, may not be applicable to other words of that very speech. There are also other good reasons why we cannot acknowledge the all-sufficiency of the rules alluded to, but it will be a digression to adduce them here. What I want to bring out prominently is that, we cannot study the phonetic changes in a speech without taking the speakers of it into account. After observing the differences among the sister dialects, we raise the question, why the parent tongue underwent different sorts of changes in different provinces, we ask why the "apabhramśa" forms in use in Hindi for example, did not become current in Bengali? What were the solvent elements in different provinces that brought about the characteristic changes noticeable in different speeches of common origin? To get to the facts, which induced different sorts of changes and modifications in different provinces, we must direct our attention to provincial racial peculiarities, as well as to the physical conditions of life, which were present in those provinces. This is exactly what is not done by many philologists. And we shall presently see how they create imaginary races to explain away their difficulties without caring to study the actual racial peculiarities existing in different provinces. This is the reason why many scientists look to the philologists and their work with much disfavour. Such an eminent man of science of our time as Karl Pearson spaeks slightingly of the philologists, as 'they do not generally pursue the scientific method in their inquiry, for they ask us to enter into the "play-room for their individual fancy," and accordingly we cannot always get into the domain of philology any classified fact or system "independent of the individual thinker" (*vide* "Grammar of Science," p. 10). Grierson's fanciful theory regarding the origin of Indian dialects may be adduced as a fitting example of this sort of philological vagaries. As the theory of this oriental scholar appears in an essay contributed by him to such a work of authority as the "Imperial Gazetteer of India," a brief discussion of it seems called for.* To show up obscurantism is to pave the way to the true scientific method of inquiry.

I set forth first of all the propositions which Grierson has asked us to accept on his authority and from which he has drawn all his conclusions. They are :—

(*i*) Modern Aryan languages were not derived from Sanskrit. "Some pastoral tribes (long before the Vedic days) found their way across the Hindukush" and spread their languages over the whole of Northern India as far as Dibrugarh in the extreme east of Assam, and Canara to the south of Bombay. All the modern vernaculars have their origin in the "patois of these pastoral tribes."

(*ii*) The latest comers of the Indo-Aryans settled themselves in the so-called Midland by forcing the earlier immigrants "outward in three directions—to the east, to the south and to the west." The latest comers would not necessarily be on good terms with their predecessors, who quite possibly opposed them as intruders, nor did they speak the same language." One particular Indo-Aryan

* Remarks I here offer are abridged from what I wrote in 1908 in criticism of Sir George Grierson's views published in the "Imperial Gazetteer," Vol. I. My criticism appeared in "Modern Review," August 1908.

dialect of these late comers may be taken to represent the archaic language of the Rigveda.

(*iii*) Sanskrit is the polished form of the archaic Vedic tongue. This polish was given to the Vedic tongue by the labours of the grammarians, culminating in the work of Pānini. This Sanskrit was never a vernacular, and even in olden times it was learnt as a second language.

(*iv*) The other languages (*i.e.*, the languages derived from the patois of the earliest settlers), namely, Mārhātti, Bengali, Oriā, etc., remain unaffected in their essence by the speech of the Midland.

It is very difficult to meet Sir George Grierson, for he has not chosen to cite authorities, nor has he adduced reasons in support of his propositions beyond what he has added at the end of his paper by way of his own signature. Where he has adduced reasons, he has rather stated new propositions in the name of reasons which stand equally in need of support. As to the original cradle-land of the prehistoric Aryans, nothing has yet been settled; and the oldest record of the Aryans, the Vedas, being far from replete with evidence as to their original home and migratory movements, the question relating to the appearance of Aryans in India is still a matter for careful inquiry and research. However, we do not hold Grierson responsible for the unscientific theory about the origin of the Aryans, which seeks to establish ethnic unity among races of men of different countries on the basis of some linguistic agreement. This is not the place for me to show that the facts established by the anthropologists tend to demolish the theory of there being necessarily any genetic affinity between the races of men speaking different Aryan dialects. We shall only notice here that Grierson has put the old theory into shadow by formulating a new theory of considerable proportions by the sheer force of his imagination.

He has mapped out the whole imaginary cradle-land of the Aryans and given a graphic description of the migratory movements of some unknown people of an unknown time. May we ask what facts justified Grierson in taking up the vague suggestion of Hoernle as an established fact and to put down with confidence that the patois of some pre-Vedic pastoral tribes had taken root in India before the Vedic dialect prevailed?

The evidence is declared to be linguistic, and, it is said, has been obtained by Grierson while pursuing his linguistic survey. The method of reasoning, the fact set forth in support of the proposition, and the proposition itself, may be briefly stated thus:—The Aryan languages in use in Northern, Eastern and South-Western countries not only differ from the languages of Mid-India, but also differ from one another; the Vedic Aryans must have occupied the Midland; hence it is established, in the opinion of Grierson, beyond any doubt that the languages other than those of the Midland originated from the patois of some pastoral tribes who preceded the Vedic Aryans. The method of reasoning is wholly unscientific. All the dialects are admitted to be Aryan in origin, but as they differ from one another, their origin has been presumed to be different. The very fact that they are so many dialects, shows that they must not be one and the same, and they must have marked points of difference, even though they might have been derived from one and the same language. Dialectic variations always take place because of distance from a centre and because of contact with other tribes or races. Facts have not been adduced to show that the dialects in question were not thus formed, as they are formed normally everywhere. On the other hand with reference to Grierson's remarks in the "Report of the Census of India, 1901" and in his monograph on the "Piśācha Languages," I am constrained to say that the learned author has built a stupendous structure with very weak materials, on the foundation of a fancy of his own. Sir Herbert Risley has very rightly remarked that without at all resorting to the theory of patois-speaking hordes, the changes in the dialects of Central India can easily be explained, with reference to the people speaking them. Need I make a statement of the well-known truth, that it is "grammar" and not "sound" or "vocabulary" which gives a dialect its character? Merely because some tribes of the Punjab frontier use some words of Aryan origin, Grierson concludes that these tribes are remnants in hilly countries of the oldest Aryan people. It is on the evidence of sound and vocabulary he has thought out different origins for some dialects of Northern India. It is such reckless assumptions that have brought philology into disrepute with all anthropologists, though philology as a branch of knowledge has a useful sphere of its own. Merely from similarity of sounds Grierson has inferred that the "Pakthas" of the Rigveda are the modern Pāthāns without caring even to ascertain if those, who are now called Pāthāns, existed in the Vedic days with such a tribal name. I would not have wondered if the Āfridis, who, to serve the convenience of a theory, may be called Āpridis, were similarly put forward as the authors of the Āpri hymns. I cannot bring myself to imagine that Grierson, who is widely known to be a great oriental scholar, has made his authoritative statements regarding our archaic and classical languages without possessing sufficient knowledge of them. But, on the other hand, it appears so strange that one having even a very common acquaintance with the languages of old India could for a moment think that Sanskrit is the polished form of the Vedic language. The grammarians, who have been given the credit of having polished the Vedic language, called this language by the name "Chhāndasa" and described what is now called Sanskrit by the term "Laukika-Bhāṣā" (or current language). Grierson could not but have noticed the matter in Pānini's book, but he has not attempted to explain it. The great oriental scholar must also have noticed in Pānini's Grammar that the Chhāndasa language was an object of reverential study, and nobody could even dare to handle it with a view to reform it. There are stringent rules that under no circumstances the Vedic form should be deviated from ; it has been stated that to do so will be to commit sin. I should not discuss the point at any further length, for later on I shall have to deal with the character of the Vedic language in an independent lecture. The reasons why the Classical Sanskrit varied from the Vedic language will be discussed in its proper place. I have only suggested here that the history of a language involves the history of the people speaking it, and as such we cannot trace it by philological research alone.

B. Preparatory.

If we exclude the recently acquired district of Darjeeling from the political map of Bengal, the entire indigenous population of the Presidency of Bengal will be found to be wholly Bengali-speaking. The district of Sylhet to the north of the Chittagong Division and the district of Manbhum to the west of the Burdwan Division, though falling outside the Presidency of Bengal, are but Bengali-speaking tracts and nearly three million souls live in those two districts. By eliminating the exotic elements from the Bengali-speaking areas indicated above, we get a population of not less than fifty million that has Bengali for its mother-tongue. It is quite an interesting history how Bengali was evolved, and how it became the dominating speech of various tribes and races who were once keen in maintaining their tribal integrity by living apart from one another, over the vast area of eighty thousand square miles.

Bengali is called a Sanskritic language by some philological scholars, but what these scholars definitely mean by the term Sanskrit is not always explicitly stated. If we can only tolerate such a loose use of the term as to make it indicate indiscriminately the Chhāndasa speech of the early Vedic days as well as the speech which Panini described as Laukika, the nomenclature of the philological scholars may be allowed to stand. I consider it, however, safer to call the Bengali speech as an Aryan vernacular to avoid the suggestion that the language in which the poets from Kālidāsa to Jayadeva composed their works was the progenitor of Bengali. It has to be distinctly borne in mind that the word "Aryan," as used by me, has not even remotely any ethnic significance; it will indicate the Vedic speech and those speeches which are allied to, or have affinity with, the Vedic speech.

Let me repeat explicitly what I have suggested above just now: that a language is mainly, if not wholly, determined by its grammar or structure and not by its vocabulary which may always swell by the process of word-borrowing. I should also add here that the accent system is a great factor in a language, and should be considered as an essential element of it; different forms of "apabhramśa" in different dialects of one common original speech are partly due to different accent systems. It will be necessary, therefore, to refer to the accent systems of our neighbouring tribes to solve some points of difficulty. In ignorance of the fact that some non-Aryan speeches exercised some influence upon Bengali, and misled by the description of our language as Sanskritic, many capable scholars have devoted themselves of late to the ingenious but wasteful work of digging out Sanskrit roots and stems for such Bengali words and inflections as are entirely of other origin. This work is conducted on the flimsy basis of feeble sound suggestions. It may interest you to know that this very unscientific method was once resorted to in Europe during the 17th and 18th centuries, and many scholars attempted to reduce all languages to Hebrew and in some cases to an original Gothic on the strength of some remote or imagined sound similarity.

If our work is not to be barren of good results, we must direct our inquiry to the solution of the following questions, as preparatory to the analysis of our language, with a view to detect and unravel all the influences which were at work in building it up: (1) We have to consider carefully the geographical limits of ancient Vanga or Bengal which has given our language its distinctive name and the character of the tribe or tribes which inhabited the area previous to the settlement of the people who brought in what may be termed a form of Aryan speech. Along with these must also be considered the ancient political or ethnical character of other tracts which, together with the ancient Vanga, constitute now the province of Bengal in which Bengali is the dominant language. (2) As far as it can be traced, we must determine what form of Aryan speech was first brought into or superimposed upon the country roughly defined above. (3) The Aryan or Aryanised and the non-Aryan hordes which made inroads into Bengal, from the earliest known time to the end of the 12th century A.D., *i.e.*, up to the time of the Muhammadan influence in Bengal, and secured settlements in different parts of the country, must also be taken into account to explain some factors which generally appear anomalous in our language.

It is too much to expect that we shall succeed in mapping out definitely how the stream of our language flowed with an unbroken continuity from a well-defined source and received in its bosom many affluents in its successive course of progress. No doubt what is true in all cases is true in respect of the evolution of our language, that nature never allowed any break to occur in her process of upbuilding, but as many earlier forms, while fading away imperceptibly into new and newer forms, were not preserved in literary records, we may only surmise their existence from a very small number of what may be termed "fossil words."

Before entering upon my subject, I set forth and discuss some propositions which are generally accepted as correct and are of such value as no one should lose sight of in such an inquiry. The first proposition, if put in the language of A. H. Keane, will stand as follows :—There is no such phenomenon as linguistic miscegenation. I fear I cannot accept the proposition as universally correct. It will be noticed later on that in our syntactical forms, that is to say, in the very structure of our language, some elements foreign to our language have accommodated themselves. This sort of mixture cannot but be recognised as miscegenation. I admit, however, that the foreign elements which no doubt change the structure are absorbed by the main organism ; this assimilation by intussusception takes place according to the active principles inherent in the organism. Consequently the new structure which becomes wholly separate and independent cannot be said to be mixed as a language in the individuated form. No language of this world can coincide with another, for every language has its own separate grammar or structure ; but it can be shown that in their growth many languages in India incorporated many foreign elements and had adopted foreign methods of expression. We can only say that no two languages are identical, but as in the case of human races, so in the case of human speeches, absolute purity cannot be thought of. I must no doubt acknowledge that we are at times misled by some instances of mixed vocabularies and wrongly pronounce a language to be mixed on that account. If Mr. Keane has emphasized upon this proposition in stating that there cannot be any miscegenation of languages I am in entire agreement with the views of the distinguished anthropologist. As an example, I may cite the case of the so-called Urdu speech—by endorsing the valuable opinion of Mr. Keane—which is wrongly supposed to be different from Hindi and is asserted by some to be a mixture of Hindi, Persian and Arabic. My suggestion to do away with the name Urdu as an additional name for the standard Hindi language was no doubt accepted by Mr. L. S. S. O'Malley during the census operations of the year 1911, but the sentiment of some people for the ridiculously unscientific term had to be, I fear, respected. The whole structure of the speech is Hindi ; the Hindi pronouns are conjugated with verbs in all tenses and moods according to the Hindi rules, yet forgetting the fact that no amount of word-borrowing can change one language into another, Urdu has been set up as a different language. That the words of Persian and Arabic origin are much in use in Hindi and more free use of them is possible, is lost sight of. Words of such foreign origin are prevalent in Bengali and Oriā as well. If we borrow European words more freely and adopt what is called Roman script in our writing, will the Bengali language be entitled to claim another name ? The vulgar people confound language not only with vocabulary but also with script. The Nāgri letters which have no better pretensions to antiquity than Bengali letters, are called even by many educated persons "Sanskrit Akṣar," merely because to serve some convenience, many Sanskrit books are published in Bengal in Nāgri character. One word more regarding word-borrowing. It must be noticed that the words borrowed from other languages have all to conform to the genius of the languages into which they are adopted. This is what takes place in the Bengali language and this is what as a matter of course takes place in Hindi even though the speakers, through whose agency the adoption is accomplished, are Muhammadans.* That an adherence to an unscientific situation has a mischievous effect on education must be duly appreciated.

(*ii*) The second proposition I should put forward is, that it is only when a new structure is gradually built with new elements on a fresh basis, a new language is evolved; but that this new language, by merely coming in contact with other languages cannot change its own structure, for such change means nothing but death or extinction of that language. The imperceptible slow change with which a new language is developed is by itself a matter for study. Never can a living people change radically or discontinuously, nor can its natural and organised mode of thinking, which expresses itself in the form or structure of its speech, be radically changed.

(*iii*) My next proposition is that what is called a patois or a rude or vulgar speech, is never a separate language. Isolation and want of culture bring about deformities, and these deformities characterise a language as a rude dialect. The language of the Māl Pāhāḍis is as much Bengali as the language of the peasants of Northern

* The sort of composition which at times our Sanskrit Pandits and Arabic scholars indulge in by introducing artificially Sanskritic or Arabic forms to make a flourish of pedantry, can hardly be classed under any dialect of the world.

Yorkshire is English. Such an unscientific term as "Sub-dialect" cannot be tolerated.

I come now to another matter of great interest and significance in this inquiry. The *shibboleth* test is usually applied to distinguish one race from another, but without duly judging its value. I cannot therefore conclude this lecture without uttering a word of caution in that direction.

That different phonetic systems do exist as racial peculiarities must be fully recognised and appreciated both by the anthropologists and philologists, though we may avoid treading the debatable ground as to whether the phonetic peculiarities imply necessarily in all cases differences in the anatomical structure of the vocal organs. For all practical purposes we can safely leave aside the extreme case of the Papuans illustrated by Miklukho-Maclay, for I shall presently show that the races I have to deal with in this book are not absolutely incapable of imitating those utterances with which we are here concerned. We may spare the vocal organs an inspection when differences may be clearly explained by climatic influences or by the long-standing habit acquired by unconscious imitation of the sounds of some neighbours.

The shibboleth test may be of practical value when two races remain apart from each other. It must, however, be borne in mind that the pronunciation of words in a particular manner does not necessarily indicate peculiarity in the structure of the vocal organs ; it may at times be wholly due to the education of the ear. If an infant born in England of pure English parents be nurtured wholly in an Indian home he will not display the peculiarities of English pronunciation, and will never mispronounce Indian names. I can speak from what I have carefully observed myself that the English baby born in India and brought up by Indians utter with perfect ease, when grown up, those words which the English people say it is impossible for them to pronounce. Bengalis who have settled in Orissa, but have not mixed their blood with the Oriās, pronounce Bengali words in Oriā fashion with Oriā pronunciation and Oriā intonation. Not to speak of the higher caste people of Bengal, there is overwhelming evidence that the very people whose environment has changed the pronunciation of even the Brahmans in East Bengal, do change their pronunciation when they settle in the district of Hooghly.

The racial peculiarities in the matter of uttering vocal sounds are no doubt very marked but my personal examination of various Indian tribes in the matter of their capacity to utter certain sounds has strengthened my view that there is no difference between man and man as far as the inhabitants of this country are concerned as to the construction of the organ or organs of speech. I have found the ears of some practically isolated tribes so trained that they fail to catch certain sounds uttered to them and accordingly they imitate them very badly; but when they are for some time with us, they do not betray any organic defect in uttering new sounds. The Muṇḍās and the Orāons are well known for their very settled phonetic peculiarities, but when employed in our houses as domestic servants they learn to speak Bengali very faultlessly, though when speaking their own tongue they do not deviate from their own path in the matter of pronouncing their own words.

The hilly accent of Manbhum, the nasal twang of Bankura and Burdwan, the drawl of Central Bengal, which becomes very much marked in the slow and lazy utterance of words by women, and the rapid wavy swing with which the words are uttered in quick succession in

East Bengal may to a great extent be explained by climatic conditions as well as by the social life of ease or difficulty ; but the influence of the tribes of different localities among whom the speakers of the Bengali language had to place themselves, must not be either minimised or ignored. It should be remembered that a man of the so-called Aryan descent may lose the power of uttering such sounds as are generated, for example, by "sh" or "bh" because of the dominant environing influence of the people of other races. That the disability is not organic and cannot invariably be considered to be a racial characteristic has been partly demonstrated.

It is desirable that I should here clearly define what I mean by a racial character of speech.

All phonetic or linguistic peculiarities that mark off one race or stock from another are not necessarily racial characters in the scientific sense of the term. By a primary racial character I mean only such of the linguistic peculiarities, or marks of a people as have an organic or physical basis in the cerebral or vocal mechanism and as are also transmitted from parent to offspring under the operation of the principles of Heredity and Variation. The capacity for speech, for example, is such a primary character for the human race. But I am free to admit that over and above such hereditary organic characters, there are secondary characters of speech, racial peculiarities, which, though not embedded in the physical conformation, are accompanied by what Wundt has called inheritable predisposition and which, therefore, appear in individuals from generation to generation under the normal conditions of existence though, no doubt, in the absence of suitable stimulus or under very marked changes of environment they do not persist but give place to acquired or induced variations. I am inclined to think that the forms and relations of thought which lie at the basis of the syntax of different families of languages, though not the grammatical structures or paradigms themselves, constitute secondary racial characters of the nature of predisposition. There is reason to believe also that accent systems, though originally acquired under persistent climatic, dietic and social conditions, have now come in many cases to be more or less stable, more or less transmittable characters and may have given rise to predispositions of the sort. But besides these primary and secondary characters there is a third sort of racial peculiarities of speech which, no doubt, distinguish one people from another but which are acquired under the influence of the tradition or of the environment, physical and social, and have to be so acquired by the individuals from generation and generation, and which disappear whenever the tradition or environment is changed. This traditional element in a speech constitutes that part of it which is a social tradition and has no ethnic significance in the biological sense of the term. Among these traditional elements of speech, which may be loosely termed tertiary racial characters, I would place the phonetic system (the vowel and consonant system) as well as the grammatical paradigm (including the tense-formatives) of a language or family of languages. But as we have seen, all the racial characters, secondary no less than tertiary, the predispositions no less than the merely traditional elements, are liable to be changed under change of environmental conditions, and replaced by newly acquired or induced characters.

The fact, therefore, stands that different sections of the Bengali people have the capacity of speaking the Bengali speech alike. But I must utter a caveat here lest a wrong anthropological use be made of this philological fact as has been done in so many cases. On the basis of this fact we cannot necessarily postulate a unity or homogeneity of race. We cannot necessarily formulate the theory that either there has been a thorough-going miscegenation of blood among all the sections, or that these sections do not represent different races of bygone days. I purposely strike this note of caution, though I am perfectly aware that there has been considerable miscegenation of blood among many races of India, for I consider it unsafe to draw any conclusion from facts furnished by linguistic investigation alone.

We are not much concerned in this inquiry with those linguistic phenomena which fall legitimately within the province of the physiologists,—though it is pretty certain that the time is not distant when to explain even the ordinary phonetic changes in a speech, the help of the physiologists will be requisitioned in preference to that of the linguists as philologists. We shall have to study carefully the settled and abiding peculiarities of some races of men in the matter of their accent systems and syntactical forms to measure the influence of those races in the upbuilding of our language, but as to how a particular race became settled in its habits to a particular mode of thinking or in a particular way of intonating certain sounds, will not concern us in pushing on our research. Practically speaking, accent being a thing of very hard growth, it survives through many changes; as such a comparative study of the accent system of different races may help us in determining the origin of many peculiarities disclosed by the people of different provinces of Bengal.

ANCIENT BENGAL AND ITS PEOPLES

LECTURE II

SECTION 1

The antiquity of the names Vanga and Bānglā

It is a fact that the Veda Samhitās and the early Vedic literature do not mention the name Vanga either in connection with the names of Indian tribes or in any enumeration of the countries owned by the Aryans as well as by the non-Aryans. The Rigveda Samhitā does not know even Anga, but this Anga country is mentioned in the Atharva Veda. In the Atharva Veda Pariśiṣṭa, however, the word Vanga occurs with Magadha as a component of a compound word; but as the scholars do not attach any value to it owing partly to the lateness of the Pariśiṣṭa itself, I advisedly leave this mention out of consideration. It will be quite unscientific, however, to come to such a positive conclusion on the basis of this silence, that the Vedic fathers had no knowledge of the country or tribe which bore the name Vanga. I cannot too highly speak of the critical acumen of the learned scholars who have attempted to reconstruct the history of the Vedic times with the materials furnished by the Veda Samhitās, but we have no patience with those who have gone the length of making this bold statement with much confidence that the state of things not disclosed by the Vedic mantras was non-existent in the olden days. The uncritical scholars do not see that, even if it be conceded that all the mantras or prayers to gods, as had been composed at different times by the Ṛṣis, were wholly collected and we get them now fully preserved in the Samhitās, it cannot be asserted that a complete picture of the Vedic times can be presented with the help of the mantra material alone. Let me take up a hypothetical case just to illustrate the force of my remarks. Just fancy that a cataclysm sweeps away all that we possess and are proud of to-day, and some historical critics arise, after the deluge, to write a history of our time with the help of such a prayer-book as the Brahma Sangīt of the Brāhmas, or a collection of Rāmprasād's songs, unearthed in the debris of some buildings, will the material be sufficient for the purpose? Will not such an inference on the basis of the hymns and prayers of the Brāhmas, that the Bengalis of our imaginary pre-deluged era were all monotheists of the Brāhma type, be a gross misstatement of fact? Is there anything in the hymns of the Brāhmas to indicate that there is such an institution as the Calcutta University or that this country is being ruled by the British people? Rāmprasād's songs may supply the information that we had such a thing as oil-pressing machine, and that machine was worked by bullocks being blindfolded; but will not this be a very poor picture of the civilization of Rāmprasād's days? We meet with an entertaining passage in a drama of our celebrated dramatist and humourist, the late D. L. Roy, which purports to be a taunting challenge to the effect—should we think that the Gopīs of Brindāban did not know the use of *jira marich*, since there is no mention of this condiment in the Srimadbhāgabatam? We cannot afford to forget that however much the Vedas relate to the general conditions of life of the ancient times, they are but ideal prayers and hymns, which, again, only a section of the Indian Aryans offered to the gods. There is ample evidence in the very Veda Samhitās, that all the Aryans of India did not pursue the religion which is reflected in the Vedic mantras.

No doubt we do not meet with the name Vanga in the Veda Samhitās and the Atharvan mentions only Anga as the outermost border country lying to the south-east of the territories of the Aryas ; but when we come upon this fact, that the later Vedic literature such as the Aitareya Brāhmaṇa mentions Vanga as a country held by a barbarian tribe, while the early Buddhistic literature (not likely of a date earlier than the Brāhmaṇa) is as silent as the Vedas are, it becomes difficult to attribute such a silence to ignorance. From these facts we can only make this plausible inference that Vanga and its adjacent parts were not colonized by the Aryans till the 6th century B. C. Let me discuss this important point of chronology by considering the value of the facts disclosed by the aforesaid literature.

It is evident from the manner in which the border tribes have been mentioned in the 22nd Sūkta of the 5th Book of the Atharva Veda that the Māgadhas and the Angas were alien barbarous people who resided outside the pale of Aryan country but it is also clear that the countries of these barbarians were in close proximity to the land of the Ṛṣis. In this Sūkta this wish has been expressed in offering a prayer to Agni that the fever called "takman" may leave the holy land of the Aryas and may reside in such border countries as Anga and Magadha which are really the home (okaḥ) of the fever. This fever which is considered to be of malarial type has been asked in the prayer to assail the barbarians and specially their wanton fugitive women (described as Sudrās) on account of their having left the Aryan protection in Aryan homes. It is rather clear from this mention that the Ṛṣis of the Atharva Veda utilised the services of the people of Magadha and

Anga and were particularly keen about keeping the 'Sudra women in Aryan villages. Looking to what has been stated of Anga we may only provisionally hold that Vanga, which lay still farther off to the south-east, was only inhabited in those days by people other than the Aryans. We get in the Śatapatha Brāhmaṇa of a much later date that the holy sacrificial fire travelled as far east as Videgha (Videha) in Mithilā. It is, therefore, pretty certain that the Aryans did not even then come in any real contact with the Vangas of Bengal. We notice in the Atharva Veda that the Kirāta people of the Himalayan region were the neighbours of the Aryans and the Kirāta women supplied such roots and herbs as were used for charms and for medicine; such a peaceful relation with the south-eastern border tribes is not indicated in any Sūkta. In the Aitareya Āraṇyaka the Vanga tribe finds only a bare mention in conjunction with the Magadha people. Some early references relating to the people of Magadha, of Anga and of other neighbouring barbarian tracts in such a fashion, that they were beasts or snakes, have been misinterpreted by some scholars. We cannot forget the fact that almost all the tribes were known by the totem names of their clans or tribes; it is therefore strongly suspected that when the Aryans knew the totem names of different tribes, they had some intimate knowledge of them. When the tribes are not made identical with the names of birds and snakes, quite another interpretation has to be given. In the history of the conquest of the rude aboriginal tribes, we get one and the same mythical account all over the world: the rude tribes in their mountain fastnesses and forest tracts are represented as giants or dwarfs with mysterious powers, or they are imagined to possess power of transforming themselves into beasts or birds. The Ṛṣis were no doubt of superior mental and spiritual powers, but they represent the Rakṣas and the Yakṣas as magicians and Māyāvīs, as invested with abiding authority over the elements. The reason is not far to seek. The aboriginal people who knew every part of their land in the hills and the forests, could appear suddenly and could escape unnoticed to places which were difficult of access to the conquering trespassers; moreover the rude tribes, who were unable to cope with the civilized intruders, took to some subterfuges which made their hostility to be dreaded in proportion to its secrecy. When the blow was struck in darkness, the awe-struck Aryans who had supreme contempt for the valour of their foes, were led to attribute it to supernatural or non-human, rather than to human agency. In any view of the case, knowledge on the part of the Aryans of the people of their country may be presumed. It has been just mentioned, that in the early Buddhistic literature, where detailed lists appear of many countries and peoples, the name Vanga is conspicuous by its absence ("Buddhist India" by Rhys Davids, pp. 23-29). The importance of this omission lies in this, that Buddha, who flourished towards the end of the 6th century B.C., had his activities mostly in Magadha which is not far off from Bengal. The story of Vijaya Simha, on the other hand, points to a pre-Buddhistic colonization of Bengal by the Aryans. How far we can rely upon the Sinhalese account, based upon a tradition merely, or rather upon a legendary account, that Vijaya Simha was a king of Bengal and that he led his victorious campaign into Ceylon the very year the Buddha attained his Nirvāṇa has not yet been critically discussed. It can, however, be asserted on the evidence of linguistic palæontology, that the early conquerors of their land went from the eastern Gangetic valley, and carried with them the speech which prevailed in Magadha at least during the 4th century B.C.

Not only the Sinhalese, but even the Vaeddas and their very wild congeners, use a large number of Māgadhi words in their speech, which are of the time I have spoken of. The use of the words "gini" for fire, "gonā" for cows, "goyā" and "goyi" (the Prākṛta forms of godhā and godhikā), "vāso" to indicate residence (as in kaeto-vaso, forest residence), "ini" from the root इ=to go (as in gamanini), etc., which occur in the old Māgadhi Prākṛta, by even such Sinhalese as lead a rude life in distant forest tracts, raises a presumption in favour of very early Māgadhi influence in Ceylon. It has to be noted that the Sinhalese are non-Aryan people, and the Tamil-speaking Hindus, who have most influence with them, are not at all familiar with the Māgadhi words noticed above. As the early chroniclers of Ceylon could always prevail upon the Gotama Buddha to visit the island off and on, it is unsafe to rely upon the dates given by them in their pious zeal for the cause of religion.

The account that Vijaya and his successors proceeded to Ceylon from Vanga, cannot also be easily dismissed, for there are indelible marks of the influence of the eastern Gangetic valley on the speech of the Sinhalese. It is a fact that many words and grammatical forms, as had their origin in the soil of Bengal at a comparatively recent time, are current in the speech of even some isolated forest tribes of Ceylon, along with the Māgadhi words of earlier date as just now noted above. This argues in favour of the proposition that the later immigrants must have proceeded directly from Bengal. Whoever the early conquerors of Ceylon may be, it will be quite reasonable to suppose that even when the old Māgadhi of .the 3rd or 4th century B.C. changed its own character considerably in farther east, lots of people of the lower Gangetic valley continued to pour into Ceylon, to exercise linguistic and other influences upon the aboriginal races of that island. As to the currency of the modern Bengali forms in Ceylon, I may just by way of illustration refer to the following words, namely—Mācha (fish), gācha (tree) (occurs also as gāha in one tribal speech), petti (small) (the Bengali word peti or pāti is used now to signify contempt). A good deal will have to be said in a subsequent lecture, regarding the accent system of our speech, by comparing the prevailing system with the systems of some Dravidian races, and the old and the modern grammatical forms will have to be similarly considered. As such we cannot do anything beyond pointing out here, that in Ceylon, the word "bhūmi" is pronounced as "bumi" or "bimi," the word "bhāt" is pronounced as "bāt" and the form "karaṇa" (to do), of which the modern Bengali form is "karā," is in use. I may only note in passing, that in some eastern districts of Bengal, "ba" is nearly the sound of "bha" and "karaṇa" is the form of "karā"; the sentence *Ār ki deon jāy* for *Ār ki deoā jāy* occurs in a humorous song composed by our poet Rajani Kanta Sen whose early death we all mourn. As to Sinhalese accent system, the remarks of Mr. R. L. Turner may be profitably quoted. He writes: "With regard to Sinhalese, it is hard to come to a decision, because, firstly, all long vowels have been shortened, and, secondly, an extensive *umlaut* has taken place." The importance of the phenomenon, noticed by Mr. Turner, will be appreciated by you when you will be treated to our Bengali accent and phonetic system. The facts relating to Ceylon, as have been discussed here rather perfunctorily, do not fail to show, that men of Aryan speech and civilization commenced to colonize Bengal from a time not later than the 4th century B.C.

Probabilities, however, seem to be on the side of the supposition, that an appreciable number of Aryans chose to make Vanga their home, even when the Aryans of the holy Midland country had neither occasion nor liking to take any notice of the eastern tracts of the barbarians. Even when the notice of the tracts was forced upon them later on, they looked down upon those of them who resided among the barbarians. Some statements in the old Dharmaśāstras warrant us in making this inference.

There are some good reasons to suppose, that the Dharmaśāstras fathered upon Baudhāyana and Vaśiṣṭha, though older than many other Dharmaśāstras, cannot be placed beyond the 6th century B.C. Baudhāyana has given the limits of Āryāvarta in the following words: Āryāvarta lies to the east of the region, where the river Saraswati disappears to the west of the Kālaka-vana (the forest region which extended over a large area to the south and south-east of Magadha), to the north of the Pāripātra mountains, to the south of the Himalayas (I Pr., I Ch., K. 2). That Bengal is here excluded from the land of the Aryans, is sufficiently clear. After stating the accepted orthodox view regarding the geography of the Āryāvarta, Baudhāyana as well as Vaśiṣṭha very grudgingly extends the limits of the Āryāvarta, on the authority of "some" who have been mentioned as "others." By virtue of the extended definition, Bengal and some other countries fall within Āryāvarta; for, according to this definition of the holy land, Āryāvarta lies to the south of the Himalayas and to the north of the Vindhya range—being limited east and west by the two oceans (Vaśiṣṭha I, 8 and 9). The conclusion seems inevitable, that the stray settlements of the Āryas, at places beyond the limits of the holy land, commenced long before the time of Baudhāyana, and the settlers were being recognized with some reluctance during the time of Baudhāyana and Vaśiṣṭha. This proposition will receive full confirmation

4

from the following facts. Baudhāyana, whom all the authors of the old-time Dharmaśāstras follow, has laid down some model rules of life for the twice-born Āryas in the second Kāṇḍikā, of the 1st Praśna of his work; I give here the purport of the whole Kāṇḍikā because of its special importance. It has been stated on the one hand, in verses XIII and XIV, that the people or peoples of Aṅga, Magadha, Avanti, and other lands lying close to the land of the Āryas, are of the mixed origin, while the lands of the Puṇḍras, the Vangas and the Kalingas are so unholy that one should go through a penance on one's return from those countries; on the other hand, it has been stated, in noting certain deviations from the model rules of the holy Madhya Deśa or Pānchāla country, that those who reside in southern countries, marry the daughters of maternal or paternal uncles, and those, who belong to some northern countries, follow the trade of arms and go to sea. As these deviations have been excused on the ground of their being special provincial customs, we cannot fail to see, that the Āryas who were of the twice-born rank, became the settled inhabitants of the unholy lands, long before the time of Baudhāyana. We notice that Puṇḍra and Vanga were separate countries in those days, and that there were Aryan settlements in Puṇḍra and Vanga, though they might not have been as extensive as in Magadha and Anga. We should further notice, that sea voyage was allowed in olden days in some northern countries of the Aryans, which fell outside the limits of the Madhya Deśa. This fact is in support of the proposition, that the Aryans of the eastern Gangetic valley proceeded to Ceylon as early as in the 4th century B.C. We thus see that however scanty be our materials, we cannot definitely assert that the Aryans did not commence to colonize Vanga, during or earlier than the 6th century B.C.

Let us now discuss some other facts for further light on the subject; let us now see what accounts we may get of the ancient Vanga people, on examining some records of non-Aryan activities of a time when the Aryans disdained to take any notice of the tribes, who were not within the pale of Āryāvarta. Recent researches in Farther India by such scholars as Mr. Phayre and Col. Gerini have disclosed these facts, that the Telegu-speaking and Tamil-speaking Dravidians of India reached Farther India both by land and sea, and established colonies and political supremacy in many parts of Farther India; and that the Hindus poured in, only subsequently, to dominate that land by displacing the Dravidian supremacy. The earliest date we get of the Hindus, who went to Burma is 923 B.C. I accept this date on the authority of some scholars, but I cannot vouch for its correctness. The Kṣatriya adventurers, who are said to have proceeded from Hastināpur and to have established an extensive territory in Upper Burma with Bhamo for its capital in 923 B. C., are reported to have displaced the Dravidians who had organised their new *Kalinga Raṭṭa* previous to the Aryan inroads into the country. This should lead us to suppose, that the Dravidian invasion in Farther India took place at least a century before 923 B. C. It is also reported of the Telegu adventurers, that they established their supremacy over Arakan and the tract of country now covered by the Chittagong Division in about 850 B. C. The accounts of Kyauk-pandang by Mr. Phayre in his history of Burma may be profitably referred to in this connection.

What concerns us principally here is that the people of Bengal formed a powerful colony in Annam in Farther India not later than the 7th century B. C., when they were being despised and not taken any notice of by the Aryans in India. The traditional and legendary accounts relating to Annam, as are reported to appear in some Chinese records, affirm that the leader of the Bengali adventurers, who became the king, of Annam, bore the name Luck-lom, and that he married one Annamese girl named Auki. It has been gathered from these records, that the province of India to which Luck-lom and his people belonged, was called Bong-long, and that Luck-lom and his followers were of Nāga Vaṁśa or rather had Nāga for their tribal totem. It becomes pretty clear, that the name of the land, which was then unknown in Āryāvarta, was Bong-long (the original form of Bānglā) and the people of Bong-long were known by the name Bong. That the term Vanga indicated the name of a tribe may be amply proved on the authority of the old Hindu literature. You may refer to Col. Gerini's accounts regarding the Bong-long kings in his work entitled "Researches in Ptolemy's Geography." Archæological research in Cambodia and Annam by Ayomounier, De la Ponte and other European antiquarians should be carefully studied in the interest of the History of India. We will presently see that those who bore the names Anga, Vanga and Kalinga, were regarded by the Aryans to have been of non-Aryan origin. I should also mention here, that the kings of Bong tribe reigned till the second decade of the 3rd century B. C., when some Buddhist Kṣatriyas of the Magadha country became supreme in Annam. It is known that eighteen kings of Bong-long origin reigned for over 350 years in Annam. We find that the compound letter or suffix "long" was added to "Bong" to signify the country belonging to the Bong people. I am inclined to think that this "long" is the Annamese form of the non-Aryan suffix "lā," and that not only the name Bong or Vanga as the name of a tribe, but the word "Bānglā" is as old as the word Vanga. I shall not be accused of giving reins to wild imagination, if I consider this non-Aryan suffix " lā " to be still persisting in our language, and that we detect this suffix in such words as " phoglā," " totlā," etc. I should, however, note that the " la " or its derivative " lā " which indicates past tense (as in *karila* or *karilā*), has nothing to do with the " lā " spoken of here. Be that as it may, we get it as a certain fact, and that is a great gain with us, that the word Bong-long or Bānglā was the name of some indefinite portion of our present Bengal, at least as early as the 7th century B. C., and the name Vanga (which originally signified a people) is of great antiquity.

We learn this good lesson from the accounts of the Vanga people, that we should not invariably make the Aryan activities in a province the sole starting point for the historic period in that province, and should not consign all pure and unmixed non-Aryan activities to the limbo of all forgotten formations, by writing the convenient term " Pre-historic time " over the events of the non-Aryan people. We see that the Vangas, previous to their being influenced by the Aryan civilisation, created a history in this world. Far from therefore being ashamed, we are rather proud of this ethnical record, that those who have to be presumed to form the bulk of our population to-day, are the Vangas, who founded once a ruling house in An nam in Farther India.

Another fact of great historical significance relating to the early migratory movements of the people of Bengal has to be narrated from the records of the Dravidians of Peninsular India. Very ancient Tamil books inform us that many Nāga-worshipping tribes proceeded from Bengal as well as from other parts of Northern India to establish their supremacy in the Tamilakam country. Of these tribes, the Marans, the Cheras and the Pangala

Thiraiyar interest us most. The Cheras, it is stated, proceeded to Southern India from the north-west of Pangala or Bengal and established the "Chera" kingdom of much historical note. It is significant that the Cheras are mentioned in the old Brahman literature as occupying the eastern tract of the Magadha country. As to the Marans, who are said to have been the neighbours of the Cheras in Northern India, it is equally important to note, that the mighty Pandya kings claim to be of Maran descent. The Marans, who were also called Maravars, are reported to have been a very fierce and warlike people, and that they worshipped the goddess Kali on the top-knot of whose hair stood an infuriated cobra snake. The Pangala Thiraiyars are recorded as the latest immigrants, and it is narrated of them, that they proceeded from the sea-coast of Bengal by boat and founded the Chola kingdom at Kānchi. As the phrase Pangala or Bangala Thiraiyar is equivalent to তীর-বঙ্গ (Tīra-Vanga), we can assert unhesitatingly, that these people had received Aryan influence in Bengal before they left for the Madras coast. These traditional or legendary accounts may not be strictly correct in all their details, but the general story must be accepted as historical truth, since the ancient Tamil writers knew nothing of Bengal and its neighbouring tracts, when they recorded these traditional accounts. We shall see later on, that these accounts are quite in harmony with what will be narrated in a subsequent lecture.

Let me mention another fact of importance in this connection. It is narrated in the old Tamil books, that when the Nāga-worshipping tribes were colonising Southern India, the Makkalas were the principal and the most influential people in the South. As this Dravidian term Makkala or Makkaḍa could be easily transformed into Markata, I suppose the poet of the Rāmāyana was pleased to make monkeys of them. To do justice to the Makkalas, it must be mentioned, that they have a very high social status in the Tamil-speaking country and many aristocratic zamindar families belong to the clan of the Makkalas. It is reported, that these Makkalas once occupied those high-lands of Central India, which are included in the Daṇḍakāraṇya of the Rāmāyana. Be that as it may, these Makkalas once freely intermarried with the Nāga tribes and brought about racial homogeneity in many parts of Southern India. We associate nothing but rudeness and barbarity with the term non-Aryan; but adverting now to the momentous activities of the high class non-Aryan people of olden days, we should do well to change or modify our notions considerably.

We have noticed that the Thiraiyars, or the sea-coast people of Pangala or Bānglā, took a sea-route to proceed to Southern India; we also notice that the Bong people established a ruling dynasty in Annam when the Telegu people were influential in Burma. It will therefore be very reasonable to conclude, that the Vangas of ancient time were a sea-faring people, and reached the coast of Tonquin Bay by a sea-route.

LECTURE III

SECTION 2

The Geography of Old Bānglā and of other related tracts

In order to fix with some definiteness the land which was the principal home of the non-Aryan Vangas, let us follow the geography of the ancient time, as we find in the Mahābhārata and in the Purāṇas. I am strongly inclined to think, that the eastern portion of the indefinite tract which was once called *Kūlaka-vana*, and which once formed the eastern boundary of Āryāvarta, came to be designated as *Jhāḍakhaṇḍa* in comparatively later times. It is pretty clear that the name Jhāḍakhaṇḍa came to be associated with the tract which lay to the south of Gaya, to the east of Shahabad, to the south of Bhagalpur and to the west of Bankura and Midnapur. The temple of Baidyanāth at Deoghar in Bengal (now in Bihar), is still considered to be situated in the Jhāḍakhaṇḍa tract, for the priests of Baidyanāth recite a mantra by indicating this geography, in worshipping the image of Baidyanāth. A portion of Jhāḍakhaṇḍa got the name Rāḍha or Lādha as we notice in the Jaina records. The Avāranga Sutta of the Jainas, though it narrates things of Buddhistic and pre-Buddhistic era, was composed at a time which may be regarded recent. According to the accounts of this book, the temple of Baidyanāth is in Rāḍha or Lādha country. The people who inhabited Rāḍha are described to be black-skinned and rude in manners, and are reported to have been fond of robbing the pious Jaina intruders.

In the Brahmāṇda section of the Bhaviṣya Purāṇa, the whole tract lying to the north of the Dārukeśvara river and extending along the Panchkot hills, has been called the Rāḍha country and the temple of Baidyanāth has been mentioned as existing in that tract.

That the main portion of the Bhagalpur Division was designated as Anga country, is well established now, and there is no need of demonstrating it here. It has also been well ascertained that the Suhma country which had Dāmalipti or Tāmralipta for its capital, must be identified with a very considerable portion of the district of Midnapur. We get in the Mahābhārata, that the five sons of Bali were the progenitors of the allied races of the Angas, the Puṇḍras, the Vangas, the Suhmas, and the Kalingas (Adi, C. IV, 4217-21). All these tribes have been so described in the Mahābhārata, as to indicate that they lived in close proximity to one another. The Puṇḍras have been mentioned as Suhmottaras in the Matsya Purāṇa, and in the Mahābhārata too, the Puṇḍras and the Suhmas have been placed near to each other (Adi, C. XIII, 24, 58). No doubt the Puṇḍras proceeded northward subsequently, and founded Puṇḍravardhan in North Bengal, but their early distribution points to the fact, that they occupied the tract of Bengal which lies to the north of Midnapur.

The account we get of Bali Raja from the Dravidian source should interest us all. The Hindu account is that Śrikrisṇa by resorting to a godly trick sent Bali, to Pātāla or Nether world. It is interesting that Bali, who was a Daitya, is worshipped in Southern India as an ideal Raja of the good old days, and there is a town by the sea-coast of the name Mahabalipuram over which Bali presides. Bali is called Mābali or Mahābali, and there is a religious festival of high importance to celebrate his memory in the Malayalam tract of the Madras Presidency; this

5

festival is called Onam. It is narrated, that no one ruled the earth with so much justice as Bali did, and all sorts of sins and iniquities were unknown in his time. The song that is sung at the Onam festival, relates these accounts; two lines of it are given here, which purport to say that in Bali's time theft and other crimes were unknown:

Māveli nadathu bajjum kalam
Kalla khedilla kalabhu milla

You can clearly see that it is the Southern country which is our Pātāla, and the Pauranic account relates to the invasion of the country by the Aryans. That Bali was considered to be the forbear of the Vanga people as well as of other allied races, shows that the non-Aryan origin of all these races was fully known to the Aryans. That Bali's queen gave birth to Anga and his brothers, was narrated to Hiuen Tsiang when he was at Monghyr. The feminine form of Bali as Bali-amma, is the name of the principal goddess of the Sinhalese and the Vaeddas of Ceylon; her consort Kande has assumed now the name Skanda because of Tamil-Hindu influence.

Let us now halt to consider a point of ethnic interest. The writer of the passages occurring in the Mahābhārata and the Purāṇas as relate to the history of the non-Aryan tribes, did not certainly make a scientific ethnological study of the tribes in question, but the facts narrated above justify us in holding that they carefully observed and noted some important points of agreement and difference between those tribes. The Angas, the Vangas, the Puṇḍras, the Suhmas and the Kalingas were noted in the first place as tribes perfectly distinguishable from one another, and in the second place as peoples closely allied to one another. It was noticed that they were all Nāga-worshippers and that they were all the sons of Bali. Regarding Nāga worship, I may remark in passing, that the story of Behulā commemorates how the new-comers in the lands of the Angas and the Vangas had to accept and venerate the religious cult of the original inhabitants. We can see from the account we now obtain of Bali, that the name of the common ancestor of the tribes under review was not the creation of a fancy of the Aryans. It has been stated in the previous section, that those who proceeded to Southern India from Bengal, and its neighbourhood, had Nāga for their totem, and we have now seen that Bali is still worshipped in the Southern Presidency. The cumulative effect of the whole evidence is in favour of this supposition, that the original inhabitants of Bengal were by race and habits allied to those who are now designated as Dravidians.

The Vangas who were always connected with the Puṇḍras and the Suhmas, must have occupied the tract of country which lay to the east of our modern Burdwan Division. The fact that the Pāṇḍavas conquered Vanga after subverting the Puṇḍras, and led their victorious soldiers to Suhma after devastating Vanga, supports this position fully (M. Bh., Sabhā, XXX, 23-25). We find also in the Raghuvamśa, that Raghu conquered the Vangas after finishing his task with the Suhmas, and planted his victorious banner in the midstream of the Ganges. The popular notion that Vanga, as described by Kālidāsā, should be identified with the modern Eastern Bengal, is erroneous. To clear up the point, I have first to note that in all old records we get the Vangas in close proximity to the Puṇḍras and the Suhmas; we may then refer to the historical fact, that when Suhma lost its old name and became a sub-province with the name Daṇḍabhukti, it became a Bhukti or sub-province of Banga. The Tirumalai inscriptions decide this point clearly and unmistakeably. It has been recorded in the inscriptions (*E. I.*, Vol. 9) that the celebrated Chola Raja first came upon Dakṣiṇa Rāḍha on crossing the northern frontier of Orissa; he then raided Vanga, and at a place in the north of Vanga (not in Barinda, nor in any other province) defeated the then Pāla Raja in a battle, and just after finishing that work came upon Uttara Rāḍha which was the adjoining country. It was from Uttara Rāḍha, *i.e.*, from the tract covered by the districts of Hooghly, Burdwan and Birbhum, that the adventurer proceeded to the coast of the greater Ganges on the other side of which lay Barinda.

What was the extent of this Vanga in olden days, has next to be ascertained. With reference to the geography of the Mahābhārata and the Purāṇas, we may say that the main portion of Northern Bengal and some portion of the district of Mymensingh were included in the Prāgjyotiṣa country or Assam, over a portion of which the Kirātas predominated. The Tripura country or the Chittagong Division was no doubt once under the sway of the Telegus of Kalinga, but as the Vangas also extended their influence over Annam in Farther India, their extension in the Tripura country in the dim past cannot be very much doubted. It is highly interesting that not knowing them to be the relics of bygone days, the present ruling chiefs of Tippera use the ensigns of those old rulers who are now almost forgotten in history. The ensign bearing the representation of a fish and the pān or betel-leaf-shaped ensign are used among other ensigns on ceremonial occasions. Let me mention, that fish has always been a subject of veneration and an emblem on the royal banner of a powerful section of the Dravidians, and a broad leaf is the emblem of the Kirātas, who now reside in the wild tracts of Cachar. As to the eastern limit of Vanga, we have obtained a rough and indefinite idea only. We have to approach this point again, after considering some other facts which are important for the history of our language.

In the Vṛhatsamhitā of Barāha Mihira (6th century A.D.), Vanga is mentioned by the name Samataṭa but no definite geography is indicated; all that we know is, that Samataṭa lay between Utkala and Mithilā. This statement tends to show, that even as early as the 6th century A.D., one general name Samataṭa could be used for all the provinces of Bengal, as lay between Orissa and North Bihar. In this connection it is interesting to learn, that in the enumeration of some tribes of minor importance, dwelling in the Rāḍha country on the Bengal frontier, the Purāḍas have designated the tribes as *Pravangas*. The extension of the name Vanga to the Rāḍha country, is clear in this statement. Let us then refer to the accounts of Hiuen Tsiang who is not much removed in time from Varāha Mihira. The celebrated Chinese traveller went from Champā in Bhagalpur to a place called Kie-chu-ho-khi-lo which was 400 *li* from Champā to the east. The traveller or pilgrim kept the hilly or jungly tracts of Rajmahal to the right, and proceeded to this place, following the stream of the Ganges. No identification of this place has yet been made, but this country or province appears to have been composed of the northern portion of the Burdwan Division, the whole of the district of Berhampore and a considerable portion of the district of Nadia, since, going from this country eastward and crossing the Ganges after trudging the distance of about 600 *li*, Punḍrabardhan was reached. At this time Kie-chu-ho-khi-lo contained six or seven Buddhistic monasteries and there were 300 Buddhist priests there.[1] It has been

---

[1] Kuchiākol is a familiar village name in this tract; it is not unlikely that such a name the capital town of this province or political unit bore in the 7th century A.D.

stated that the people were fond of learning and were simple and honest. It is reported that the people spoke a dialect of the Midland language. By "Midland" the Magadha country is meant. Existence of ten Hindu temples was also noticed by the traveller. It appears from his description, that the country had then only recently lost its independence and was being governed by the king of a neighbouring country, before Śilāditya Harṣavardhan annexed it to his kingdom. It will be presently seen, that the Rāḍha country was at this time being ruled by Raja Śaśānka or rather by his descendants who were sworn enemies of Harṣavardhan. I think therefore, that the neighbouring Raja who then dominated Kie-chu-ho-khi-lo was, of the family of Śaśānka *alias* Narendra Gupta. The description that somewhere on the northern portion of this country, not far from the Ganges, was a high tower made of bricks and stones, and that this structure was ornamented with rare sculptures, and on the four faces of the tower there were sculptured figures of the saints, Devas and Buddhas in separate compartments, is of great archæological interest. Looking to the fact that wild elephants roamed about on its southern frontier, it may be supposed that between Samataṭa (which stretched along the coast of Bay of Bengal) and Kie-chu-ho-khi-lo, lay a tract covered with wild vegetation, which could invite the wild elephants of Rajmahal hills. Who knows that Banagrām (now the headquarters of a sub-division) does not carry in its name the memory of the old physical aspect of the locality?

The description given of Puṇḍravardhan of rather vast area, shows that a very considerable portion of Northern Bengal was then under the influence of the culture of Magadha country, and that this country extended to the frontier of Assam. It is to be noted, that the culture of

Magadha which prevailed over all parts of Bengal, was absent in Assam, where Buddhism could not make any impression. This phenomenon partly explains why the Assamese speech was not then exactly identical with that of Northern Bengal. The people of Assam of those days are reported by the traveller to have been "of small stature and of dark-yellow complexion"; this description leads me to think, that the Mongolian element predominated then in Assam, and because of this ethnic character, the language of mid-India became slightly different in Assam. Hiuen Tsiang then goes to Samataṭa of Bengal, after travelling a very long distance from Kamrup. As particulars of that route are not on record, the geography remains incomplete as to the extent of Vanga to the east. But it seems to be implied in a statement, that the hilly tracts of Tippera and Chittagong which were not visited by the traveller, were included in the Samataṭa country, for the traveller speaks of those tracts, when describing the Samataṭa country, as a wild country difficult of access. Another fact is quite clear, that just to the west of Samataṭa was the Suhma country. This tallies exactly with what we inferred regarding the geography of old Bengal from ancient Indian records. It must be specially noted, that the influence of Buddhist priests and Magadha culture were as extensive in Samataṭa as they were in Suhma, Kie-chu-ho-khi-lo, Puṇḍravardhan and Karṇasuvarṇa. The Puṇḍras, the Suhmas, and the Vangas, who were kindred tribes, were dominated by one and the same cultural influence, during the seventh and very likely during the sixth century A.D.

Śaśānka or Narendra Gupta who annexed some portions of Orissa and Ganjam to his empire, had his principal seat at Karṇasuvarṇa in the seventh century A.D. This Karṇasuvarṇa was no doubt located somewhere to the south of the wild tract which stretched forth from the Rajmahal hills, since going 700 *li* north-west from Tāmralipta, Karṇasuvarṇa was reached. Having narrowed down the limits of different provinces with the help of Hiuen Tsiang's topographical survey, it may be safely asserted that Karṇasuvarṇa was the capital of the Rāḍha country, in the seventh century A.D. The records of moral and intellectual advancement of the people of Karṇasuvarṇa, as left behind by Hiuen Tsiang, justify us in making this inference, that all over the country which forms now the presidency of Bengal, the influence of the Magadha civilization of the seventh century A.D. did effectively and extensively prevail.

I have related several facts which have some bearing upon the province which is now known by the name Orissa; it will be necessary also to relate what relation subsisted between Bengal and Orissa, to explain some points of linguistic unity between the languages of those provinces. I have just now mentioned that Śaśānka *alias* Narendra Gupta annexed some portions of Orissa, but it must be stated that his influence can only be traced in Kongada (*i.e.*, over the Puri district) and in some parts of Ganjam, where Oria language now prevails. It must be made clear, that the Kalinga country of historical note and the territories of Śaśānka had no connection with the land, which was possessed in ancient time by the tribes which got the names Oḍra and Utkala. With reference to the people of that part of Orissa, which was within the range of Śaśānka's influence, we get this account from Hiuen Tsiang, that with respect to their written characters, they were the same as those of Mid-India, but their language and mode of pronunciation were quite different.

It is a significant fact, that we do not get a well-defined country bearing the name Utkala in the Mahābhārata though the situation of Kalinga to the south of Suhma and Vanga, is rather well defined in many parts of that work. In the Viṣma Parva for instance (IX, 348), the Utkalas have been mentioned as rude people, and nothing has been stated regarding their owning any country in an organised form. Vanga seems to have been in olden times connected with Anga on one side, and with Kalinga on the other; for the Angas, the Vangas, and the Kalingas are found constantly linked together in the Mahābhārata, as people closely allied by race and position. [*Vide* for instance Drona Parva (Chap. LXX).] In the Purāṇas also the Utkalas have been distinctly mentioned as a rude tribe of very early origin, having no affinity with the races around them. (*Vide* Mārkaṇḍeya Purāṇa, Canto LVII, Hari-vamśa, X, 631-32.) From the description given by Kālidāsa in the 4th Canto of the Raghuvamśa, it becomes clear that just on crossing the river Kapisā, the country of the Utkalas was reached. Here too, there is mention of the Utkalas, *i.e.*, of a tribe but not of any country possessed by that tribe. The river Kapisā is the modern Kasāi or Kānsāi, which flows through the southern parts of both Chutia Nagpur and Midnapur. The Utkalas in Kālidāsa's days, had no political organization, for Raja Raghu had not to conquer the country of the Utkalas, and the people only showed the soldiers of Raghu their way leading to Kalinga. Again, in the Purāṇas the Utkalas have been mentioned in the east, near about the Bay of Bengal, and in the west, in connection with the wild tribes of Mekhala of the districts of Raipur and Bilaspur in the Central Provinces. It is also to be noted, that in the Purāṇas, the river Vaitarani is described to be flowing right through the Kalinga country. All these facts taken together lead us to suppose, that the hilly and wild tract of the Utkalas, extended from Nilgiri and Mayurbhanj to the borders of Bilaspur and Raipur, and that the Utkala country lay to the south of the river Kānsāi, and did not extend much to the south beyond the northern portion of the district of Balasore. The sea-board districts of Orissa were then within the Kalinga country, and the whole of the Kalinga country as far as the Godāvari to the south, had the designation of Muḍu (three) Kalinga. This Muḍu Kalinga became Trikalinga in the language of the Aryans, and the people who had their sway over the country, got the name Trikalingas or Telingas or the Telegu people. Thus we see, that a very long and narrow strip of land, extending mainly through hills and forests, was recognised in olden days, as the land of the Utkalas. But about 200 years after the time of Kālidāsa, the political situation was much changed. A considerable portion of the district of Midnapur to the south, was no doubt still then a part of Utkala or Oḍra, but the bulk of the population continued to be the rude Utkalas, whom Hiuen Tsiang describes as uncivilised, tall of stature and of a yellowish black complexion. Some portions of the districts of Balasore and Cuttack, seem to have been included at this time in the Oḍra country, and the Rajas having their seat somewhere in the district of Midnapur (J. R. A. S., N. S., Vol. VI, p. 249) presumably governed the newly formed Utkala country, during the seventh century A.D. That the capital town of Utkala, during the earliest days of Hindu influence, was in Midnapur, is fully supported by the statement of Hiuen Tsiang, that the capital of "U-cha" (Utkala) was over 200 miles to the north of "Kongada" country. It has now been established by the discovery of old inscriptions that, the district of Puri bore the name Kongada in the seventh century A.D., and Śaśānka *alias* Narendra Gupta of Karṇasuvarṇa was about then its mighty lord. The country of Kalinga became limited at th time to the territories where Telegu is now spoken

LECTURE IV

SECTION 3.

Gauḍa, Rāḍha and Vanga

It is regrettable, that it is too often assumed by some Bengali scholars devoted to historical research, that in the tenth century and earlier, the name Gauḍa signifies Bengal. That the name Gauḍa is of comparatively recent origin, and that we do not meet with the name during the time of the Imperial Guptas, must be admitted by all. In the Calcutta edition of the Matsya Purāṇa (Ch. XII, 30), it has been stated that Śrāvasti, was founded in the Gauḍa deśa by Rājā Śrāvasta, son of Yuvanāśva of the Ikṣāku family.* The date of this passage is unknown, but it can be said that for the well-known town Śrāvasti to have been founded by the Rājā in the Gauḍa deśa, Gauḍa must have been lying to the north of Kośala and to the north-west of Mithilā. That this was the geography of Gauḍa in the eighth century A.D., is perfectly clear from poet Vākpati's description in his Gauḍa-vaho Kābya. The hero of the poem first proceeded against the king of Magadha who was also the Lord of Gauḍa, and after having slain him, led his army against the king of Bengal, whose territory lay far to the east near the sea coast (verses 413, 417, 418 and 419). On noticing the fact, that Yaśovarman did not proceed to any other part of Bengal, and some time

* On reference to the text of the Purāṇa, it will be unmistakably seen that the old Kośala country of the Ikṣākus, has been described and place names in Oudh and its neighbourhood, have been strictly discussed; there will then be no room for supposition, that this reference to Śrāvasti is to any other Śrāvasti of any other province lying outside the Oudh territory.

after his return home at the termination of his warlike expedition, went straight to Oudh to erect a pillar at Ayodhya, to signify his already accomplished conquest of Magadha *cum* Gauḍa, we cannot but be inclined to hold, that Gauḍa at this time lay to the north of Magadha.

The meaning or import of the word Gauḍa is not very clear. Those who keep cattle and sell milk are called Gauḍa in Orissa; here this term must either be the Apabhraṁśa form of Gopāla or a slightly changed form of the Vedic word Gaura which meant wild ox as well as buffalo. If the origin of the name has anything to do with the term Gopāla, we may identify Gopāla Kakṣa of Mahābhārata with the Gauḍa country of our inquiry, since Gopāla Kakṣa is placed near about Kośala, and not far away from the Kauśīki Kaccha or the valley watered by the Kuśī (M. Bh., Sabhā, XXX, 3). The evidence of the Purāṇas is in support of this identification. We get the name of a tribe called Gomanta (those who keep cattle) just after the name of the Magadha people, in the enumeration of the eastern tribes in the 44th verse of the 57th chapter of the Mārkaṇḍeya Purāṇa. In the Vāyu Purāṇa (XLV, 123), after enumerating the tribes of Assam and North Bengal, the Videhas and other tribes of north Bihār have been mentioned; in this enumeration the Govindas come after the Magadhas, while we get Gomanta for Govinda in the Mārkaṇḍeya. The geography of Gauḍa as indicated above and the presence of a tribe near about that Gauḍa with the name Gomanta or Govinda, persuade me to believe, that the word Gauḍa is derived from the name of a tribe who grazed cattle and kept dairy.

When Alberuni visited India, Thāneśwar was included in the Gauḍa country. Mr. Jackson has rightly observed with reference to this extension of Gauḍa country, that "this explains why the Sārasvat Brāhmaṇas of the holy Sarasvati are the Gauḍas *pare..cellence*, and why Gauḍa and Vaṅga are mentioned separately in the Barodā grant of 812 A.D. We find in the second volume of the Cochin tribes and castes by Mr. A. K. Iyer, that the Brāhmaṇas in that country who claim to be Gauḍa Brāhmaṇas, and have now no manner of knowledge of the geography of northern India, assert on the strength of their family tradition, that a place called Trihotrapur was their original home. This Trihotrapur must be identified with Tirhut or Terhot, which also once fell within the limits of Gauḍa. Mr. Iyer says, that these Brāhmaṇas still use some words in their speech, which belong to the Prākṛta of Magadha and Mithilā. I myself noticed, that the women of this sect of the Brāhmaṇas, wear a single Sāree like the women of Mithilā and Bengal, and do not dress themselves like the other Brāhmaṇa women of the southern country.

The political condition of Bengal from the latter half of the eighth century to the twelfth century A.D. during the supremacy of the Rājās, who on account of their having compounded their names with the word Pāla, are known as Pāla kings, has been clearly set out by Babu Rakhaldas Banerjee, in two easily available works. I shall therefore refer briefly, to those facts alone of that period, as have direct bearing upon my subject. The early Pāla rulers were principally lords of Gauḍa and Magadha, and ruled Bengal from their headquarters in Bihar. As a dependency or as an annexed province of Magadha *cum* Gauḍa, Northern Bengal which lies between Mithilā and Assam, could at this time be called Gauḍa or a part of Gauḍa, but it must not be forgotten, that in the Geography of the Purāṇas, Northern Bengal has always been mentioned as a tract lying outside the limits of Gauḍa and Mithilā. Let me cite an analogous case to explain the situation. When Orissa constituted a part of the Presidency of Bengal, the term Bengal could be found, in some works of history and geography, to signify Orissa along with Bengal proper; if because of such political inclusion of Orissa in Bengal, no portion of Orissa could be confounded with Bengal proper, no one will be justified to identify any portion of the Barinda country, with the Gauḍa Deśa of the 10th century, or of earlier times.

When the Westerners such as the Gurjaras and the Rāṣṭrakuṭas became supreme all over Bihar, the successors of Nārāyana Pāla, ruled over a limited area which is supposed to be the Rāḍha country, having lost Gauḍa and Magadha. When these successors of Nārāyana Pāla, lost their real dignity, Northern Bengal came into the possession of a Mongolian tribe, known in History as the Kāmbojas. Very likely these Kāmbojas came from Farther India, but no discussion on the point is here necessary. When Mahīpāla regained the possession of Northern Bengal, he styled himself as Gauḍeśvara in memory of the past glory of the family. True it is, that Mahīpāla and his successors regained subsequently a footing in Mithilā and Magadha, but the good old time did not return. Constant invasion of Bihār by the Westerners and the permanent domination of the province by some of them, wrought such changes as had far-reaching effect both in Bihār and Bengal.

We have seen that in Rāḍha, Puṇḍrabardhan, and Vaṅga, that is to say all throughout the country of Bengal, Māgadhi culture including the Māgadhi speech was prevailing since long; and now we see that at the transfer of the capital of the Pāla Rajas from Magadha to Bengal, the chance for a very free development of Māgadhi civilization in Bengal became very great. If we compare to-day, the eastern Bihāri speeches with Bengali on one side, and with what is called Western Bhojpuri on the other, we find that the Eastern Bihāri speeches, in their colloquial and vulgar form, agree in many essential points, with Bengali, and differ much from Western Bhojpuri. This fact has been noted by Hœrnle and Grierson. The fact is, that Bihār of to-day is altogether a changed country on account of the mighty influence of the Westerners, while Bengal continues to be the real heir and representative of old Bihar.

Incessant migrations and displacements of various tribes, make it uncertain as to which people formed the substantial lower stratum in Rāḍha, when the civilisation fostered in Karṇasuvarṇa, was humanizing the frontier lands of Vaṅga. The Puṇḍras are found mentioned in the Purāṇas, once in conjunction with the Suhmas and another time in North Bengal, on Assam frontier in the company of two other tribes, namely the Pravijayas and the Bhārgavas. It seems that the Puṇḍras thrived better in North Bengal, while in Rāḍha they could not secure any prominent position. Of the other tribes mentioned in the Mārkaṇḍeya Purāṇa, either under the general name the Pravangas (*i.e.*, the tribes of Vaṅga frontier), or as stray tribes such as Māla, Māhiṣika, and Mānabattika, we get to-day the representatives of the Māl people in Bānkura and Mānbhūm, and the Mānas or the Mānabattikas may only be surmised to have been the originators of the geographical name Mānbhūm.

The epigraphic records of a line of rulers of some parts of Orissa and Dakṣina Kośala, during the tenth and eleventh centuries, disclose some facts which are of real interest in the history of Bengal. I have given elsewhere these rulers, the designation Kośalendras, as their political activities lay principally in the Sambalpur tract.

These Kośala Guptas, though they originally came of the family of Śiva Gupta cf Rājim and Ratanpur (Chattisgarh Division, C. P.), their immediate ancestors, or rather the branch of the Kośala family to which they belonged, got something to do in ruling some parts of Bengal. It is found recited in the plates of Yayāti, who is the second ruler of this line (*vide* my paper in J.B. & O., March, 1916) that his father Janamejaya, and after him he himself, became Kośalendra as well as the lords of Trikalinga or the sea-board tracts of Orissa and Gañjam, and that the family to which they belonged, was a ruling family somewhere in Vaṅga, as clearly distinguished from Rāḍha and Varinda. These Kośala Guptas had a large number of Bengali Kāyasthas in their service (*vide* my paper Ep. I. XI), and in the course of their inroads into the Sambalpur tract, helped lots of Bengali people to settle permanently in Sambalpur, Sonepur and Bolāngir-Pāṭuā. The Tewars (or Tivaras or Dhivaras) who migrated from Bengal in large number, call themselves Boṅgālis, though in language as well as in other matters, they have become Oria, and do not even know where Bengal is. The Orias call it a Baṅgāli Paḍā, where the Tewars live. It is amusing to note that the Tewars who live now over 400 miles away from the farthest limit of Bengal, and do not know even a syllable of our language, returned Bengali as their language at the census of 1911, to the census officer of Bolāngir Pāṭnā. As we meet with the Kalitās in Northern Bengal, and also get a very large number of Kultās in the Sambalpur tract, and as the widely apart Kultās and Kalitās agree in many social customs, I throw out this suggestion, that a clan of the Puṇḍras bore the caste name in question, and those of them who did not proceed to North Bengal, got into the Sambalpur tract, in the time of the Kośalendras, as Śūdra cultivators.

That a large number of Aryanised people was necessary for the new Rājās in a backward country, full of aboriginal tribes, cannot be much doubted.

I shall show what indelible marks our language put upon the Oria speech, as prevails in the Sambalpur tract, when in a subsequent lecture, I shall take notice of the old forms of our language. The epigraphic records of Bengal proper, of the Kośala Guptas and of the Chola kings, have amply proved that even during the time of the later Pālas, the different parts of Bengal bore different country-names of Varendra, Uttara Rāḍha, Dakṣina Rāḍha and Vaṅga, though the general name Vaṅga prevailed as the country-name over all the tracts. It is only to be noted that, Suhma which lost its name long ago, became then a province of Vaṅga, and the tract covered by the Kantāi subdivision, got th name Daṇḍabhukti and became a Bhukti or subdivision of Vaṅga.

Some facts which reveal the plasticity of the society of Bengal, during the time of the Pālas and Senas, may be noted, to examine the old formative elements of our population. I have just spoken of the Bengali Kāyasthas, as were in the service of the Kośala Guptas; these Kāyasthas with their surnames Ghosa, Dutta, and Nāga, have described themselves as Rāṇakas, that is to say, as descendants of the *Anabhiṣikta* families of the Rājās of Kośala, who must be regarded as Kṣatriyas. The Kośala Guptas were Kṣatriyas, even though their remote ancestor comes of a clan of the Śabaras, since from Tibaradeva downwards, the Rājās of this line formed their marriage alliance with the recognised Kṣatriya families of Northern India; the Rājās of Kośala and their descendants, assumed the title Gupta from the time of their connection with the Magadha Guptas. I may mention here that the rule or custom still continues in the Rāj families of Orissa, that the descendants of the Anabhiṣikta members of the Rāj family, become Bābus,* and these Bābus are employed as ministerial officers.

More interesting seems to me the history of the Vaidyas of Bengal, who like the Kāyasthas are in no way inferior to the Brahmaṇs, in intellectual powers and moral virtues. The term Vaidya, we all know, is singularly peculiar to Bengal, to indicate a *caste*; this term for medical profession may be assumed, by any man of any caste from Brahmaṇ downwards, in other parts of India. It is an interesting history, how a high class of people got Vaidya as a caste-name in Bengal. As the Vaidyas acknowledge universally, because of their family tradition, that their origin has to be traced from the Sena Rājās of Bengal, we should see what history we may get of the origin of these Senas.

That the Senas described themselves as Karṇāṭa Kṣatriyas, *i.e.* the Kṣatriyas of the Dravidian country, is well known. Referring to these Senas and the rulers of their kin, who once became supreme in the Northern Mithilā, Mr. R. D. Banerjee writes in the Memoirs of the Asiatic Society of Bengal, Vol. V, No. 3 :—

The invasion of the Coḷa King did not change the political divisions of the country, but it left one permanent mark in the shape of a body of settlers, who occupied the thrones of Bengal and Mithilā, as the Sena and Karṇāṭa dynasties, during the latter days of the Pālas (p. 73). To unveil the mystery of the warlike people who came with Rājendra Cola and settled in Western Bengal,

---

* The term Bābu is a diminutive of Bābā and is a term of endearment generally ; the Bengali word Bāpu to signify this meaning is of similar origin being derived from Bāpā ; Bāpā is another variant of Bāpu.

we have to peep into the history of some castes of Southern India.

Regular Brāhmaṇic supremacy and the settlement of new Brāhmaṇs in Southern India, commenced no doubt from the 10th century A.D., when Jaina supremacy came almost wholly to an end, but Brāhmaṇic ideas had commenced to prevail over Jainism nearly a century earlier, to pave the way for the new condition of things, which dates from the 10th century A.D. Very likely those who had priestly functions in the Jaina temples, assumed Brāhmaṇic rank during the earliest period of Brāhmaṇic influence, for we get such genuine Dravidian sects as the Kammalas and the Visva-Brāhmaṇs, who though not recognised by the modern Brāhmaṇs as men of Brahmaṇic order, do return themselves as Brāhmans, and perform priestly functions, in the houses of many people of lower order. The Vellālas, who were superior to the sects named above, and who were known for their military prowess, became Brāhmaṇs some time earlier than the 10th century A.D. As to the derivation of the term 'Vellāla,' there are two views; according to one it comes from 'Vellam' (flood) and 'alam' (ruler). According to the other derivation the word comes from 'vel' the god of war. Both these derivations suit the Vellālas who were once dominant people in the country. It is a historical fact, that these Vellālas of warlike disposition, studied the Vedas and performed fire-rights, when Brāhmaṇic influence commenced to grow in the land; on account of their knowledge or rather the study of the Vedas, they got the designation Vaidya in southern country. This term Vaidya does not signify or relate to medical profession. That besides being engaged in Vedic studies, the Vellālas or the Vaidyas, became military leaders and high civil officers of the Rājās, is what we know from the old records. Many

Vaidyas are known to have become the priests of the Dravidian Kings, and their occupying the situation of high class officers of the Coḷa as well as the Pāṇḍya Rājās, is also on record. It is also very significant to note, that the Vaidyas or the Vellālas who were not employed in the Rāj service as mentioned above, followed very generally the medical profession, though this profession did not give them the name Vaidya. In Southern India, the physicians were called *Ambaṭṭans* and not Vaidyas. The barbers once took largely to the medical profession, and now the barbers in general are called by the honorific name Ambaṭṭan, though the term does not really indicate the barber caste.

I strongly suggest that the Vaidyas of Bengal, owe their origin to the Vellāla Vaidyas, on reference to the above facts, which may be summarized as below :—

(*a*) The Vellālas were Vaidyas because of their Vedic studies, were recruited as high officers of the Rājās and were physicians very commonly.

(*b*) The Vellāla Vaidyas are known to have been in the service of the Coḷa Rājās.

(*c*) Those who came in Bengal at the time of the Coḷa invasion, described them as the people of Karṇāṭa.

(*d*) Those who claim to be the descendants of the Senas, are physicians by profession, wear Brāhmaṇical thread, call themselves Vaidya, and assert the right and privilege to read the Vedas.

(*e*) The term Vaidya as the name of a caste is unknown elsewhere in Northern India and is peculiar to Bengal alone.

Though the surname Sena can be easily explained without referring to any caste-name in the southern country, I may mention this fact that a section of the Vellāla Vaidyas in the Tamilakam country is known by the name Shānan. If my suggestion is not a bad one and may at least be considered arguable, I point out the fact that an early Rājā of the Sena dynasty had the name Ballāla, which is meaningless in a sanskritic language but is honorific in the South Indian speech, according to the derivation already given. I may consider another fact along with it. The name of the ancestor of the Senas, who first settled in Bengal is not known, but the claim of the Senas that they belong to the Candra Vaṁśa, has some reference perhaps to the name of their ancestor; that the first military leader, from whom the Senas trace their pedigree, bore the name Candra, appears pretty certain from what the poet Gobardhan Ācārya has written in his Āryā Saptaśati; the word রাকা (full moon) as occurs in the 39th verse is what I allude to here. The line of the verse stands as :—

সকল কলাঃ কল্পয়িতুম্ প্রভুঃ প্রবন্ধস্য কুমুদবন্ধোশ্চ।
সেনকুলতিলক ভূপতি রেকো রাকা প্রদোষস্য॥

To complete my survey of the races and tribes of different parts of the presidency of Bengal, who after adopting the speech which flowed in from Magadha and Mithilā, developed some provincial peculiarities in the language, I should mention, that the Indo-Chinese people of Farther India, raided Bengal from time to time. The sway which the people of the Mekhong Valley established once in Eastern Bengal is perhaps still commemorated in some geographical names. I suspect that the river Meghnā in eastern Bengal is the changed form of the name Mekhong. As to the Indo-Chinese origin of the name Dacca I do not entertain any doubt: the word Ḍhakkā means "old Ganges" in the language of the people of the Mekhong Valley, and we get the river Buḍi-Gangā, flowing past the town called Dacca.*

Lots of geographical names in the Bengal Presidency as well as in other parts of India, remain unexplained, and such names as Hooghly, Bentra, Tāki, Jāguliā, etc., appear meaningless to us, though it is perfectly certain that our meaningless geographical names had some meaning, in some forgotten speeches of past time. That the anthropologists and the philologists have collected a deal of information, regarding the old races and their languages, by rightly interpreting the seemingly meaningless geographical names, is perhaps too well-known. In Bengal it is a huge task fraught with numerous difficulties. In the first place, many old tribal dialects have now died out altogether; secondly, many names have been partly transformed into other names, because of the altered pronunciation of them, by people who speak now quite a different speech; and thirdly, in our mania to Sanskritise the old names, we have intentionally effaced the history which was impressed upon the old geographical names. As this subject requires a separate and independent treatment, I need not dilate on it any further.

---

* The Lāos have been the principal people of the Mekhong Valley; this induces me to suppose that the name Lāo Sen as a name of an old time Emperor of Bengal, is only a generalised form to indicate that the Lāu people once came into Bengal. The curious form of the name is altogether non-Indian, for Lāu (a gourd) is not likely to be the name of an anointed Hindu Emperor.

LECTURE V

The Influence of the Dravidian Speeches on Bengali

The Vedic or the Chāndasa speech was very much changed when the Brāhmaṇas were composed; the language of the Brāhmaṇas again differs widely in many essential particulars from what is called the classical Sanskrit, as well as from the speech which has unfortunately come to be designated by the name Pāli. That the later Prākṛtas and the provincial vernaculars, differ similarly from one another, as well as from the earlier speeches, is a well-known fact. Even the scholars who are mere linguists, and have only made a comparative study of all the speeches of N. India, without any reference to the characteristics of the speakers thereof, have not failed to notice, that the changes and deviations from the norm cannot be wholly explained by those laws, which the philologists have formulated, to account for all sorts of linguistic changes and modifications. The orthodox philologists have however been forced to admit, either directly or by implication, that the influence of some people other than the original speakers of the Aryan tongues, must have been at work in bringing about the aforesaid changes, though no particular non-Aryan people has been pointed out, from whom this influence emanated. Looking to the fact that cerebral sounds prevail very much in the Dravidian speeches, it has been vaguely asserted that some Dravidian people, as speakers of the Aryan speeches, induced dentals to be changed into cerebrals. Mr. Stenkonow's remarks on this point, as appear in the IVth volume of the Linguistic Survey of India, are very correct in my opinion. Since such a change of a dental into a cerebral is not wholly unknown in some Indo-European languages, Mr. Stenkonow considers quite possible, that the Indo-Aryan cerebrals developed quite independently, without there being any special inducing cause. Referring then to the phenomenon in the later Prākṛta speeches, that there is almost a wholesale change of dentals into cerebrals, the learned scholar offers a very reasonable suggestion which I quote in his own words :—

"The cerebral letters, however, form an essential feature of Dravidian phonology, and it therefore seems possible, that Dravidian influence has been at work, and at least given strength to a tendency which can, it is true, have taken its origin among the Aryans themselves."

It has not, however, been noticed by the philologists, that even though cerebral letters prevail very much in Dravidian speeches, these letters are never initials of genuine Dravidian words. No doubt, we observe this very peculiarity in the Vedic as well as in the earliest classical Sanskrit, but we notice that in later Sanskrit as well as in the Prākṛta speeches, there are many words, which though not onomatopoetic in origin, have cerebrals for initials. টঙ্ক (the top of the hill), ঠকুর or ঠাকুর (a word of respect), ডমরু (a musical instrument), and ঢুক (to signify entering into) are some examples. As India has been the home of diverse races of men, since remotest antiquity, it is difficult or rather unsafe to particularize definitely the influence of any special non-Aryan race, as the sole cause of any unusual linguistic change.

I must, however, notice in this connection, an important peculiarity of Bengali phonology, which has not to my knowledge, been noticed hitherto by any philologist. I have made it sufficiently clear in a previous lecture, that the people closely allied to the Dravidians, or rather who have to be presumed to be pure Dravidians, form the bulk of our Bengali-speaking population ; yet it is to be noted as a fact, that the cerebral letters are not so much cerebral as they are dental in our speech. If we carefully notice our pronunciation of the letters of the 'ট' class, we will see that we articulate 'ট' and 'ড,' for example, almost like English T and D without turning up the tip of the tongue much away from the region of the teeth. We can detect this peculiarity very clearly, if we compare our. sounds with those of the Mahrattas. As we articulate ড and ঢ more as dentals than cerebrals, we have been required to introduce two new consonants ড় and ঢ় to produce special cerebral sounds ; that for the latter sounds the letters ড and ঢ quite do in other Indian spęeches, is well known. This natural organic aversion to articulate cerebral letters with distinctness explains why the cerebral ণ is uttered wholly as dental ন, and why in some eastern districts ড় and ঢ় are wholly pronounced as র and হ্র ; in Eastern Bengal the letters are not articulated by the learners of the Alphabet, but their physical appearance is described as ড—এ শূন্য and ঢ—এ শূন্য letters.

I am perhaps creating new difficulties without seeking to explain things by a Dravidian influence. To be able to face all difficulties properly, is better than offering a plausible solution.

The phenomenon I have spoken of, may be partly explained by postulating a Kirānti influence ; but since when and to what extent this influence has been in existence, need be inquired into. The earliest reference to the Kirātas occurs in the Atharva Veda which discloses a good deal of knowledge of the eastern lands, from where the original form of our speech flowed into our country. We find in the Atharva Veda (X, 4. 14) that the Kirāta women were employed to dig out medicines for use as charms in the Himālayan region. That the Kirātas were mountaineers, is clear from some statements in the Vājasaneyi (XXX, 16, etc.) and in other later Saṁhitas. These hilly people have been mentioned however in Manu (X, 44) as Vrātya Kṣatriyas. We get in the Brāhmaṇa literature, in connection with the story of Asamāti, that the Kirāta priests, who knew charms came into prominence in the Aryan society. I cannot say if the dark yellow colour of skin ascribed to the Kṣatriyas in the Kāṭhaka (কাঠক) Saṁhitā, has anything to do with Kirāta (কিরাত) intermixture. The Kirāta cult of magical charms and mystic mantras being universal in Northern India, a special influence of the Kirātas in Bengal cannot be formulated.

It is true that in Eastern as well as in Northern Bengal, direct Mongolian influence can be formulated from some known facts of history. It is also true that the inability to articulate ড় and ঢ় occurs in some eastern districts only, but not in Northern Bengal. The consonants of চ class, however, are made very much palatal in Eastern Bengal, unlike what the Mongolians do, while these consonants are made semi-dentals or rather pronounced by almost closing the teeth, in Central Bengal. This question, however, will be discussed in a subsequent lecture.

It is really very curious, that some peculiarities which are doubtless due to Dravidian influence, have been sought to be explained by some eminent philologists by a cause other than the real one. Such an eminent scholar as Sir Ramkrishna Gopal Bhandarkar considers such changes in the oldest known Prākṛta, as ধম্মো for ধর্ম, সঙ্কপ্পো for সঙ্কল্প, সিলোক for শ্লোক, etc., to be due to the natural vocal tendencies of the Aryan speakers themselves. Explanation for these changes was not sought anywhere outside the mouth of the speakers, as the influence of the Dravidians who now reside far away from the limits of Northern India, could not be thought of forty years ago, when the Wilson

Philological lectures were delivered. The fact that the Dravidians could once be the neighbours of the Aryans in the Northern country, did not suggest to the scholars. I have mentioned before, that according to the Dravidian traditions, all the dominant tribes of S. India migrated from Northern provinces to Peninsular India. It is a distinct and a definite characteristic of essential nature, in the Tamil language, that an initial of a word can *never be formed of double consonants*, and compound letters formed of consonants of different Varga *can occur nowhere in a word.* If we refer the changes under consideration to the essential peculiarities of the Tamil speech, our problem will be solved. Compounding of র with ম as in ধর্ম and ল with প as in সঙ্কল্প cannot be tolerated according to this rule, and to maintain the long sounds of the compound letters in question, the very letters have to be doubled. This is how at first in Prākṛta, the consonants joined unto র were doubled by dropping the র or ´(রেফ), and then in giving Sanskritic form to the changed words additional ´(রেফ) was added, and the new rule was formulated that a consonant may be optionally doubled if it is joined unto a র in the shape of a ´(রেফ). If we compare the early Prākṛta forms or the so-called early Pāli forms with the later Prākṛta forms, we can see that as time went on, the Dravidian influence went on increasing; the early forms such as ব্রাহ্মণ, স্নেহ, etc., as have been considered to have been exceptions by Sir R. G. Bhandarkar, were reduced to বরাহ্মন or বেরাহ্মন and to সিনেহ or নেহ, etc., at a later time.

When, by about 1865, Bishop Caldwell suggested that the Tamil কু as a dative-denoting suffix was identical with Oriya কু, Bengali কে, and Hindi কো, denoting exactly the dative case, a host of critics rose up to throw away the right suggestion of the Bishop. Sir R. G. Bhandarkar clearly saw the mistake of Trumpp and Beams, but could not accept the suggestion of Caldwell, as he thought that a Dravidian language could not possibly influence the Aryan speeches in that manner. Trumpp suggested that কে of Bengali came from কৃতে and Beams rightly rejected the derivation, as কৃতে could not signify the sense conveyed by কে. Beams himself, however was wrong, when he sought to derive the suffix denoting the dative from old Hindi কহঁ. Sir R. G. Bhandarkar showed that as in no Prākṛta, either কৃতে or কহঁ (derived from কক্ষ according to Mr. Beams) signified any dative sense, the proposed derivation could not be accepted. Sir R. G. Bhandarkar is right that for many case-denoting suffixes we have to look to pronouns and pronominal roots, but his imaginary case that কেহি as well as তেহি *might have been in use* to signify instrumentality, and কেহিঁ might have been subsequently used to denote a dative case cannot be accepted, or rather may be easily rejected, by using the very argument with which the learned scholar himself has rejected the theory of Mr. Beams. Sir R. G. Bhandarkar's suggestion that কহঁ in a phrase as রাম কহঁ might mean at first " Rama's somewhere," and thence the sense " to give to Rama," might have originated, is very faulty as the old time forms do not warrant such transformation. The derivation would not have been sought in such a roundabout manner, if the cause of such changes as ধম্ম, সক্কপ্প and সিলোকো could then be rightly detected.

How the Dravidian people could influence the speakers of the Aryan speeches in dim past, should be a subject of special research. Many ethnological problems, relating to the Dravidians, have not yet been solved. The ethnologists of our time agree in the main, that the Dravidians have been autochthonous in India: even though this proposition is not free from doubts and difficulties, the situation of the Dravidians in India as neighbours of the Aryans, since the earliest time of Aryan activities, cannot be denied. Again, adverting to a list of the races of man, made out either by the ethnologists or by the linguists, we can see that the representatives of all races in greater or smaller number came to live in India, and did not find the country an uncongenial home. How the jetsam and flotsam of the floating races of the world were absorbed in the main body of the Indian population, is impossible now to ascertain. I cannot discuss all these questions here; but one fact relating to the range of influence of the Dravidians during the days of early migrations of peoples will be noticed here to draw the attention of scholars to some hither-to-neglected facts of great importance.

The ethnologists agree to some extent in holding that the old inhabitants of Etruria in Italy proceeded to the latter country from some parts of Asia-Minor. It is also very reasonably supposed that the language of the Etrurians did not belong to the family of speech which is generally known by the name Indo-European. Mr. Stenkonow has shown in his essay on "Etruscans and Dravidian" (J. R. A. S., 1912) that there are many interesting points in which the language of the Etruscan follows the same principles as that of the Draviḍas. It is interesting to note, that the plural-forming suffixes 'gal' and 'ar' of the Dravidians are in existence in Italy, the Etrurian verbs like those of Malayalam do not change for number, and words in genitive case are freely used in Etrurian as adjectives. We shall see that all these Dravidian and Etruscan characteristics, are distinctly noticeable in Bengali language. If the Dravidians have been autochthonous in India, their migration to western countries indicates a state of their early social condition, which has not been hitherto considered. The influence of this people upon the proud Soma-pressers and their successors cannot make us wonder. I am concerned, as my subject indicates, with the Dravidian influence on the Bengali language; as such I give a few examples only to show that our early speeches were not also free from the Dravidian influence. Patanjali's Mahābhāṣya proves that much was done to maintain the purity of the classical Sanskrit: yet borrowing of words from Dravidian sources could not be altogether stopped. (1) In genuine colloquial Tamil (which is called Kudam) the word মালা signifies flower; this word to indicate a garland, does not occur in the Vedic speech and we first meet with মালা or মাল্য in the Upanishads, which were written in the land of the Kosalas and Videhas. (2) গুররা—মু properly গুররা of Telegu speech became ঘোড়া as a deśi word; this ঘোড়া was no doubt Sanskritised into ঘোটক for such a synonym of অশ্ব is unknown not only in the Vedic, but also in old Sanskrit. In the district of Barisal the Telegu pronunciation of the word as গুর্‌রা is maintained. (3) মলৈ signifies a mountain in the Tamil as well as in the Malayalam language; very likely in the 3rd century B.C., when the Aryans after some acquaintance with the people of the south, confounded the general name for a mountain, with the name of a particular mountain, a মলয় গিরি (tautology) was made the seat of the spring breeze flowing from south. (4) মীন as a word to signify 'fish' was unknown not only in the Vedic speech but also in very old classical Sanskrit, but this মীন or fish which was on the ensign of the Pandyas and was the name of the Dravidian tribe Minavar, became a synonym for মৎস্য and fish-god as well, very likely when the Pandyas established some relation with the northerners. 'Mina' of Tamil is also Min in the Kui dialect of the Kands, and Minu in the Canarese tongue. We meet also with many Dravidian words in Pāli; I cite only two examples here:

আ—ম indicates 'assent'; this is exactly the meaning of the Tamil word আম, ইঙথ signifies 'come here' in the imperative mood. Compare Tamil ইঙ্কে, Mahrati ইংকড়ে and Telegu ইক্ড়া indicating the same meaning. But occasional word-borrowing does not signify much. I proceed to notice now such Dravidian words as are in use in Bengali, as imply a very close and intimate relationship, between the Dravidians and the so-called Aryans of Bengal. Those words which may be borrowed in consequence of the existence of a trade, or on account of some occasional social touch, will not be included in the list; for example we have got ঝিঙ্গা (S. জ্যোৎস্নী, Oriya জহ্নি) and বঁইটি (kitchen knife) of Mundari which can be explained by occasional touch in market places. Some words, common to Bengali and Dravidian, however, which are extremely indecent, and which cannot be traced to any classical origin, and which one people can learn from another if both of them happen to be close neighbours, are of importance; but they cannot certainly find a mention here. I think the list of words I append below, will go a great way to establish the social influence of the Dravidians upon us, in a past time.

N.B.—In the following list T. stands for Telegu, Tm. for Tamil and B. for Bengali.

(1) আকালি (Tm. and T.) hunger, Gondi আকাল (famine). B. আকাল (famine); that it is not from Sanskrit অ+কাল will be presently discussed. (2) কল্ Tm. stone is also pronounced as খল্; it is গল্ in Ceylon; there is only one letter in Tm. for ক খ গ and ঘ; our খল্ (a mortar) was originally of stone only and hence the name. This word occurs in Sanskrit as an inseparable portion of the word উদুখল. (3) কাই (Tm.) vegetable in general, as in কাই—কারি (from কারি comes B. তরকারী and Anglo-Indian curry); or as in পুলি—কাই (tamarind); we can see that from পুলি—

কাই came the simple obsolete Bengali word কাঁই to signify tamarind; কাঁই রিচি still signifies tamarind seed. (4) কুদ (Tm.) to leap; this word is of general use in northern India. (5) কোকা and কোকি son and daughter as in কোকাই—হাড়, কুক্‌কি—হাড়, B. খোকা and খুকি are derived from them. The E. B. equivalents are exactly কোকা and কুকি. The Mundari কোড়া and কুড়ি are perhaps in existence in Eastern Bengal in the form of কোদা and কুদি. (6) খাড়াল sea in Tm.; it is very significant that our বঙ্গ উপসাগর is called খাড়ি. The very word খাড়াল is in use in some parts of Bengal to indicate the stagnant portion of a river which may fitly be called a pool. (7) খুট্টা (Tm.) to pick up or gather = খোঁটা to pick up in B. (8) খাট্টা Tm. to bind, the upper edge of our lower garment when tightened around the waist and a portion is tucked in to fasten the tie is called খেঁাট্. (9) খাট্টাই (Tm.) a piece of wood or fuel; compare B. খোঁটা a peg and E.B. খাটুয়া (pronounced in Jessore as খাট্ উ অ) a log. Compare E.B. খড়ি fuel or fire wood; there is also another word খাড়ু in Tm. to signify forest. (10) গান্ড্রা গোল T. a tumult or noise = B. গণ্ডগোল. (11) গোন্দু (Tm.) Gum = B. গঁদ. (12) গোড়া T. wall, hence basis or foundation. B. গোড়া indicates beginning or lower or base portion of a thing. (13) চাপা (T.) a mat (is pronounced as scāpā; there is only one letter for চ and শ in Tm. = শপ of B. as in শপ চাটাই. (14) চক্‌কণি T. beautiful = চিকন of B. as in 'চিকন কালা' or চেকনাই (15) চিন্না T. and Tm. = small. The old use of this word may be noticed in চিনাজেঁাক or চিনেজেঁাক a tiny leech. In certain parts of Bengal the form has been wrongly reduced to ছিনেজেঁাক. The Oria form of the word is সা—ন and in Nepalese also the word is in use in that sense and form. In the district of Sambalpur the third brother who is next below মাঝিয়া (lit. middle) or the second brother is called সান মাঝিয়া and sometimes in the contracted form সান—জিয়া or সাঁজিয়া which corresponds exactly with সেজো of B. as in সেজ দা, both in form and meaning, and so the word সান্ is imbedded in the word সেজো. (16) চোল্লাম (Tm.) maize, in T. common name for grain of gram class; ছোলা of B. comes from it, the Sanskrit name for which is চণক. (18) তা—লা T. and তালৈ Tm. head, we get in such a phrase as মাথার তেলো, Sanskrit তালু bears another meaning and has no connection with it. (19) তাল্লি T. and তায় Tm. signifies mother or one of the rank of a mother. It is interesting to note that the word আম্মা is also used to signify the same meaning. We have the words তালই or তাওয়ই in masculine and আমৈ or মাঐ in feminine to indicate respectable persons who are of the rank of father and mother. (20) নিজ্জম্ (T.) true, compare নিজ্জস্ of B. (21) পালু (T.) or পাল্ Tm. milk, in the word 'পালান্' signifying 'udder' of a cow, this word is retained in B. (22) পট্টু T. and Tm. silk and silk cloth. *Cf.* পাট, পট্ট বস্ত্র (23) পিল্লই Tm. or পিল্লা (T.) a child; occurs in some compound words in B. as in ছেলে পিলে, in E. B. পোলা is in use. (24) পিল্লি (T.) cat = বিলেই Oria and Kui = E. B. বিলাই (even in old Sanskrit বিড়াল is unknown, the word was মার্জ্জার ; বিলার or বিলাল or বিরাল of Pāli comes from Dravidian; in B. বিড়াল and বেড়াল are in use). (25) বা—ন (T.) rain = B. বান flood. (26) বা—না Tm. flag, same in Oria and same in old B. as in Chandidāsa. (28) মো—ট (T.) (pronounced, as it should be as মোটা, মোটই Tm.), a heavy bundle of luggage, same in B., in the district of Sambalpur it is pronounced as মোটা following Dravidian pronunciation. (29) তাণ্ডু as in ওয়ালে—তাণ্ডু the central stem like solid portion of banana plant. B. থোড় seems to be derived from 'তাণ্ডু.' It is curious that banana flower and this তাণ্ডু or থোড় are used as vegetable food in Bengal and in the Madras Presidency only.

Those who try to trace all our words to some Sanskrit origin, may on reference to the foregoing list suggest some Sanskrit words for the Dravidian words depending upon very remote sound similarity; for instance the word আকালি may be rejected, as the Sanskrit word কাল may anyhow be made to be a component of আকাল. With a view to point out the right method that has to be pursued in such an enquiry, let me show that the suggestion of the Sanskritists on the point will be wrong. We do not get any word, either in Sanskrit or in the old Prākṛtas, which has 'কাল' for stem to signify the idea conveyed by দুর্ভিক্ষ (famine). What led our ancestors then, to coin a new word in Bengali agreeing with Tamil and Gondi, to express an old and familiar idea, is difficult to imagine. It is curious that the word which was current in Prākṛta was given up and an unidiomatic expression was introduced in a slovenly way by joining আ and কাল together. If আকাল be said to be a corruption of অকাল the argument will not be stronger, for no Sanskrit or Prākṛta lexicon will give us the word অকাল to signify famine. A word may anyhow be made to look like a Sanskrit form, but it is to be seen whether such a form or its prototype was at all in common use in old time. In their zeal to derive all Bengali words from Sanskrit roots and stems, such old and obsolete words are at times drawn out of the Sanskrit Dictionary as were not even in use in Sanskrit for centuries previous to our time. We cannot avoid looking to the people and their antecedents in our inquiry relating to language. Let me also cite an example of contrary character to illustrate the right method of getting a derivative. The word সাঁকো (bridge) looks like a deśi word and is treated as such, for it is difficult to see that the word comes from সং+ক্রত. With our knowledge of Oria we can see that সঙ্ক is the Oria word for a bridge which is in a less decayed or অপভ্রংশ form. One who knows Pāli cannot fail to notice that the Pāli word সংখত derived from সং+কৃত is the adjective form from which সঙ্খ as noun came out; সংখত in Pāli signifies 'put together' 'constructed,' 'prepared.' That we are not to follow sound alone, but have to look to many other facts in this sort of research, is what I want to impress upon you all.

I have spoken of some essential grammatical peculiarities of the Dravidian language as have been detected in the Etruscan speech of Italy; that these very peculiarities are noticeable in Bengali, is a highly interesting fact to take note of. As to this phenomenon that as in Dravidian and in Etruscan, the Bengali verbs do not distinguish between singular and plural, nothing beyond a mention of the fact seems necessary; as to the use of genitive forms as adjectives such idiomatic expressions as এক—এর নম্বর জুয়াচোর (first-rate cheat), তিন—এর ভাগ (third part) সুখের খপর (happy news) গোলের কথা (a complicated affair) ঝালের মাছ (a dish of fish hot in preparation), etc., may be referred to. The use in Bengali of the Dravidian plural forming suffixes 'gal' and 'ar,' must however be explained carefully. That গুলি or its variant গুলা (in use in Beng. and Oriya only) comes from গল্ will be evident from the following facts: (1) In the Jataka stories composed in old Māgadhi Prākṛta or Pāli, we get পুপ্প—গল্ (lit. many flowers) to signify a nosegay; (2) in the Prākṛta works of later days, we notice such expressions as মত্ত—গল মাত্রা সমূহ বিষ—গল ম-অ গল, etc., as plural forms; (3) গুলি or গুলা of Beng. and Oriya signifies plurality exactly as গল্ does in Tamil and as it did in old Prākṛta as noted above. We notica that গুলা has assumed the form গিলা or গিলাক্ in that Bengali-speaking tract which is quite close to Assam; Mr. Laxmi Narayan Bejbarua has suggested to me that the Assamese বিলাক্ is very likely a variant of গিলাক্, since that Assamese form cannot be traced to any Mongolian sonrce.

That our plural-forming suffix রা originates from Tamil অর্ need be discussed next. We have to notice first that the plural form with রা is peculiarly Bengali as distinguished from Māgadhi, Oriya and Assamese. We have next to notice that neither any Prākṛita form, nor any provincial idiomatic use can be cited in support of the view that the possessive case-ending 'র' became the plural-forming suffix 'রা.' That this suffix was adopted in Bengali on the soil of Bengal, is quite evident; being a new suffix of vulgar or popular origin it was not much used in the literary language of olden days; the Editor of Sree Kṛṣnakīrtan has noted only three instances of its use in the whole book. One early use of the suffix exactly in the form of অর্ may be noticed in the formation of the word পয়ার (পদ=পয়+অর্) which signifies a couplet or verse of two lines. We will see that 'আ' became once a plural-denoting suffix in প্রাকৃত; that this 'আ' could naturally be compounded with অর্ to give rise to the suffix 'রা' can be easily formulated, since such compounding of different suffixes in the formation of one new suffix is noticeable in other cases: for example, 'ক' of অম্হাকম্ (অস্মাকম্), তুম্হাকম্, etc. was joined with honorific দীয় of মদীয়, তদীয় etc., and the whole portion (*i.e.*, দীয়+ক) was compounded with possessive-denoting 'র' to form the suffix দিগের. I shall have to discuss this question, over again, later on.

The position of negative-indicating particle না in a sentence in Bengali seems also to be due to Dravidian influence; in Chāndasa, in Sanskrit, in Pali and in later Prākṛitas, the negative-indicating ন has its place before the verb, and this idiomatic use is current in Hindi, while in the

Sanskritic Vernaculars of the tracts bordering on the lands of the Dravidians, this particle has its place after the verb; that Assamese is naturally expected to agree with Bengali and Oriya in this respect as well as in many other points of significance, will be explained in a subsequent lecture.

I have made out a list of hundred words which may be called দেশী and which cannot be traced either to any Sanskritic origin or to any other non-Aryan origin. On reference to this list as appears in the form of an appendix to this lecture, you will notice that in their physical appearance they do not look either like Dravidian words or like the Kirānti words. As many tribes have lost their original speeches and speak one form or another of the Aryan speech, it is difficult to get to the origin of these words. It is not the place where I can discuss the ethnological problems but I can say on the strength of some known facts of Southern India, that the word Dravidian does not cover the whole ground, when we take even those tribes into consideration, who speak uniformly one Dravidian speech. I purposely avoid here the question of fusion of races in Bengal. I notice here a very familiar saying of the Tamil country, that an *Akallan* became a *Maravan*, the *Maravan* became an *Agambadiyan* and an *Agambadiyan* became a *Vellalan*. That the tribes who are quite mixed up now spoke once different speeches, may be detected from such a phenomenon that, in the Tamil language there are 34 synonyms for the word 'wind,' 50 for 'water,' 35 for 'cloud,' 62 for 'earth' and 60 for 'mountain.'

We cannot dissolve a thoroughly mixed-up people into their original elements, but we can push on our research to see if the words of unknown origin and the terms of expressions not in agreement with the idioms of Aryan speeches or the idioms of the known Dravidian speeches, can be traced to some other origin or origins. I shall consider the influence of the Dravidian accent system in my next lecture when a comparative study of all the accent systems, Aryan as well as non-Aryan, will be specially dealt with.

Appendix to Lecture V

The following words of uncertain origin are given in two lists as owing to their nasal sound, the words on the first list (left hand side) seem to be different from those on the second list (to the right hand side), in the matter of origin.

List I.

(1) আঁচড় (a scratch), (2) আঁটকুড়িয়া, (in Bengal and Sambalpur, a man not blessed with progeny), (3) আঁটি, tight আটা (gum) seems to be connected, since আঁটা (to stick or to paste) is the verb form. (4) আড়ং, a market (আড়ং seems connected as it signifies a farm), (5) ইঁচড় or এঁচড়, a green or unripe jack fruit, (6) উরচুঙ্গ (in eastern parts of Jessore and in some parts of E.B. it indicates a cockroach), (7) ওঁৎ (as in ওঁৎ পাতা—said of an animal, addressing itself to swoop upon the object of prey), (8) কঞ্চি=branch of a bamboo, (9) কাঁড়া (the form is কাড়ণ্ড in Hemchandra's দেশী নামমালা)=husking or

List II.

(1) অজ্ (veritable as অজ্-পাড়াগেঁয়ে), (2) আলি, in Bengali and Oriya, a female friend of a female, (3) উই, white ant, (4) উলু, thatching grass, (5) কিল, a blow, (6) কুটা, a straw, (7) কুড়ি, twenty (is it connected with কপর্দ্দ কড়ি in its counting to the number making up a score unit ?), (8) কুলা, winnowing fan, (9) কোট্ (জিদ্) perverse or strong determination, (10) কোটি (used in Sanskrit but not in use in Vedic; it is to be noted that কোটি in vernacular form used as Crore, though normally a word made up of compound consonants is reduced to simpler form and not *viceversâ*), (11) খালুই,

APPENDIX TO LECTURE V—*contd.*

LIST I.	LIST II.

polishing, (10) কেঁচো, earthworm, (11) খাঁচা (a cage), (12) খেংরা, a broom, (13) গুঁড়া (a variant of গুণ্ডা)= dust-like particles, (14) গেঁড়, the stump or rather the hard upper portion of root. (15) চেংড়া (bearing almost the sense of a flippant); in E. B., a young boy, (16) চাঙ্গাড়ি (a basket, চাঙ্গোড়ি in Pāli), (17) চোঙ্গা, a pipe, (18) চোঁচ, a thin bamboo slip with sharp cutting edge, (19) চোঁতা (worthless), (20) জঙ্গল in Sans. also, (21) ঝাঁক, a multitude as in a flight of birds, (22) ঝাঁটা (a broom), (23) ঝাঁপ, a screen, and a sudden falling in water; (Oriya ঝাম্ in the latter sense and ঝম্প in pseudo-Sanskrit); Is ঝম্প an intensive variant of কম্প? (24) টেংরা as in হেঁটা (হেঁট=down) টেংরা (টেঙ্গর indicates high mound in Assamese; compare also টং, or টুঙ্গি, or টোঙ্গ a raised bamboo platform), (eel to

keep fish), (12) গড়ান, (to roll), (13) গাছ (গচ্ছ or গছ and গুচ্ছ or গোছা in Prākṛta and in vernacular equally of non-Sanskritic origin), (14) গাদা, a heap and also the dorsal portion of a fish, (15) গুটি or গুঁটি or ঘুঁটি (in Assamese and in Nepalese গুটি means a fruit, a fruit in its early stage is so called in Bengali; a small piece of hard clay or stone is also called a ঘুঁটি), (16) গোদা, a head or a leader as in পালের গোদা, (17) ঘুম (sleep) in Bengali and in old Oriya) may be from to dose which is *Dhama* S.; compare নিঝুন্ গেলা (he has slept) in Marathi, (18) ঘাড়, shoulders or neck. (19) চাল, a roof, (20) চাড় (compare Oriya চাণ্ড quickly) eagerness as in এ কাজে চাড় নেই, (21) চারা (young plant), (22) চুবড়ী (basket), (23) ছোট (may be a variant of খাট,—from খুদ্র we get খুল্ল as well as চুল্ল in old Prākṛt, from খুল্ল

APPENDIX TO LECTURE V—*contd.*

LIST I.	LIST II.
(25) ঠেঙ্গ, a leg, Hindi টাং, (26) ঠোঙ্গা, a cup made of leaves or of paper, (27) ডাঙ্গা, land as opposed to water (may be connected with either টেঙ্গর of Assamese or ডুঙ্গরি, a hillock of Gondi), (28) ডিঙ্গা or ডোঙ্গা, a boat (ডিগ্ is to leap as ডিঙ্গান or in ডিগ্‌বাজী), (29) ঢং, a fashion or a queer mode, (30) ঢেঁকি, husking machine, (31) ঢোঁড়া, (hollow) hence inoffensive as ঢোঁড়া সাপ, (32) নোংরা, unclean, (33) নাবস্তা (used in E. B. only=sham kindness), (34) পাঁটা, a goat (in Oriya the feminine form পেঁটি is in use), (35) পোঁটা (entrails of an animal), (36) ফড়িং, a grasshopper, (37) ফেচাং (a disturbing obstruction), (38) বেঁওং, also in Sambalpur, a careful handling, (39) বোঁচা, snub-nosed (40) বাঁকারি, a bamboo slip used, say for the thatch of a house, (41) বোঁচ্‌কা, a bundle, (42) ভড়ং, a show of	we may get খুট্টি or খাট and so from চুল্ল, ছোট্ট and then ছোট, (24) ছড়া a verse and sprinkling of water, (25) ছিপ্ (a fishing rod), (26) জড়, root, (27) ঝাড়, forest, (28) টাক, baldness, (29) টোপ, a bait, (30) টোল a school, (31) ঠাকুর (pseudo Sans. ঠক্কুর, a term of respect), (32) ঠাট্টা, jeering (Oriya থট্টা), (33) ঠার, a gesture, (34) ডেক্‌রা, a shameless bold fellow, (35) ঢাকা, a cover, (36) ঢোকা, to enter (ঢুক্ also in pseudo-Sanskrit), (37) তড়্‌কা, a fit in a fever, (38) তাড়া, a bundle, (39) তুলসী, (a plant in general in পালি ; Hem Chandra simply mentions as a দেশী word ; now a special aromatic plant), (40) থাবা, the paw of an animal, and one handful. (41) দোপ, used in E.B. only to signify 'down,' (42) ধামা, a basket, (43) ধুকড়ী (beggar's bag), (44) নুলা, a paw, or one having the arm paralysed,

APPENDIX TO LECTURE V—*concld.*

LIST I.	LIST II.
vanity, (43) ভেংচান, to imitate one by gestures, to irritate that one (may be from ভঙ্গ), (44) ভুচুং, as in ভুচুং দেখান, to hold out a false hope, (45) ভোঁতা, dull-edged, (46) রাঁড়, widow (রাণ্ডী, a bad woman in Hindi), (47) হেঁয়ালি, a riddle, (48) হেংলা, meanly craving for food.	(45) নেকা, a pretender or one who shams, (46) নেটা as a নেটা হাত, one who cannot use his right hand. [In E. B. the word ডেবরা is in use, which is also in use in Oriya and Nepalese.] (47) পেট (পোড় in Marathi), the belly; (48) পোকা, a worm, (49) পোড়া (burning), (50) ফোগ্‌লা (without teeth), (51) বোকা, a goat, or a silly fellow [বোক্কড় is the form in প্রাকৃত as noticed by Hem Chandra] (52) ভাটা, down stream, shallow water in Sambalpur, (53) ভিড়ান to bring to the shore as a boat, (54) ভিড়, crowd, (55) ভুল, mistake, (56) মন (40 seers), (57) মাগি, a woman (মাউগি a wife in Behari), (58) মিহি (thin), (59) লোশা, to dose, as in ঝুরি লোশা, (60) লক্ষ, as the word কোটী, so is লক্ষ a non-Vedic term, (61) শাট্‌, secret signs, (62) শট্‌কান, to slip away unnoticed, (63) সাড়া, (alarm), (64) হাট্‌, market.

BENGALI PHONOLOGY

LECTURE VI

An analysis of the character of our vocalic and consonantal sounds can only lead us to form a definite idea regarding our provincial accent system. As such, a comparative study of Bengali phonology should be carefully pursued, though this sort of study involves a detailed consideration of the phonology of not only the ancient Vedic and the post-Vedic languages, but also of the Drāvidian accent system. It is a hard work to do; but I must make an attempt in this direction, in the hope that my failure may lead to success, by attracting the attention and calling forth the energies of worthier scholars.

The letters of the ancient alphabet, which are not articulated in our pure Bengali speech, and which we keep in stock for the only purpose of representing the words of the ancient languages of India, will be dealt with only briefly.

অ.—(*i*) The usual sound of this vowel may be represented by 'o' as it is pronounced in pot, not, hot, etc. The sound of it in ancient times, may be presumed to have been like 'u' in but, cut, hut, etc., and so the long sound of this short অ may easily be made into আ (as 'a' in part, calm, large, etc.). This may explain why আ is the long form of অ, as ঈ and ঊ are the long forms of ই and উ. In Marathi, Canarese, Tamil and Telegu, অ is pronounced as short আ; this sound is exactly similar to our short unaccented আ sound as in আমার, আন্দাজ, আচার, etc. The Mundās and the Orāons of Bengal frontier do also pronounce অ as আ short. The Bengali sound of অ, as verging upon the sound of 'ও,' is naturally subdued when it is in the beginning or in the middle of a word, but it is distinct at the end of a word, when the final vowel, as a matter of course, is not হসন্ত in sound. Forgetting this natural mode of pronunciation, some writers unnecessarily write মতো for মত (like), ভালো for ভাল (good), কোনো for কোন (certain), etc. This process may be called wasting the black paint to paint a Negro black. The spelling reformers, moreover, fail to see that the sound of অ as a final, only approaches the sound of ও, and it will be creating confusion, if this sound be made identical with 'ও'.

(*ii*) The pronunciation of অ in Oriyā is midway between the Bengali and the Tamil pronunciation. The sound in Oriyā is similar to 'a' in ball; while we pronounce রবি as Robi, the Oriyās pronounce it as Raw-bi. This Oriyā pronunciation of অ is the highest exercise we make in producing the ancient sound, when reading Sanskrit, and this is the sound we produce, when accent is put upon অ not followed by ই or উ sound in a word. For example, when there is an accent on অ of অত (so much), the অ sounds like 'aw' in raw or like 'a' in ball. অ in অতি, however, does not change the normal Bengali sound, even though accented, as the ই sound follows it. Our spelling reformers may also take notice of the fact, that even when we attempt to maintain the purity of the sound of অ, as in অত, the sound is almost an 'ও' to the men of other provinces of India.

The Vedic sound for অ may no doubt be presumed to be our short আ, but we notice in the Atharvan Prātiśākhya (*e.g.*, 1,36) that besides the open sound, there was also a close or, saṁvṛta, sound of অ, which it appears, we have only inherited in Bengal. It is difficult to say, if this saṁvṛta sound has come down to us through Pāli and other later Māgadhi Prākṛtas, for we have no Prākṛta Prātiśākhyas to bear evidence to such a transmission. No doubt in Pāli, *i.e.*, in the old Māgadhi Prākṛta, all nouns ending with the vowel sound of অ are found in the form নরো, ধম্মো, etc., in nominative singular, but this cannot perhaps be said to have been due to the peculiarity of the pronunciation of অ at the end of a word, for though there was no visarjania in use in Pāli, it may be said that, in its origin the sound came out of an elision of visarjania. It is, however, worth noting, that besides a general saṁvṛta sound for অ, we can detect in the Vedic itself a tendency of অ (as final) to be reduced to the sound of ও when joined to the visarjaniya: we first notice it very unmistakably in several euphonic combinations, where the final অ sound with the conjoined visarjaniya is reduced to ও; we again may notice that the dual form of দেবঃ, for example, is দেবৌ; the word দেবঃ must have been pronounced as দেবো (as in Pāli) for, to create a dual form by the lengthening of the final sound, the long sound of ও (which is ঔ) was reached, and this became the dual denoting suffix. It should be mentioned here, that the dual with ঔ is later in date in the Vedic language, and that the earlier বিভক্তি is noticed as আ in Chāndasa.

In consequence of their settled habit of pronouncing অ with its long and open sound, the people of Upper India, when pronouncing such words as 'long,' 'follow,' etc., by half adopting them in Hindi, utter those words as লাঙ্গ, ফালো, etc. The Bengali boys on the other hand, not being accustomed to emit the sound of 'i' and 'u' as in 'bird' and 'cut,' pronounce them as বা-র্ড (bard) and কা-ট, etc.

We gather from the works on Vedic phonology, that both অ and আ carried in their full-bodied open utterance, a half-distinct nasal sound. We can detect that the half-distinct nasal sound developed into a full-bodied nasal letter, when the sound in অ and আ was very long drawn to create, for instance, the plural form; this is why ভবতি became ভবন্তি, and we get in the Vedic speech জুহ্বন্তি as an additional plural form by the side of জুহ্বতি. How a দীর্ঘ sound naturally evolves a nasal, will be noticed presently. For want of any work on phonology, relating to the old Māgadhi speech, we cannot say, if the Prākṛta speakers of old Magadha displayed the peculiarity noticed in the case of the Vedic speech. It is, however, a fact that in the district of Bankura, as well as in the western portion of Burdwan, a final half-nasal occurs at the ends of such words as করিয়া, খাইয়া, etc., and they are pronounced as করিয়াঁ, খাইয়াঁ, etc. We also find that in some cases of our অপভ্রংশ words, where আ or any other vowel is accented to maintain the long sound, occurring in the original word, we put a half-nasal ˇ on the accented vowel, though the derivation of the word, does not justify the nasal. আঁটি (from S. অস্থি or অট্ঠি), জোঁক (from জলৌক), and সেঁতা (from সিক্ত) are some fitting examples. That in old Māgadhi Prākṛta a nasal was introduced in similar cases, can be presumed from some অপভ্রংশ forms; for example, from বক্র comes বঙ্ক, and from Vedic কুথ comes the form কন্থা; our vernacular forms বাঁকা and কাঁথা, I need hardly say, are from বঙ্ক and কন্থা respectively. We may note that বঙ্ক and কন্থা were adapted in Sanskrit from Prākṛta. সাঁপ from সর্প in Hindi may be compared with the above forms.

The nasal *of* আ.—I proceed now to show, that there is a natural basis in our very organ of speech, for the occurrence of this phenomenon, that আ carries at times a nasal sound with it. To do this, I have to also notice that আ is sometimes transformed into ই in the lengthening of the voice, as will also be pointed out presently.

To serve our purpose, the results of a scientific research touching the origin and character of the vowel sounds, may be briefly stated here. Helmhotz and Koenig made very accurate and delicate experiments, in the mouth of men, and thereby accomplished a nice analysis of the natural sounds, produced by our vocal organs; it has been established by these experiments, that U (উ) is musically speaking the lowest, I (ই) the hightest, and A (অ) the central of all the vowels. This scientific evidence in support of this proposition, that অ, ই, and উ are the three cardinal vowels, shows with what degree of accuracy, the old grammarians of India, analysed and classified the vowels, as well as the consonantal sounds, many centuries before the Christian era. We all know that অইউণ্ is the first মাহেশ্বরী সূত্র, with which the old Sanskrit Grammar starts. It will not now be difficult to see, how আ becomes ই in the Vedic speech in the lengthening of that long vowel, some examples regarding which will be presently adduced. It has also been established by physical experiments, referred to above, that if অ or আ sound is lengthened without allowing the sound to reach a high pitch, that is to say, without allowing it to develop into ই sound, the lengthened voice is sure to become nasal; this is why আ carries with it a nasal when the sound is lengthened.

আ.—(*i*) Generally speaking our আ is a short vowel and it becomes long only when there is accent upon it. In respect of all long sounds, it has however to be noted, that there are different grades of them, and one sound, though long, may not be so long as another long sound may be. It is difficult to symbolise these grades of length, but we may formulate at least a 'half-long' sound, as intermediate between short and long. When আ is followed by a হসন্ত consonant, that is which does not carry a vowel sound, it becomes a half-long vowel as আ in আজ্, রাত, ভাত, পাত, etc. In the words আপন, কাপড়, পাতা, বারুই, বাড়ি, etc., আ is short; this short sound of a long vowel may be termed as the normal long sound in Bengali. We do not make any distinction between long and short sounds of vowels according to Sanskrit rules. As a rule, the single letters when uttered separately, as independent syllables or words, are uttered long; our children, unlike those of Upper India, pronounce অ—অ, আ—আ, ই—ই, ঈ—ঈ, ক—অ, খ—অ, etc., when learning the alphabet. Words of one letter are pronounced long, as it is the case in the Tamil speech. In Tamil, there are 42 one-letter words and they are all sounded long. The Bengali one-letter word 'না,' to indicate a reply in the negative, is rather long, while it is short in না জানি, যাব না, etc., where it has been joined to, or compounded with other words. The initial letter of a word of two letters is pronounced long, when the final letter is হসন্ত; *cf.* ফল, শিব, গুড়, etc.; it is to be noted, that here the words of two letters are words of one syllable, and as such, the rule regarding one syllable is applicable.

(*ii*) I have spoken of the nasal sound which আ develops at times; it may be noticed that when আ carries a nasal sound in Bengali, it has the tendency to be pronounced long, no matter whether it is followed by a হসন্ত consonant or not; the long sounds of আঁ in আঁশটে, আঁচড়, কাঁঠাল, বাঁশী হাঁটু are examples.

(*iii*) In the Vedic speech, আ when made very long, was at times transformed into ই sound; compare সিধ্যতি and সাধতি (succeeds), শাস্তে (teaches) and শিষ্ট (taught); this is especially marked in final আ, as স্থিত from স্থা, গীত from গা, গীথ as a variant of গাথ, দীর্ঘ from দা and হীন from হা (Macdonell's Vedic Grammar, p. 4). We may notice in this connection, that in the অপভ্রংশ formation of আখ্ from ইক্ষু,

the ই sound of the original has been reduced to আ in Bengali.

It will be noticed that in a large number of cases, the final আ followed by ই sound is changed into এ, as it is in the Vedic speech. Here the rule of law is, the preceding vowel sound influences the one coming after. This is the inverse of 'umlaut.' In our pronunciation মিঠা becomes মিঠে, রিষড়া becomes রিষড়ে, বিশ্বাস becomes বিশ্বেষ, etc.* If however, the final আ comes after the উ sound, the আ is changed into ও, কুটা, পূরা, বুড়া, etc., are pronounced as কুটো, পূরো, বুড়ো, etc. If the final আ is attached to য় (which is pronounced as অ in Bengali) in a word of more than two letters, the whole of the final letter য়া is changed into এ or ও as the case may be, and this এ or ও takes the place of ই or উ of the next preceding letter; নদীয়া becomes নদে, বাঁশবেড়িয়া—বাঁশবেড়ে, করিয়া—করে, পড়ুয়া—পড়ো, লিলুয়া—লিলো, etc., গিয়া, দিয়া, ধুয়া, জুয়া, etc., being words of two letters they will be changed into গিয়ে, দিয়ে, ধুয়ো, জুয়ো (জুয়োচোর contracted into জোচ্চোর), etc. We thus see, that though 'য়' is seemingly pronounced as 'অ' the ই-অ sound is partly in our ears, to effect the phonetic change described above. Since the words are sure to be pronounced in the manner indicated above, even though they are spelt correctly in their original form, our spelling reformers may give up the attempt of spelling the words by representing all sorts of change of sounds, caused by phonetic decay. The writers, I speak of, want to introduce the verbs only in their contracted forms, but not the nouns, adjectives, etc. With what logic this distinction is sought to be made, is not easy to see. Why should we not write ইন্দিরে, ঈশেন, কৈলেশ, মিথ্যে, বিচের (as in আচায় বিচের), etc.,

* As in Eastern Bengal the last syllables are accented, the final আ of মিঠা and such other words, does not change into এ.

if করে, গিয়েছে, etc., for করিয়া, গিয়াছে etc., may be introduced with propriety.

Having enunciated the rule regarding the change of final আ into এ, I must further note that the change spoken of, takes place even though other words are compounded with the words ending with আ, and even when suffixes or inflections come after the final আ; মরেছিল from মরিয়াছিল, এল from আইল, বেঁধেছে from বাঁধিয়াছে, যেতে from যাইতে, etc., may be noted. No one should confound the forms গাইতে, নাইতে, চাইতে, etc., with যাইতে, পাইতে, খাইতে, etc.; in the former series, the letter 'হ' of the verb stems, has only lost the sharp aspirate sound, and as such গাহিতে, নাহিতে, and চাহিতে have been reduced to the softened down forms; it will therefore be ridiculous, if one would attempt a further contraction of the words of the first series into গেতে, নেতে, চেতে, on the analogy of যেতে, পেতে and খেতে, which are the contracted forms of যাইতে, পাইতে and খাইতে. We shall see from other examples later on, that even where we use the letter 'হ,' our tongue glides over the sound of 'হ' almost unawares, to allow the letter to perform its physiological work.

ই, ঈ.—I have said that there is no vowel in Bengali which has an inherent long sound; as such, ঈ and ঊ are used only to spell the words of Sanskrit origin. I have also noticed, that the vowels are sounded long, when we put accent or emphasis upon them, and they are all short when not accented. In pronouncing the Sanskrit word ঈশ্বর we do not really make ঈ long, but only a slight long sound is uttered as the result of our pronunciation of the compound letter which follows ঈ; all letters become slightly long in our pronunciation, when it is followed by a duplicated or a compound letter, no distinction can be made between the sounds of ই and ঈ

when we pronounce ইচ্ছা and ঈশ্বর. Since we cannot indicate by phonetic representations, the long or rather accented sounds of অ, আ, এ, and ও, and since ঈ has not got a long sound in Bengali, it is hardly correct to write কী for কি to indicate accent or emphasis; for example, when we put emphasis upon the word তুমি (you) in such a sentence as আমাকে কে মারবে? তুমি? no one can seriously think of spelling the word as তূমি.

I have shown under the heading আ how this sound is changed into এ; it is also to be noted that when as a general rule, the aforesaid change takes place in our pronunciation, one exception is observed in some parts of Eastern Bengal. In the district of Dacca, the ই sound without being changed into এ, a metathysis in the sound occurs; for example করিয়া becomes কইরা, বালিয়া becomes বাইলা (বেলে=sandy), etc. It is to be further noted, that this phenomenon also occurs when the compounded ই-অ sound which is represented by what is called য-ফলা is taken by a consonant after the অ or the আ sound, and so মধ্য and বাধ্য are pronounced in some eastern districts, as মইধ্ ধ and বাইধ্ ধ. As a letter with য-ফলা is pronounced in Bengali as a duplicated letter, the ই sound comes before a compounded letter, specially when there is an aspirate sound at the end of the compound letter; thus the word ব্রাহ্ম will be pronounced ব্রাইহ্ম in Dacca. I must point out in this connection, that we meet with the forms কইল and ধইল for করিল and ধরিল, in our old Bengali books which were composed in the Rāḍha country. I have shown in a preceding section, that the Puṇḍra people, who inhabited the Rāḍha-land, proceeded to North Bengal in early times, and a large number of them migrated also to the Sambalpur tract, during the time of the Kośala Guptas. There may be or may not be any causal relation between this fact and what I am going to state now; it is curious, that unlike their neighbours on all sides, the people of Sambalpur reduce পানি, বালি, মালি, etc., to পাইন, বাইল, মাইল, etc.; a line of a song composed in the vulgar speech of the Rangpur district, will disclose the above peculiarity in that far off locality in Northern Bengal: আমার মইন্সা (মিন্সে—husband) ছিল ঘরতে (ঘরে) কি সতে (কি কারণে) আগ্ (রাগ) কইরা (করিয়া) গইছেন (গিয়াছেন) বাহে (মহাশয়) একনা (একটা) কথাতে (কথায়).

We utter the ই sound in some cases to prepare the ground as it were, for pronouncing a compound letter, of which sibilant is a component part. The English word school is pronounced sa-kul in the Punjab, e-skool in the U. P., us-kul in some parts of Orissa and is-kul in Bengal, in the sea-board districts of Orissa, and in the Madras Presidency. I may remark in passing, that the disinclination to pronounce a compound letter as an initial, is India-wide; as the speakers of Aryan speeches in Europe pronounce the initial compound letters aright, and as it is a rule in the Dravidian speeches, that the initial letter can never be a compound letter, I am inclined to formulate a widespread Dravidian influence since a remote past, to explain this peculiarity in our pronunciation. It will be noticed later on, that this inclination to drop the letter 's' as a first part of a compound initial letter, is noticeable in the Vedic speech as well. In the U. P., the introductory vowel sound becomes আ, when the initial compound letter terminates with আ sound, and so স্নান is uttered as আস্নান; in the case of other terminal vowel sounds, এ becomes the introductory sound. In the Punjab, the compound letter is split up, and one letter is pronounced after the other; in the Tamil pronunciation however, ই must be pronounced not only before the compound letters of the class spoken of above, but even before other initial compound letters; if even the second letter of a word is a compound letter, and the initial letter is a simple one, the ই sound is uttered by the Tamil people ; the Tamil Apabhranśa of রাক্ষস is ই+রাক্কধন; this is also a rule in the Tamil speech, that an introducing vowel is added to a word beginning with র.

উ ঊ.—I need hardly repeat that ঊ has got no place on the list of pure and genuine Bengali vowels. উ is changed into ও, when as a pure vowel it is followed by আ or accented অ, in a word of two syllables ; we may notice this change in ওঠ, ওঠা and ওড়া. In the Chittagong division, ও is changed into উ sound in some cases ; I could not obtain a sufficiently large number of words to frame a generalised rule for this peculiarity of pronunciation in Chittagong.

In our vulgar Bengali pronunciation, a compound or duplicated letter with final অ sound, takes ই or উ when followed by ই or উ in the syllable, and so ইষ্ট, কৃষ্ট (কৃষ্ণ), মিষ্ট, etc., become ইষ্টি, কিষ্টি (in কেলে-কিষ্টি), and মিষ্টি, and পুষ্ট, তুষ্ট and উচ্চ become পুষ্টু, তুষ্টু and উঁচু; it will be noticed that at the dropping of one চ, the long sound of উ has generated the half nasal চন্দ্রবিন্দু. Consideration of the sound of ঋ will follow after taking notice of the sounds of য, র, ল and ব (v).

এ, ঐ, ও, ঔ.—These vowels or dipthongs have lost their original sounds and are pronounced as 'e' in met (or as 'a' in mate), as অই, as 'o' of the English vowel, and as অউ. The original sounds of these vowels have been partially retained in Tāmil and Telegu ; or rather, the Dravidian sounds of those letters nearly approach the ancient Aryan sounds of them. We learn from the remarks of the ancient Grammarians (*e.g.*, Vārtika of Kātyāyana, VIII-2, 106 ; under Mahābhāṣya, I-1, 48), that এ is equal to অ+ই and ও is equal to অ+উ, and ঐ and ঔ

being respectively the farther long sounds of এ and ও, the sound আ for অ has to be prefixed to ই and উ respectively, to obtain the proper sounds generated by ঐ and ঔ. The following examples collected by Prof. Macdonell in his Vedic grammar, may be profitably cited. We get in saptami singular অশ্ব+ই=অশ্বে, পদ+ঈ=পদে, and ভব+ঈঃ =ভবেঃ; notice also যমা+ঈ=যমে (twin sisters). When we get অনূপ (pond) from অনু+আপ, we see that উ has become long under the influence of succeeding আ. The two examples তস্ম+এ=তস্মৈ and দেব্যা+এ= দেব্যৈ are illuminating. I may notice in passing, that in Orissa, ঐ is pronounced as এই and ঔ as আউ. It is clear that our Bengali pronunciation is wholly peculiar to us. ঐ and ঔ being merely long or augmented forms of এ and ও respectively, they ceased to be in use in the Prākṛta speeches.

এ.—(*i*) The sound of the vowel as indicated above is after the ancient Aryan sound of it, and this sound is uttered only in pronouncing the words which are at times designated by the technical term তৎসম. The initial sound of এ in indigenous Bengali words, can be represented by 'â' in mât. This normal sound of Bengali এ is so very exclusively peculiar to Bengali, that no letter or letter-signs of our ancient script, can represent it. It took me full six days to make a boy of the U. P. to pronounce the English word 'bat' correctly; the sound was altogether new to his ears and he was constantly varying his pronunciation from bet to bate. It is very important to note, that this â sound, as it occurs in bat, mat, etc., exists in the Dravidian tongue of Tamil; the pronunciation of the word কল্ (stone) as Kâll or of অন্বু (cajoling) as ânbu, are examples. Some Bengali writers, who do not know what the real sound of য is, make at times the unscientific and useless attempt to represent the sound by য+আ to convey the peculiar Bengali sound to the ears of the foreigners. They do not know that the spelling গ্যাল for গেল is highly misleading to the people all over India, for ই অ is the sound of both য, and য ফলা,—outside the presidency of Bengal. The Indians of all other provinces, as well as the Europeans, who come to learn Bengali after studying Sanskrit or Hindi, are sure to pronounce গ্যাল as গিয়াল. This method of representation will therefore be of no help to the outsiders, and will have the mischievous effect of teaching the Bengali boys a very wrong sound of য, which they have to deal with in their Sanskrit text-books. The Bengali boys learn the normal sound of Bengali এ even when they commence to lisp in their early infancy. All that we should do, is to frame rules regarding the normal and Sanskritic pronunciation of the vowel এ. As we have to learn the sounds of the vowels of the foreigners from the foreigners, our special Bengali sound has to be learned by those who are not Bengalis. To indicate this special sound of এ, we shall put a circumflex upon it.

I have stated that the initial এ in the তৎসম words, does not become the normal Bengali এ̂. I could notice only four words, namely, এ̂ক, ফে̂ন or ফে̂না বে̂লা and হে̂লা, which only seemingly form exception to the rule; we see that the old এক became এক্ক in the Prākṛta, and so the newly formed Bengali word এক, is not, inspite of its physical identity, identical with the original Sanskrit form; the words বে̂লা and হে̂লা are not of ছান্দস origin, and they were only adopted in Classical Sanskrit from Prākṛta; words with ফ initial are suspected to be non-Aryan in origin; ফাল, ফেন and ফল are the only words which occur in the Vedic language, of which ফেন

alone belongs to the Aryan stock, being perhaps a decayed form of spena. I notice here that in the Northern and Eastern Bengal, the general tendency is to pronounce the initial এ of even the তৎসম words, as এ̂, and so কেবল, কেশব, দেশ, দেবতা, শেষ, etc., are pronounced with এ̂ initial.

এ as a single letter, and as an adjective, taking indicative particles as টি or টা, or particles of emphasis ই or ও, or being joined to other altogether separate words as রূপ, সকল, etc., retains its Sanskritic sound. The initial এ sound in a monosyllabic word, where the final consonant is হসন্ত, is pure; compare টের (to perceive) and টেঁরা̂ (one who squints) and ঢের (much) and ঢে̂রা (clumsy as in ঢে̂রা সই). When however the final হসন্ত consonant is nasalised, the normal এ̂ sound will prevail, as কেঁক (a sound), খেঁক-শিয়াল, খেঁট (sumptuous feast), বেঙ্, চেঙ্ (a fish), টেঁক্, ঠেঙ্, পেন্ পেন্ (slow teasing murmur), etc.

The words which are designated by some as তৎভব, including the অপভ্রংশ words, are subject to the rule governing the indigenous words. In Sir Rabindranath Tagore's highly suggestive work শব্দতত্ত্ব, the rule regarding the Sanskritic sound of এ, where normal Bengali sound might be expected, has been very nicely enunciated. His statement, that the এ sound when followed either by ই or উ sound, does not change into এ̂, is quite correct, the other rule formulated by him as noted below, should also receive universal acceptance. When the Prākṛta or অপভ্রংশ or দেশী root or stem of a word has an initial ই, the word derived from it with an initial এ will be pronounced with pure এ sound; কেনা begins with pure এ sound as the original stem or root is কিন্ (compare the forms কিনিলাম, কিনিয়াছিল, etc.), while বেচা having বেচ্ and not বিক্রয় for its origin, is pronounced otherwise; ঘেরা from ঘির্ (*cf.* ঘিরিল, ঘিরিলাম), চেরা from চির্ (*cf.* চিরিল), মেশা from মিশ্ (*cf.* মিশিতে) and মেলা from মিল্ (*cf.* মিলন, মিলিতে) are some examples. মেলা from মিল্ may be contrasted with মেলা (many) which claims no root having the ই initial. This will give us a clue to see that এমন, কেমন, খেলা, etc., are not the direct descendants of ইদম্, কিম্, ক্রোড়্, &c., but are derived from the Prākṛta forms এমং, কেমং and খেল respectively. It is to be noted that when 'ই' as a particle of emphasis, comes after the এ sound (এ-ই), the normal pronunciation is not changed; in এ, কি ? however, এ is an independent word and so it retains the Sanskritic sound. Those who resorting to an unscientific method, do not keep ই and ও, indicating emphasis, distinct and separate from the words to which they are joined, must see on looking to the two foregoing forms, what a confusion may be created by their wrong spelling; if ই of emphasis is joined to হসন্ত-ক—final of the word এক in the shape of ই-কার, the two forms illustrated above will be identical. It becomes physically impossible to make ই or ও indicating emphasis, an inseparable part of such following words as তুমি, সে, আলো, etc., and one is bound to write তুমি-ই, তুমি-ও, সে-ই, সে-ও, আলো-ই, আলো-ও, etc.; why then such an exception should be made as to spell কোনো for কোনও when the emphasis itself is drowned in the new spelling, is difficult to understand. It must be pointed out, in this connection, that though য় is not pronounced as ই+অ, the sound ই is in our ears unconsciously, as it were since the general rule governs our pronunciation of such following words as কেয়া, খেয়াল, চেয়ার্ (chair), তেয়াগ, দেয়াল, ধেয়ান, পেয়ালা, শেয়ান্, হেঁয়ালি, etc.

Visarjaniya.—Neither the sign nor the sound of it was in use either in Pāli or in the later Prākṛta speeches; properly speaking, we do not use it in Bengali, and only three or four Sanskrit words as are spelt with visarjaniya, have been adopted in Bengali; these Sanskrit words again, are pronounced in the very fashion in which they were pronounced by the speakers of the ancient Prākṛta tongues; দুঃখ is pronounced as দুক্‌খ and নিঃশ্বাস as নিশ্‌-শাস্‌. Some of our Paṇḍits in their zeal and eagerness to give the Bengali language the sort of dignity which Æsop's jackdaw sought in the land of fables in dim backward of time, persuade us in vain to believe, that it is not মন but মনস্‌ which is the original word with us. They forget that we have borrowed মনোহর, মনস্তাপ, etc., in their entirety from what is called the Sanskrit language, and not that we have made euphonic combinations of মনস্‌+হর, etc., in our current speech, following the stringent Sandhi rule. The Sanskritists of the olden days borrowed মন্মথ ungrudgingly from a Prākṛta speech, and মনচোর is not found fault with, though চোর is a Sanskrit word; why should then our Paṇḍits shy at মন-কষ্ট or similar other forms in Bengali? Our natural sound has a history, and it cannot be obliterated. I may notice by the way (even though it is a digression) that in the Vedic speech we can notice a simple মন by the side of মনস্‌, as disclosed by such a term as আমনঃ signifying—having the mind or disposition to be friendly.

The nasal sound—The sound of the full-bodied final nasal is what may be represented by অনুস্বার; it is something like অ-ঙ্‌ in Bengali while it is অম্‌ in Sanskrit. In Telegu and Tamil there is an indigenous অম্‌ which is articulated as a final nasal at the end of all words, which are nouns. The Andhras and the Tamil people have not got the half-nasal ˇ in their script, and they do not also utter the sound involved by it; they have an abundance of 'am' and 'un' as terminal endings, but the half-nasal is altogether wanting. As the Mongolians are notorious for their excess of nasal sound, we cannot attribute the inability of the people of Eastern Bengal to utter the half-nasal sound to Mongolian influence. I may note that the half-nasal or ँ is freely used by the people of Assam. The absence of the half-nasal must therefore be due to excessive Dravidian influence, in Eastern Bengal.

ঙ *and* ঞ—which are not strictly speaking independent letters, but indicate only the sort of nasal sound which must be generated, when occurring in conjunction with the letters of ক-বর্গ and চ-বর্গ respectively, have now lost their original sounds. সঙ্গ and বঙ্গ are pronounced almost as সং-অ and বং-অ; the full sound of গ is always subdued in গঙ্গা, রঙ্গ, সঙ্গ, etc. When ঞ sound comes first and the letters of চ-বর্গ are pronounced next, ঞ is pronounced as ন; অঞ্চল, বাঞ্ছা, অঞ্জন, ঝঞ্ঝা are pronounced as অন্চল, বান্ছা, অন্জন and ঝন্ঝা. When ঞ comes after জ, the sound becomes peculiar; জ which is no doubt a variant of গ, is replaced by গ, and the final nasal is uttered as half-nasal; আজ্-ঞা আজ্ঞা and প্রজ্-ঞা প্রজ্ঞা are pronounced as আগ্-গেঁ and প্রগ্-গাঁ in Bengal and Orissa.

ণ.—ণ is never sounded correctly in Bengal, and it is useless as a letter to spell the indigenous Bengali words. The use of ণ is limited within the sphere of spelling the Sanskrit words. It is worth noting, that though in the sea-board districts of Orissa, and in the eastern Garjat states, ণ is pronounced with considerable distinctness, the Oriyas in the Sambalpur tract, do not pronounce this letter, unless they are forced to produce the sound in schools, by abandoning their natural ন sound. Though we get enough of ণ in the script, representing Māgadhi speech of old, we notice the rule in the Prākṛta Grammar by Hem Chandra that ন takes the place of ণ in the Māgadhi Prākṛta. This is a very good evidence of the fact, that we have been pronouncing the cerebral ণ as ন since long. খোঁড়া (to dig) comes from the Prākṛta word খণণ, and hence a half-nasal and the cerebral ড় have evolved out of ণ sound. In কেষ্ট and বিষ্টু or বিষ্টু for কৃষ্ণ and বিষ্ণু the cerebral ট has been substituted to represent the cerebral sound. The initial এ of কেষ্ট, comes from the tendency to pronounce এর্ for ঋ; it is no doubt a rare tendency, but it is noticeable in the pronunciation of ঘেরৃত for ঘৃত, by some villagers, who attempt at Sanskritic pronunciation. I may notice, that the Iranian pronunciation of ঋ was এর্-অ in near approach of the old Vedic pronunciation of the vowel ঋ.

As we do not pronounce অন্তস্থ ব and identify it with ব of প-বর্গ, we do not keep the অনুস্বার separate from it, and compound it with ম which is the nasal sound of the letters of প-বর্গ; we write and pronounce বশম্বদ, কিম্বা and এবম্বিধ; this practice has been in vogue since long, as we meet with the above sort of spelling in ancient epigraphic records; I think this wrong use should be avoided, as it is necessary to know, which nasal sound is appropriate to which class of letters. We meet with such wrong spelling of words as তাম্ব and আম্ব in the old epigraphic records of East Bihār, Bengal and Orissa. The people of Orissa, pronounce আম্ব and not আম, and even now write তাম্বু for তাম্র in rural districts; it is noteworthy, that in some parts of Bengal আম is pronounced as আঁব and তামা as তাঁবা.

It is significant, that when ম becomes a ফলা or nasal adjunct of a consonant, it is not at all pronounced in Bengal, and the consonant with which it is compounded, is pronounced as if it is duplicated; পদ্ম and লক্ষ্মী are pronounced as পদ্দ and লক্‌খি, while our silent ম is distinctly pronounced in all other parts of India including Orissa. In some cases, it is noticed, that the consonant to which ম is conjoined, is dropped altogether, and ম is alone articulated; as from শ্মশান the word মশান has been derived. It is worth noting here, that this particular word "মশান" as the অপভ্রংশ of শ্মশান, is in use in some parts of Western India as well; the Pali apabhranśa form was "সুমান," from which our "শশান," has originated. I may notice one অপভ্রংশ of this class, which is in common use all throughout Northern India: শ্মশ্রু was first reduced to মশ্রু and then to মস্সু in old Prakṛta, and from this মস্সু the forms মোচ্ and মোছা came into use, and are still in use in some modern Vernaculars. I have shown in a previous lecture, that the peculiarity here noticed, is fully in accordance with the rule of grammar, as obtains in the Dravidian speeches; according to this rule, the initial letter of a word can never be a compound letter, and that double or triple consonants of different vargas, cannot occur anywhere in a word. The word জ্ঞান (জ-ঞান) has the pronunciation of 'gân'; but when the compound letter is a medial as in ধর্মজ্ঞান, the pronunciation will be 'Dhamma-ggân' without any nasal sound.

য, র, ল, ব.—Though these letters are regarded as consonants, their real character as compound vowels, has always been admitted by the old Sanskrit Grammarians. That য is a compound sound of ই + অ has been pointed out before. As য is pronounced as জ in Bengali and Oriya, special mark has been added to the letter to signify the 'y' sound. It is worth noting, that in old Prakṛta speeches, we get জ for য and যৌবন for instance was pronounced as জোব্বন.*

---

* In Bengali as well as in Oriya, য as an initial or taking another য as a ফলা is uttered as জ and in any other situation, it is য as a rule. In Oriya, I could notice a single exception to the rule in the pronunciation of মযূর which is pronounced as মজূর. That this general rule, I have stated obtained in old Prâkṛta, is pretty well known. It is noticeable in later Mâgadhi speech, that the name জালি for example has been spelt with the usual জ initial, while this word occuring after উপ or rather compounded with উপ, উপযালি has been the form adopted.

র, ঋ, ল *and* ৯.—The reason why I take up to discuss the sounds of the vowel ঋ and ৯ along with the discussion of the value of র and ল will be clear from the remarks I offer hereunder.

র.—I should explain that র originated from the compounding of ঋ+অ. It may be gathered from the Prātisākhyas (Rk. Prā-8-14; Atharvan. Prā-I. 37, 71) that the sound of a liquid was the final sound which ঋ produced. Again we get in the Vājasaneyī-Prātisakhya (IV. 145), that the initial half of ঋ had almost an অ sound. The Punjab frontier tribes pronounce ঋ as অর্-অ; the old Iranian pronunciation of ঋ, as may be detected in Āvesta literature, was অর্-এ and এর্-অ at times. We may notice that in ancient Prākṛta, বিকট became a variant of বিকৃত, কৃত became কত and মৃত became মত; this shows that ঋ had once the initial অ sound. The vulgar tendency to reduce ঘৃত to ঘের্ত and the pronunciation of কৃষ্ণ as কেষ্টো, and of বৃষ as বের্ষো (as in বের্ষো—ছুগ্‌গু) remind us of the old Iranian pronunciation of ঋ. In the Rangpur district, the letters অ and র are interchangeable, when they are initials; this tendency is not wholly unknown among the populace in central Bengal as well. That the Prākṛta forms with অ and উ finals, were reduced to forms with র and রু finals may also be noticed, though in this case, the flat and boneless Prākṛta forms were really given stronger or more easily-pronouncible forms; thus we get মুনির, from মুনিঅ (gen.) and গরু, from গউ (গো). We may further notice, that when র is the adjunct to an initial letter of a তৎসম word, the sound এ is induced in pronunciation: প্রণাম, প্রসন্ন, প্রহ্লাদ, ব্রজ, etc., are reduced to পেন্নাম (পরণাম in H.), পেসন্ন (পরসন্ in H.), পেল্লাদ (পহ্‌লাদ in H.), বের্জ (বর্জ in H.); contrast the forms মিত্তির, সমুদ্দ্‌র, বস্তর্, etc., from মিত্র, সমুদ্র, বস্ত্র, etc., where the letters with র-adjunct are not initials.

ঋ.—It becomes perfectly clear from the Prātisākhyas, that the Aryans in India were settled in their pronunciation of ঋ as 'ri.' Adverting however to such apabhraṁśa forms as বুড্ডি from বৃষ্টি, উতু from ঋতু, etc., some scholars have wrongly asserted, that the Dravidian pronunciation 'Ru' for ঋ was in vogue in Northern India, when Pāli prevailed as a Northern Prākṛta speech. They have failed to see that only when the sound of ঋ had to be harmonised with the dominating উ sound in a word, that this vowel sound উ took the place of ঋ; we get ঘিয় or ঘি from ঘৃত where neither ই nor উ sound has to be assimilated; from ঋষি however, we get ইসি, while from ঋতু we get উতু because of the final উ sound. ব (v) is compounded of উ and অ; so the vowel ঋ conjoined to the accented ব (v) changes into উ; thus we get রুক্থ, বুড্‌ঢ or বুড়া, উষভ, etc., from বৃক্ষ, বৃদ্ধ, বৃষভ, etc. When however the final উ is not accented, and the letter joined with ঋ is accented, ঋ is not reduced to উ; for example, মৃত্যু has been reduced to মচ্চ়, because of the accent on ঋ of মৃ preceding a compound letter.

ঌ—Grammatically considering ৯ generated ঌ, but this vowel never got any prominence. We should not forget to notice, that there was a field of a very free interchangeability of র and ল in the Vedic as well as in the post-Vedic speeches of the Aryans; this being an essential feature of the Dravidian speeches, the Dravidian influence in this matter as well is generally formulated. An additional 'ল' as a mixed sound of 'ল'+'ড' occurs in all the Dravidian speeches; this 'ল' producing a cerebral sound, is in full use in Oriya and Mahrathi. Though this letter did not get admittance into the Vedic alphabet, the transformation of ল into 'ড' is recognised in the Vedic Grammar; we meet with the Vedic phonetic rule, that when 'ল' occurs between two vowel sounds, the letter may be optionally pronounced as 'ল' or 'ড' and so 'ঈ' লে may be uttered as 'ঈডে.' We have not got this cerebral in Bengali, but there are a few words in Bengali, which disclose the transformation of 'ল' into 'ড়'; তাড়ি (to-dy) the juice of Tāl (palm), may be an imported word, but কুঁড়ি from কলি (bud), মুড়া (extremity) from মূল, পাড়া from পল্লী (village), শিকড় (on account of the chainlike ramifications of the roots) from শিকল (—Sk. শৃঙ্খল, Pr. শিঙ্খাড় and শিঙ্খাটক) etc., are pure Bengali words. These forms, however, should not be confounded with those in which 'ড' or 'ড়' has originated from 'দ' or 'ত.'

Though ব (v) has lost its position in the Bengali alphabet, its উ-অ sound is retained in many words of ca origin; গুয়া from গুবাক, দেঅর from দেবর, ডুয়ার from দ্বার, ধাওয়া from ধাব, জোয়ান from যুবন্, and সোয়াদ from স্বাদ, are some instances. It must be familiar to the students of Prākṛita, that at times no distinction is made between 'b' and 'v' and that in the later Māgadhi, 'v' as an adjunct to a consonant, drops out altogether; such as, দ্বি is reduced to simple দি. The reduction of 'v' to 'b' cannot be said to be due to Dravidian influence, as distinction between 'b' and 'v' is strictly mantained in Telegu, Tamil, Malayalam and Canarese; but the dropping out of 'v,' when it is an adjunct to a consonant, can be explained by the rule of the Dravidian Grammar, which does not allow consonants of different classes to form a compound. According to this rule, দ্বি and স্বা of স্বাদ have to be reduced to দি or দু and to সো or সা, if they are initial letters; but if they occur as medials, they have to become দ্দি and স্সা respectively; compare the forms দুই, and সোআদ, স্বাদ or সাদ on the one hand, and the pronunciation of the words অদ্দিতিয় (অদ্বিতীয়) and বিস্সাদ (বিস্বাদ) on the other.

Consonants.—As the question of Dravidian influence is being considered all along, I should add here a few remarks regarding the Dravidian alphabet system. In the Tamil script, we get only ক to represent all the consonants of ক-বর্গ and this ক is uttered with slight variations to pronounce খ, গ and ঘ. The usual Tamil sound of ক is almost খ to our ears. Similarly there are only ট, ত and প for all the letters of their বর্গ or class. There is only one letter to represent চ and শ and the sound of চ is peculiarly sibilant in all the Dravidian languages. In connection with the phonetic value of the Tamil consonants, a few remarks relating to the consonants of the Aryan speech, may be fittingly introduced.

From the admirable scientific analysis of the sounds of our letters, in old grammatical works, we get considerable information, regarding the genesis of the consonants. Professor Sayce, after considering the value of the grammatical works of the Greeks and other peoples, has rightly made this remark, regarding the Sanskrit grammar and phonology: "Far more thorough-going and scientific were the phonological labours and classification of the Hindu Prātisākhyas.........The Hindus had carefully analysed the organs of speech, some centuries before the Christian era, and composed phonological treatises which may favourably be compared with those of our own day."

That ক changes into গ by slightly raising the accent (বাক্+অর্থ=বাগর্থ) and that খ and ঘ are but aspirated sounds of ক and গ, need not be demonstrated; that চ is a variant of ক, ছ is an aspirated sound of চ, that জ and গ are always interchangeable, may be detected even on reference to the Sandhi rules. To serve the purpose I have in view, let me adduce here some examples from the Vedic or Chāndasa speech. From শুচ্ (glow of light) we get শুক্র and শুক্ল, both of which are identical in form and meaning, as র and ল are one and the same ; we get also চিত্ (to perceive), কেত (desire) and চেত (=চিত্ত) lined together in one series. We may also notice, that from রোচ্ (bright with light) রোক (light) was derived; the later word আলোক owes its origin to রোক or লোক with an addition of আ as a prefix to the word. I draw the attention of the readers to the words ভোজ (ভোগ), রুজ (রোগ), বিজ (বেগ) and ওজ, (উগ্র). Thus we see that the ক of Tāmil may fitly represent the whole series of letters of the ক-বর্গ; similarly ট, ত and প may be made as the sole legitimate fathers of the letters of their class. That শ is the same as চ may also be shown by phonetic analysis ; in the old Iranian ছ, শ and স were interchangeable.

The pronunciation of the consonants of চ class is nearly as sibilant in Eastern Bengal, as it is in the Dravidian speeches; to represent this sound in letters I write here চ, ছ, জ and ঝ as—scha, ssa, dza, zha.

That the letters ছ, জ and ঝ were imported into the Tāmil script, some time after the introduction of what is called the 'Vatteluttu alphabet,' can be detected on comparing the modern Tāmil alphabet with the 'Grantha character' (prevailing now in Malabar) as well as with the Telegu script. The Telegu script, which agrees in the main with the Canarese, came into existence, at least as early as the 7th century A. D., since Hiuen Tsang speaks of the script, in the accounts of his travels in India. The epigraphic records show, that in the 6th century A.D., northern script was in use in the Tamilakam country, and that the modern Vatteluttu cannot be traced to a time earlier than the 8th century A. D. The Granth character was introduced in the 10th century A. D., to represent the North Indian Alphabet completely. At this day, the speech of Malabar was identical with the Tāmil speech, and some letters from the Grantha script were adapted in the Vatteluttu. These remarks will be sufficient to show, that when the Dravidian people first adopted the Northern script, they could, if they liked, introduce all the letters of the North Indian script; they elected to adopt a limited number of letters, so as to represent their natural sounds, they did not require all the letters for their use.

What I have stated in the previous lecture, of the origin and character of the cerebral letters, may just serve the purpose we have in view. I proceed now therefore, to consider the sound value of the sibilants and of the letter হ.

S.—It appears that ষ was derived from sibilant ছ which is intimately connected with খ in the matter of origin; লক্ষ্মী is pronounced লছ্মী in the U. P. and in Orissa, and খ represents ষ in many speeches in Western India; in the Canarese script ষ is written by giving one additional stroke to খ. Since ক্ষুদ্র, which is identical with ক্ষুদ্ল in the Vedic speech, became খুল্ল in early Sanskrit, to signify small (as in খুল্লতাত=খুড়া), we may safely assert, that ক্ষ was pronounced as খ in very early times, and this peculiarity is not due to corrupt pronunciation in Bengal. We must not forget, that in Pāli and in the later Prākṛtas, ক্ খ was written to represent ক্ষ as well as খ, occurring after a বিসর্জ্জনীয়. ষ is clearly pronounced as শ in Bengal and is never reduced to the sound of স. The sound of শ prevails in our speech, and this শ is pronounced as স, only in some cases where compounded with র and ল, as in শ্রী, অশ্লীল, etc. স is pronounced as a dental only when compounded with ত and থ. For purely Bengali words শ is the only sibilant that can be used.

Let me notice here some words of onomatopoetic origin, in which besides other sounds, ষ and ড played a good part. ষ indicated a heavy and solemn sound, while ড (ড় included) signified a roaring sound; বৃ and কং also conveyed or were made to convey a sonorous sound. বৃহ, বৃংহ, বৃংহতি signified the sound of a horse or an elephant; ঘোষ comes from ঘঃ (a heavy dull sound)+ষ; ঘণ্টা is composed of ঘং+টা (টা being the sound produced by striking something which is hard). Compare also the words মেষ ('মে'+ষ indicating sound), মেঘ, বৃষ, হ্রেষা, হর্ষ, ভাষ, মহিষ, রোষ (রু+ষ), কাংস্য (কং or কণ্ sound+য), and শুষ্ক (from the sound শুষ্ occasioned at the drying-up of water on fire).

In the Sanskrit language of a comparatively later time, as well as in the Prākṛtas, ড may be pointed out as the letter which has been used to indicate an awe-inspiring sonnd; ষং+ড=ষণ্ড of the later Vedic speech, may also be noted. Our ঝড়, তোড়, দৌড়, কড় কড়, হুড় হুড়, মড় মড়, etc., are examples in point.

হ *and* শ.—The aspirate sound of হ which has created the extra consonants খ, ঘ, ছ, ঝ, etc., is not as is very distinctly marked, fully pronounced in Eastern Bengal; the subdued sound of it is something like অ—অ which cannot be properly pictured; হ as an initial letter, is very clearly pronounced in other parts of Bengal, but that there is a tendency to soften its sound when it occurs as a medial or a final, is to be duly noted. It is a peculiarity all over Bengal, that মহাশয় is pronounced almost like মশাই by dropping হ and by retaining a portion of the sound of the final য় or ই+অ; মহিষ is pronounced as মোষ by introducing the long ও sound compensating the loss of হ, and কহা appears in our speech and script as কওয়া. Even when we omit to write হ in such a word for example as তাহার, our tongue glides a little over the হ sound, and thus we can distinguish this word in our pronunciation from তার to signify either 'wire' or 'taste.' When হ takes a য-ফলা, it is pronounced as জ-ঝ in Bengali as well as in Oriya.

The pronunciation of ঘর or ভাত is not exactly গর or বাত in Eastern Bengal, but is something like গঅ-র or বাআ-ত, while in Dravidian pronunciation, they are uttered as গর্ and বাত্. The non-aspirated pronunciation of ঘ, ধ, ড, etc., seems therefore due to Dravidian influence. I remind you, that I noticed previously, the similar pronunciation of the people of Ceylon. In the Chittagong division of Eastern Bengal, however, the Mongolian influence has been so very much predominant, that in some points, regarding the articulation of sounds, the Dravidian peculiarities (though not obliterated) have been drowned; unlike their neighbours of the Dacca division, the people of the Chittagong division, breathe the 'h' sound into ক, চ, ট, ত and প, and pronounce ফাক্ (পাক্), খলম (কলম), ছুপ কর, (চুপ কর), etc.; not having done away with the original Dravidian influence, they do not pronounce ঘর and ভাত, but they pronounce them as গ্গর and ব্বাত by doubling the initial letters as it were.

Though the letters চ to ঝ are made markedly sibilants in Eastern Bengal, as they are done in the Dravidian lands, শ is seldom rightly pronounced by the ordinary people of Eastern Bengal; the reduction of শ to হ in Eastern Bengal (or more properly to a half হ with a wavy swing) cannot wholly be attributed to Mongolian influence, since such a change of sound, may be noticed in other parts of Bengal as well; the word গোশাল has been changed into গো-হাল or গোয়াল all throughout Bengal. In the Sambalpur tract, we hear হেইঠি (there) for সেইঠি of standard Oriya; this substitution of হ for শ is noticeable in Marhatti as well. I have already stated, that the sound of 'শ' predominates in Bengali; I should mention also, that Hem Chandra has noted in his Prākṛta Grammar, that 'শ' takes the place of 'স' all throughout, in the Māgadhi speech, though the representation in script of the Māgadhi Prākṛta, shows the use of dental স for the palatal শ.

*Non-*হসন্ত *final.*—We cannot conclude without noticing a peculiarity in the pronunciation of a simple consonant occurring as a terminal in a word. On reference to the list of words arranged in pairs below, it will be observed that final letters of the first words of the pairs are pronounced as distinct syllables, while those of the second words of the pairs are হসন্ত or silent. ভাল and ঝাল, ব্রত and মত (opinion), কাল (black) and লাল, ঘৃত and শীত, প্রমথ and শপথ, নিহিত and মোহিত, constitute the short list in question, to illustrate roughly this peculiarity. Let us frame tentative rules, regarding the pronunciation of the simple consonants, when they are final. We must first note, that as a rule, the final simple consonants are হসন্ত in Bengali, unlike what the case is in Oriya ; the following are the rules for what form exceptions.

(1) When the penultimate is হসন্ত, no matter whether the penultimate and the final are made into one compound letter or not in spelling, the final is bound to be pronounced as a distinct syllable, unlike what is the case in Hindi ; শক্ত, জব্দ, কষ্ট, etc., are examples. (2) The final simple consonants of the verbs in the Imperative mood, second person, are distinct syllables as in কর, বল, চল, etc., where the imperative-indicating final হ has now been dropped ; when the expression is either non-honorific or highly honorific, হসন্ত sound prevails,—as কর্, বল্, চল্, etc. and করুন, বলুন, চলুন, etc. (3) (*a*) When the final letter is the representative of a compound letter of the original word, or (*b*) where the final letter of our vernacular word has become final by the decay of a syllable or of some syllables, স্বরান্ত pronunciation prevails. It is not asserted, that in all cases of such origin of words, the final simple consonant,

must as a rule be pronounced as non-হসন্ত; what is pointed out is, that where the normal হসন্ত pronunciation is deviated from, the words disclose the history of their origin as formulated above. ভাল (from ভদ্র=ভদ্দ), এত (from এতাবৎ), বার (from দ্বাদশ=বাড়শ), etc., are some examples. Contrast খাল, ঝাল, এক, তিন, সাত, দশ, etc. Notice also মত (like) decayed form of our vernacular মতন and মত (opinion). It has also to be noticed, in the history of such words as ছোট, বড়, ভাল, etc., that their earlier forms were ছোটা, বড়া, ভালা, etc. কাল=black is pronounced as কালা in Eastern Bengal, and this form কালা obtains in Upper India. It is further noticeable, that আ, like ই-আ and উ-আ is found conjoined to many noun stems, to indicate the adjective forms of the nouns; we are not, however, concerned with that phenomenon here. (4) The participle-forming ত (but not ইত) is pronounced as a distinct syllable, as কৃত, ক্রীত, প্রীত, আগত, etc.; contrast with them রহিত, মোহিত, সহিত, etc. (5) The past-indicating ল suffix, which owes its origin to participle-forming ত, is pronounced non-হসন্ত, as করিল, গেল, হইল, etc.; the ছ-ending of the suffix আছ (occurring in second person only) is also similarly pronounced, as আছ, করিয়াছ, গিয়াছ, etc. (6) When the initial letter is compounded with র or ল, and (*a*) vowels other than অ, do not come between the initial and the final, and (*b*) the consonant হ or ব does not intervene, the final letter is pronounced as a distinct syllable; *e.g.*, ব্রজ, ব্রত, প্রমথ (contrast with শপথ of হসন্ত ending), শ্লথ, etc.; but notice the হসন্ত finals of (*a*) গ্রাস, গ্রাম, ঘ্রাণ, প্রাণ, প্রসাদ, প্রদীপ, শ্লোক, ক্লেশ, সু-গ্রীব, etc., where vowels other than অ intervene; mark again, (*b*) প্রহর and প্রবল, where হ and ব intervene. As an exception to the general rule, we get first, the word ধ্রুব, the final of which is uttered as a syllable; we notice the general exception, where ম is final; as ক্রম, ভ্রম, শ্রম, etc. (7) The simple finals of the words of two letters are স্বরান্ত, when the initial letter has ঋ for its adjunct; *e.g.*, কৃশ, ঘৃত, নৃপ, মৃগ, etc.; contrast with them the হসন্ত sounds of the finals of কৃষক, কৃপণ, পৃথক, etc. (8) The finals of only a few re-duplicated words develop into স্বরান্ত sounds, wheu emphasis is put upon the words, as খচ-মচ in "কি খচমচই করছ" and পড় পড় in ঘরখানি পড় পড় হইয়াছে.

In the uame of framing rules, the cases where স্বরান্ত pronunciation prevails, have been set out in a classified order; to frame regular rules, we have to find out the essential underlying cause or causes, governing the phenomenon. In rule No. 1, we observe convenience in the matter of pronunciation. In rule No. 3, we notice, that to compensate the loss of letters at the end, a স্বরান্ত sound is drawn long; this is virtually the guiding cause in rule No. 2, since কর, চল, বল, etc., are the reduced forms of করহ, চলহ, বলহ, etc. As to other cases, I fail to enunciate any natural law, which causes the occurrence of the স্বরান্ত sound.

The scope of my subject did not allow me to notice the allied and cognate sound peculiarities as occur in other Aryan languages; I refer you however to a few Iranian peculiarities, just to suggest how wide our field of research is. In the first place we may notice, in connection with the sound of the vowel ঋ, that in Iranian, the radical 'ar' (ঋ) is reduplicated by ই; that the Indian sound of ঋ has always been 'ri' and not 'ru,' is clearly demonstrated by it. In the second place, we may observe without any reference to the ethnic composition in Iran, that 's,' is generally reduced to 'h,' which has been noticed as a special peculiarity in Eastern Bengal. In the third place, we may refer to the phenomena of Epenthesis and Prothesis, as occur in the old Iranian speech for comparison with similar phenomena, noticed before. As an example of Iranian Epenthesis, we may notice that the Vedic ভবতি stands as Bava-i-ti in Iranian ; by Epenthesis, I mean the introduction of anticipatory ই or উ in the middle of a syllable. As to Prothesis, *i.e.*, regarding the introduction of an anticipatory ই or উ, initially before a consonant, we may cite the example of ই ঋণ ইতি which corresponds to Vedic ঋণক্তি. Many other Iranian peculiarities, as agreeing with some provincial peculiarities in India, may be studied very profitably by the Indian students of Comparative Philology.

SOME FACTORS RELATING TO PHONOLOGY AND ACCENT

LECTURE VII

SECTION I

A Comparative Study of Accent

The term *akṣara* (literally "undying," *i.e.,* the ever-living and essential factor in human speech) signifies a letter as well as a syllable in the Vedic and so also in the later Sanskrit language. Different sounds of letters coalescing themselves in euphonic combination, and consonants unvitalized by vowel sounds, being joined to other consonants, generate compound letters; these compound letters, as well as the simple letters, being so many independent syllables in a word, must be separately pronounced. No doubt, in this method of pronunciation, we find the Vedic in agreement with the Sanskrit speech, but we have to notice that in the matter of accent, Vedic language differs very widely and radically from Sanskrit. In the Vedic language, the vowel sounds were not so very rigidly and unalterably fixed as long or short, as they are in Sanskrit; though, no doubt, a definite value is found assigned to each and every vowel, we can clearly see, on reference to the *pada-pāṭha* system, that the accentual stress of উদাত্ত, স্বরিৎ, and অনুদাত্ত, change what may be called the normal sounds of the vowels.

We have to first notice, that the final vowel of many flexional endings and of several adverbs, is given by the text, sometimes as short, sometimes as long. We have to notice next in the Vedic accent system, that not only the syllables, the words, and the phrases, but even many sentences are found accented. This fact, which discloses the living character of the speech, may be studied in the excellent analysis and discussion of the matter, in Prof. Macdonnel's Vedic Grammar. It may no doubt be said of the Vedic verses, that the general rythm of versification is not affected by accents; but that because of musical stress and accents, the verses are not lifeless quantitative ones (as in Sanskrit), should be duly appreciated. Since it is a fact, that natural gestures and modulations of voice, which contribute to the growth of the human speech, do survive as living factors in some proportion in each and every developed speech,—since it is undeniable, that every *real and living speech* must have an accent system of its own, a few examples of the Vedic accent should be adduced here, to form some notions regarding the Vedic, as well as the post-Vedic classical languages. Before citing the examples, I should note that উদাত্ত (as the meaning of it indicates) is the high accent in the Sāma Veda, while as a later innovation, স্বরিৎ of the next grade, is the high accent in the Ṛg veda; it will therefore be convenient to name the grades of accent by high, middle and low pitch or accent.

The first example I cite, is to show how by change of accent, a Vedic word changes its meaning. If the high accent be put upon রা of রাজপুত্র, the word will mean (being constructed as বহুব্রীহি) 'a person who is the father of sons who are or became kings'; but if the last letter ত্র is accented, the meaning will be, in the তৎপুরুষ compound, 'the son of a king.' For a similar change of meaning in Bengali, let me cite a few examples: if the Bengali word কলম is accented on the first syllable ক, the meaning will be 'a graft,' but with accent on the last syllable লম্, it will mean 'a pen.' How because of change in pronunciation, occasioned by difference in stress, a word varies in meaning, should be studied to realize the importance of accent in Bengali. *Cf.* আটা (flour) and আটা (gum), কড়ি (beam) and কড়ি (shell), কানা (blind) and কানা (edge), খোলা (open) and খোলা (tile), ছোঁড়া (boy) and ছোঁড়া (to throw), গেরো (a knot) and গেরো (as derived from গ্রহ signifying ill luck), চান (a bath, derived from স্নান) and চান্ (he wants), ঘাট (bathing place) and ঘাট (dereliction of duty), etc. Notice again, a case of accent where gesture becomes partly prominent. If a smell be pleasing, the word for our agreeable sensation will be normally accented, and the word গন্ধ will be accented on the first syllable, but our feeling of disgust about bad smell, will be expressed by putting a long accent upon the last letter, without any qualifying adjective being added : the utterance গন্ধ-অ-অ is sufficiently expressive. To express agreeableness, the particles of interjection in Bengali, are accented closely on the letter when the particle is of one letter, and on the first syllable, when the word is of more than one syllable; while on the other hand, in expressing our painful feeling or feeling of disgust, the accent is on the last syllable, and when the interjection is of one letter, the accent is put in such a manner on the letter, as to generate an additional syllable with a drawl sound upon it. For example, in expressing the feeling of admiration, the first syllables of বাহবা and বাপ্‌রে will be accented, and a close accent will be put upon the letter বা ; on the other hand বাপ্‌রে (not as exclamation of admiration), is accented on the last syllable, to express the feeling of pain. Similarly আ! gets a broad accent, generating a drawl, to express pain or disgust. It may again be noted, that বাহবা! will be something like বা-হাও-বা, with accent on the second syllable, when there is a banter in the tone; to signify such a sentiment, the interjection বা will be so modulated, as to make it a word of three syllables, with two আ sounds. This is difficult to express in script. We may consider also, that the emphasis-indicating 'very much' tends to duplicate the final consonant of a word; অত্ত from অত and এত্ত (so much!), এট্টু (very small), কোত্থাও, গোচ্ছা from গোছা, ছোট্ট, ঝক্কি from ঝুঁকি or ঝোঁক, ধাক্কা and ধক্কল, ফক্কা from ফাঁকা, বড্ড, বক্কেশ্বর from বকা, রগ্গা from রোগা, রত্তি, as in একরত্তি, from রতি, and সক্কাল বেলা (very early in the morning) are examples. We may compare similar forms in Oriya of Sambalpur, as খড্ডা (to fry) to indicate বেশী খড় খড়ে করে ভাজা (to make crisp by overdoing), and মেচ্ছা (for মোছা=moustache) মুরুছি (twirling) to express one's defiant attitude.

For my second example, regarding Vedic accent in metrical composition, I quote a Vedic verse, which is full of emotional sentiments. In this verse, the mixed feeling of eager solicitude and despondency has been expressed. The first portion of the first verse of the 95th Sukta of the 10th Mandal, which is addressed by Pururavā to his fugitive wife Urvaśi, on meeting her accidentally, stands with accents as follows :—

" হয়ে জায়ে মনসা তিষ্ঠ ঘোরে
বচাংশি মিশ্রা কৃণবাবহৈনু "

We cannot fail to notice, that many long vowels have been made either short or semi-short, with accents of lower grade upon them, and the short syllable ন in মনসা has a high accent on it. How on account of the subdued utterance of 'হয়ে,' and a high accent on the final syllable of 'জায়ে,' the feeling of coaxing with fervour, has been expressed, may be explained and appreciated, if in the first place, the verse is correctly recited, and in the second place, we carefully consider, how to express this very sentiment, we accentuate our words and modulate our voice to-day. If we translate হয়ে জায়ে by ওগো উর্ব্বশী or by ওগোও, we can see that to express anxious solicitude or cajoling, we have only to half accentuate ওগো, but have to fully accentuate শী of উর্ব্বশী, or the last ও of ওগোও, with a peculiar modulation of voice. This thorough agreement of Bengali accent, with the Vedic, in this particular instance, may be merely a chance agreement, but all the same, it is interesting to note, that in Hindi, as well as in Oriya, the method of accent is different. In the corresponding Hindi form of the expression, as য়ে উর্ব্বশী or ইয়ে পিয়ারে, the interjection ইয়ে will be pronounced with high accent or great emphasis ; similarly 'এ' of এ উর্ব্বশী or এ ধন of Oriya idiom, will require the high accent to be placed on এ. Even though ও comes before a name in the vocative case in Bengali, the name itself is modulated peculiarly, to signify address, and the interjection portion is not so vigorously pronounced, as it is done in Hindi ; the forms, রাম হো (Hindi) and হৈ হো রাম (Sambalpur Oriya) may be compared with our corresponding Bengali form. In the Nepalese, এ must invariably come before a word in the vocative case. When thus noticing different accentual peculiarities in the vocative case, I should note, that in the Dravidian speeches, interjections do not occur before the words in the vocative case.

The third example, I cite for Vedic accent, relates to the pronunciation of the word Agni, as occurs in the Sāma Veda, the Maitrāyani Samhitā, and the Kāṭhaka Samhitā ; we find the high accent placed upon the compound letter গ্নি (*i.e.*, to say upon the final নি) and not upon the initial অ, which alone should be pronounced long in the Sanskrit language. That with this very accent on the second syllable, the word অগ্নি was pronounced in our oldest-known prākṛta (misnamed Pali), may be gathered from some facts which I should notice here. We get গিনি and অগ্‌গি, as two different decayed forms of অগ্নি in the aforesaid Prākṛta ; they represent presumably, two different provincial forms of the old time. We can clearly see in the history of the word গিনি, that on account of accent on the last syllable, the unaccented first syllable dropped out, following the natural rule of phonetic decay. In our consideration of the form অগ্‌গি, we first notice, that according to our previously formulated rule (stated in illustrating the Dravidian influence), গ of the second syllable has been doubled, as letters of different বর্গ cannot form a compound; the word is therefore, more in a changed form than in a decayed state. As to the pronunciation of it, I refer to a line of a verse composed in ইন্দ্রবজ্রা, as occurs in the Thera Gāthā:—অগ্‌গি যথা পজ্‌জলিতো নিসীথে (like the fire blazing in the midnight). The metre here is only seemingly faulty, as the second syllable of অগ্‌গি is not long; but if we accept the proposition, that the short syllable in question has a high accent on it, it will be admitted that the accent makes up for the shortness in question.

We notice, both in the so-called Pāli and the later Prākṛta dialects, that their speakers changed the spelling of the words according to accent and pronunciation, but did not introduce like the Dravidians, such additional vowels as short এ and short ও. The fact however, that long and short vowels were articulated short or long, following the natural accent, can be easily determined by referring to the prose composition with which the Prākṛta literature abounds. Professor Pischell has rightly asserted in his work on the Prākṛta. Grammar, that the Vedic accent or tone did not die out, but existed in the so-called Pāli Prākṛta. The learned scholar came to this conclusion, by looking deep into the causes, that led both to the phonetic decay and the accretion of new letters in the Pāli words. Professor Jacobi, misled by the modern artificial method of reading Pāli, has criticized this view, and has asserted, that the Vedic tone did not survive in the Pāli speech, but only it was a sort of *stress*, that was in use in the utterance of words. We must remember, that accent is a thing of hard growth and cannot die out easily. By the introduction of new racial elements, the old accent system of a speech may undergo some change, but the system itself is not wholly effaced.

We have seen, that a very regular and thorough-going accent system prevailed in the Vedic speech; we have also seen from an example of a Vedic verse, that emotions were freely expressed in the Chāndasa speech, and in consequence thereof, the vowels could not be kept rigidly fixed in their long or short pronunciation. It is on the other hand perfectly clear, that the Vedic text for illustration (beginning with হবে ক্ষাবে, etc.) will be a lifeless quantitative verse in Sanskrit, requiring artificial and meaningless raising and lowering of vowel sounds in the following form:

⏑ —, — —, ⏑ ⏑ —, — ⏑ — —, etc.

We should not however overlook, that inspite of rigidity of rules, we have to put different stress upon different words occurring in a Sanskrit verse, when there is a feelingly recitation in contradistinction with what may be called metrical articulation. No doubt, we can see, that this sort of putting emphasis upon phrases, is not due to the living character of the language, in which the poems are composed; there are many good Sanskrit verses, wherein we find, that their poets by virtue of their skill, have arranged the words of long vowels in such a manner, that the feelingly expressions may be appropriately brought out, by putting emphasis upon the long vowels only: The example of the verse in the নীতিশতক, beginning with নিন্দন্তু নীতি নিপুণা যদিবা স্তবন্তু, is in point. This is rather infusing life in dead bones.

I have judged here the Sanskrit language, by taking the question of accent only into consideration; other facts, as are necessary to be discussed in determining the character of a language, will certainly be discussed relevantly in a subsequent lecture, but we should not forget, that accent is the life breath which vitalizes the words, and a speech without accent is a contradiction in terms. We have seen from the accent point of view only, how unnaturally rigid the Sanskrit language is; we will see on references to other facts, that this artificial rigidity is due to the fact, that Sanskrit had to accommodate itself within a frame-work of generalized rules, which some mighty grammarians constructed in their zeal to perpetuate linguistic purity, when in consequence of a natural change, the speech of the holy Vedas was transformed into a new popular speech.

I should mention in this connection, that some persons are very wrong in their opinion, that such a living speech as Oriya, is without an accent system. The misconception is due to the fact, that in Oriya, as in Sanskrit, all the letters are pronounced as distinct independent syllables. That inspite of it, the letters and words are accented by the Oriyas, without any reference to the long or short sound of a vowel, is instructive. I cannot deal with the Oriya accent system here; I adduce only one example to serve my purpose. গলা (gone) as an exclamation of surprise, will be articulated with accent on the first syllable, which is short, and the word will sound like গ-অ-অলা (Oh ! it is gone), while the accent on the second syllable in similar feeling of surprise will bring in another গলা as প্রচয় or accumulated unaccented letters, like a tag to the word, and the sound will be like গলা-আগলা. I should inform you in this connection, that in Oriya the final syllable of a word is generally accented and this is why, (*a*) the final simple consonants are not pronounced হসন্ত, (*b*) রাজা has been reduced to রজা and the Apabhranśa form of কাংস্য is কঁসা, and (*c*) the half nasal ঁ is placed on the final letters of such words as কাহিঁ, যহিঁ, etc.; it is noticeable, that when the Bengalis write the Oriya words কাহিঁ, যহিঁ, etc., they represent them as কাঁহি, যঁহি, etc.

In my general criticism relating to the question of accent, I have noticed many peculiarities of ours; I proceed now to consider some other marked peculiarities, as should engage the attention of all scholars. As a general rule, in our standard Bengali speech, the first syllables are accented, while curiously enough the last syllables are accented in Eastern Bengal. Mr. J. D. Anderson, late of the Bengal Civil Service, has written of late some very suggestive and learned notes in the J. R. A. S. on the character of Bengali syllable and accent. To the students of philology these original notes are of very high value. Misled by the wrong idea or information, that the people of the districts of Mymensingh and Dacca, have the tendency to make the first syllable accented, Mr. Anderson has compared the Assamese mode of pronunciation with that of Eastern Bengal, and has subjected the Eastern Bengal accent system to Assamese influence. As the case is quite the contrary, we must look to some other influence for this phenomenon. Let me just give a few examples as to how the words are accented differently in Eastern Bengal and Central Bengal. In Central Bengal, মাথা having the accent on the first syllable, the unaccented syllable is pronounced soft, and থ sounds like ত; in East Bengal, however, মাথা́, কথা́, কেরে́, etc., are the accented forms. With accent on the first syllable, the final য় of কোথায় is wholly or partially dropped in Central Bengal, while the accent on the last syllable in Eastern Bengal brings out খা and য় distinctly. As a result of accent being placed on the first syllables, the unaccented second syllables of many words, have undergone a natural phonetic decay, in the common speech of the people of Central Bengal, and thus the unaccented ই sound in the second syllables of করিব, করিয়া and করিলাম have become extinct, and the forms করব, করে and করলাম have prevailed. As in Eastern Bengal the last syllables of আইল, আইস, etc., are accented, and the first portions must be uttered to come to the last syllables, almost no change takes place in those words; but when the first portions are accented, the two vowels আ and ই, coalesce and long এ, which is the combination of আ and ই takes the place of the first two letters; thus এল and এস take the place of আইল and আইস. In Manbhum and in some parts of Bankura, which are contiguous to the lands of the Dravidians, the last syllables are mostly accented; in the sentence তোমার বেটা বটেক্? (Is he your son?) the last syllables of all the three words are accented. Because of change of accents, বেটা is pronounced বেটা in Central Bengal. কুথ, the old Prākṛta or proto-Bengali form of কোথা still survives in Manbhum, partly because of the hilly accent, and partly because the accent is placed on the last syllable. It is notorious, that the last syllables of words are generally very much accented by the Dravidians. The final আ of foreign nouns are for this reason made into āi, as for example মণিমেখলা becomes মণিমেখলৈ. This is why the vulgar people in the South, pronounce the English words 'government,' 'and,' etc., as governmen-ta, an-d, as, etc. I have spoken before of the Dravidian element in Bengal; it is the excess of this element which I suppose to be the cause of Eastern Bengal peculiarity. In the Chittagong Division however, where the Mongolian influence is considerable, the first syllables are mostly accented vigorously, by almost duplicating the accented syllables, and thus পাক, তোমার, etc., are reduced to ফাক, থোমার, etc.; but in other respects the wide-spread Dravidian influence of basic character, peeps through the thin Mongolian veil.

I have spoken before of the general disinclination in Bengal, of not fully articulating হ, when it is not an initial letter, and that thus we have got such forms as গাইতে, সইতে, রইতে, etc., for গাহিতে, সহিতে, রহিতে, etc. When the tendency to put the stress of accent upon the first syllable is coupled with this phenomenon, we see how তাহার and তাহাতে are reduced to তার and তাতে. That in spite of the decay of হ, the sound of the letter is partially retained in our tongue, can be detected in the mode of our pronunciation of those words, in contrast with the pronunciation of তার meaning taste or wire and তাতে, a verb which signifies "becomes hot." Really speaking therefore, হ is not dropped, but its sound fades into indistinctness, after the accented তার; as such, it is improper and useless to leave out হ in our spelling in these cases; those who elect to pronounce তার for তাহার will do so in spite of the letter হ, for accent on the first syllable will soften the sound of the letter হ. The so-called reformers should see, that if হ is retained, it will not be sounded much because of the accent on the preceding syllable; again presence of হ will maintain the right pronunciation of the words concerned.

SOME FACTORS RELATING TO PHONOLOGY AND ACCENT

LECTURE VIII

Section 2

Bengali Metrical System

We should do well to proceed now to ascertain the character of the Bengali accent of olden days, by examining the metrical system, preserved in the poetical works of old Bengal. Adverting to the fact, that the early Vaiṣṇava poets of Bengal treated each and every letter as a syllable, and made the final consonantal sounds non-hasanta, by imitating the old fashionable poet Vidyāpati of Mithilā, many people have formed two wrong notions; one is that Bengali was derived from Maithili, and the other is that our mode of pronunciation and of counting syllables, was of the type presented by those poets. Mithilā became no doubt, at one time, a portion of old Gauḍ which extended to the foot of Nepal if not into Nepal itself, but the Maithili speech of the days of the Vaiṣṇava poets, had nothing to do with our Bengali language. As to elements, common to Bengali and Maithili, we have to look to the older Māgadhi speech of which, notice will be taken later on. From the earliest known time, our Bengali poets (excepting those who followed the Maithili fashion) ḥave uniformly composed their poems, not by counting letters but by counting syllables. Looking to the fact, that the fourteen letters of the পয়ার verse for example, are the same as fourteen mātrās of fourteen syllables, the পয়ার may be seemingly regarded as composed of fourteen letters; but that it is a *syllable* (which may consist of more than one letter) and not a *letter* which is the *unit* in a Bengali word, should never be lost sight of. How is it that consistently with or rather in harmony with the phenomenon, that our metrical system is grounded on a syllabic and accentual basis, a fixed number of letters come in a chanda, will be explained presently, after considering some facts leading to the point.

To explain the character of Bengali syllables, let me set forth some words with their syllable divisions by marking the syllables off, by the sign hyphen : মা-নুষ, আ-মা-মের, বন্-ধু (বন্ধু), অ-হং-কার, etc., will show that there may be less number of syllables than the number of letters in a word. Mr. J. D. Anderson has rightly remarked with reference to our phrase accents as well as in respect to the syllables in a word, that this special aspect of phrase accent in a word, "is sufficiently dominant to be the basis of accentual verse in Bengali." Mr. Anderson has very successfully demonstrated what I once feebly pointed out in a Bengali essay, that the assertion of our Paṇdits, that the পয়ার metre is not composed of syllables but of fourteen letters, is wrong. The two lines quoted by Mr. Anderson from Kṛttivāsa in J. R. A. S., 1913, 861, may be cited to show, that the lines of fourteen letters consist of twelve and thirteen syllables respectively, and that the verse moves on with syllables and not with letters. The lines, as accented by Mr. Anderson stand as :

এ'ক-দিন শু'-ক্র গে-ল ত-প'-স্যা ক-রি-তে
হে-ন কা-লে' দ'ণ্-ড রা-জা গে-লে'ন প'-ড়ি-তে।

It will be noticed that it is the accent on লেন of গেলেন in the second line. which has given the easy motion required by the rhythm, and by virtue of accents, lines of seemingly unequal syllables have agreed in the metre. I adduce now another example, to illustrate our metrical system.

Take first a line of verse which accommodates fifteen letters which coincide with fifteen syllables :

তুমি অতি শিশু ছেলে কোথা যাবে একাকী ?

Let us then notice, that maintaining this very metre, lines of fifteen syllables may be introduced in a verse, though counting by letters, the lines may contain twenty or twenty-two letters :

আ-শ্বিন মা-সের ভো-রের বে-লায়
বা-গান ত-খন ফুল-প-রা
স-তেজ শ্যা-মল ত-রুর ত-লায়
গ-ঙ্গা ছি-ল কূল-ভ-রা ।

To indicate cæsura, I have divided the lines above keeping eight syllables in the first foot. The first line of the verse contains twenty-two and the second twenty letters. Refer to whichever poet of the past time you please, excepting the Vaiṣṇava poets, who imitated non-Bengali forms, you will find that our verses are all based on accentual basis. I quote here only some lines from Dāsarathi Ray and Iśvar Gupta, who preceded our immortal poet Madhusudan.

খেয়ে কিনা মোচার ঝাল ঝাল লেগে বানরের গাল
আপ্‌নার গাল আপ্‌নি চড়া চড়ি ।

If read according to the natural accents of the words, it will be seen that the syllables being taken as units, there are eight distinct sounds of eight letters in each of the first two feet, and sounds of ten letters occur in the third, fulfilling the requirements of number of letters for such a ত্রিপদী metre. Next after this verse of Dāsarathi, a verse of Iśvar Gupta in our indigenous রেক্তাছন্দ may be noticed.

" নানারকি নানা কেলে
নানারকি নানা কেলে রাজ্য পেলে
তাতেই এত জারি !"

Before proceeding to show, how from our indigenous songs which unmistakably disclose our accent system of old times, not only the literary Bengali verses but the Sanskrit verses as well originated, let me notice here the wrong opinions of some eminent Bengali writers, regarding the character of our versification. It has been wrongly held by some, that in the old poetry of Bengal, হসন্ত words practically do not exist. It has been wrongly asserted, that in our old poetry, natural accent was not cared for and the "unnaturalness of recitation was made up for by chanting the verses to a tune." This is only true of those writers, who imitate the old Vaiṣṇava poets in the matter of their versification and diction, that an adventitious artificial jingle has been introduced.

In addition to what I have quoted from the old poets, I quote below another verse from Kṛttivāsa to substantiate my statement and to show the incorrectness of the opinion just referred to.

অতিকায় পড়ে রণে রাবণ চিন্তিত
যোড়-হাতে বাপের আগে কহে ইন্দ্রজিৎ।

The word চিন্তিত rhyming with ইন্দ্রজিৎ leaves no room for even a careless reciter to articulate its final ত with a vowel sound; that যোড় and বাপের carry normal pronunciation, is absolutely clear. The supporters of the contrary opinion are found even to name অন্নদামঙ্গল of Bhāratchandra in the list of the delinquents, without noticing that if we leave a few artificial Sanskritic verses out of consideration, Bhāratchandra must be given the credit of having composed verses with words of common use with their natural accent. অন্নদামঙ্গল as well as his other works, abounds with verses like :

"ঝাঁকড় মাকড় চুল্, নাহি আঁদি সাঁদি,
হাত্ দিলে ধূলা ওড়ে যেন কেয়া-কাঁদি।"

When, more than fifty years ago, we read Madanmohan's poem পাখী সব, etc., we were not asked by our village teachers to deviate from the usual pronunciation, and did never read সব, রব, কুসুম, রাখাল, গরুর পাল, শিশুগণ দেয় মন, etc., with final অ sound.

Despite the fact that Madhusudan has drawn largely upon the Sanskrit vocabulary for some effect in the blank verse, his verses have to be read by putting proper accents upon the words. Is it not true, that far from imposing an adventitious artificial jingle upon our verse, and far from throttling our natural accented words to death, Hemchandra has made the Bengali verse to move with natural accent, with uncommon vigour and rapidity? I think I have made it clear, that Bengali words with their accent have always been used in our Bengali verse, and the exception to the rule has only been occasional, where there has been an imitation of the forms of some Vaiṣṇava poets. The imported metrical system of some Vaiṣṇava poets could never take root in Bengal.

I proceed now to show from the history of evolution of our metrical system, that the accent system which now prevails, has been the accent system of the Bengali-speaking people, from the time about which faint suggestions can only be made, by taking a stand at the shadowy threshold of dim past. The history of the evolution of human institutions has made us familiar with this phenomenon, that our verse with our metrical system owes its origin to tribal festive songs, which in their turn originated from primitive expressions of emotions. In its normal condition, therefore, no metrical system of any race, can have any other basis than an accentual one.

To ensure convenience, I refer first of all to such Sanskrit metres as are of undoubted late origin. মানবকা-ক্রীড় is a ছন্দ of late origin and its origin in Magadha-Gauḍa cannot be seriously doubted. The hemistiches of one line of this verse are divided below by partition lines :

আদি গতং। তুর্য গতং। পঞ্চ মকং। চান্ত্য গতং।

Each hemistich is really a complete foot, and the characteristics of it are repeated in subsequent hemistiches. A portion of our nursery rhyme will be seen to be exactly in accord with it. It is as follows :

হাত ঘুরুলে। নাড়ু দেব। নৈলে নাড়ু। কোথা পাব।

The apparent inaccuracy in the second hemistich of the first foot disappears if the সুর or tune underlying the Sanskrit as well as the Bengali verse is rightly caught. Uniformity in Sanskrit metre is maintained by the fixity of long and short sounds, while without following the Sanskrit rule, mere tune may maintain the purity of the metre with natural accent in the Bengali verse. Compare the same ছন্দ in another nursery rhyme :

ডালিম গাছে, ফিলপু নাচে ; তাক্ ধিনাধিন্ বাদ্যি বাজে।

It will be seen that how the four akṣaras required in each hemistich in Sanskrit, correspond exactly to the four syllable-unit of Bengali. No one will venture to say, that our village girls or matrons imitated the মানবকাক্রীড়; that the Paṇḍits utilised the indigenous chhanda for a Sanskrit metre verging upon মাত্রাবৃত্ত, cannot be doubted. When songs were composed with mātrās, numerous chhandas cropped up in Sanskrit, and the verses were set in indigenous tunes. To illustrate this properly, I take a verse of a very familiar song from the গীতগোবিন্দ. I divide the lines for the purpose of my analysis, and put the tag portions in brackets.

বদসি যদি। কিঞ্চিদপি। দন্তরুচি। (কৌমুদী)

হরতি দর। তিমিরমতি। (ঘোরং)।

ফ্‌ুরদধর সীধবে। তব বদন। (চন্দ্রমা)।

রোচয়তি। লোচন। (চকোরং)॥

প্রিয়ে চারুশীলে etc., as ধুয়া or refrain.

It is first to be noticed, that each portion divided by partition lines consists of either five letters or five mātrās. The beginning of the refrain portion if divided similarly, a great artificiality will be noticed, since the first division will take in only the first three letters প্রিয়েচা ; but if sung according to the tune, this unnaturalness will disappear, and the whole refrain will be found to be set in music with all regularities. Compare with it the line composed in Bengali রেক্তাছন্দ, already quoted above, and is quoted again, for facility of reference :

নানারকি নানাকেলে—

নানারকি নানাকেলে। রাজ্য পেলে।

তাতেই এত। জারি।

If we exclude the introductory নানারকি নানাকেলে which is pronounced as অনুদাত্ত, and if we set apart the word জারি as a tag, the essential agreement between the Bengali metre and the Sanskrit metre, will be obvious ; the word জারি if pronounced with lengthening sound as is done in reciting a verse of the রেক্তাছন্দ, its agreement with ঘোরং, will also become clear. In রেক্তাছন্দ there is an introductory portion which is of peculiar nature; the first portion of the first line becomes the independent introductory portion of the verse. The introductory line সে যে গো পুষ্যি এঁড়ে, must first be articulated as অনুদাত্ত, and then it is to be repeated as উদাত্ত with the other portions of the verse. The verse then will stand thus—

সে যে গো পুষ্যি এঁড়ে—

সে যে গো পুষ্যি এঁড়ে দস্তি ভেড়ে

নস্তি কর তাকে।

That the refrain portion, therefore of the Sanskrit song, originates from the introductory tag, becomes rather clear. No doubt there has been some lengthening of the tune in Sanskrit in the refrain portion, but this is because a uniformity of the metre has been maintained. To explain the matter more clearly, let me notice here a verse which has been composed by exactly adopting the metre of Jayadeva's song বদসি যদি, etc.; it will be observed in this verse that the essential character of the chhanda has not been affected, even though there has been either a little lengthening or a little shortening of some mātrās, in conformity with the genius of the Bengali metre. The Bengalicised Sanskrit verse runs as :—

তেমন-ইকি আসে উষা সে সোণালি সুষমায়,
সাজায়ে শ্যামল দেহ শরতের ?
শুনি যবে পাখীদের আনন্দের ঘোষণায়
ভেঙ্গে যায় নীরবতা জগতের ?

If the portions হরতি, etc., and রোচয়তি, etc., of Jayadeva's song, and the corresponding lines of the Bengali verse be put aside, the following Bengali verse composed after an indigenous Bengali metre, will be found to be in perfect agreement with the chhanda in question :

ঠাকুরমা, সেই ছেলে বেলায়, ঘুম পাড়াবার ফন্দিতে,
এক যে রাজার মজার গল্পের হুঁ হুঁ জোড়া সন্ধিতে
এম্‌নি ক'রে ঢেলে দিতেন নিদ্রালসের আবর্লি,
নেতিয়ে পড়্‌তে হ'তই ঘুমে, রাজারাণী যা বল্লেই ।

For an example of a Sanskrit metre, corresponding to or agreeing with the Bĕngali লঘুত্রিপদী, which may easily be conceived to have evolved the longer or দীর্ঘত্রিপদী, I lay again the poet Jayadeva under contribution. In his

চল সখি কুঞ্জং সতিমির পুঞ্জং
শীলয় নীল নিচোলং ।

if নিচোল be separated from the third foot, the three feet will be found to be of equal length in quantity. We can therefore see, that the final নিচোলঃ comes in as a tag to break the monotony. Consquently, to trace the origin of the chhanda, we may safely take into consideration, the three feet of the verse leaving the tag portion out. Corresponding exactly to these three feet in form and tune, we get the lines of a country song, which is sung in a game, that may be fitly described as choral dance. In this game a boy usually stands in the centre of a ring, formed by a number of little boys and girls standing hand in hand: the boy in the centre seeking slyly the opportunity to break through the circle to run away, goes on singing an action song—এতৃত টুকু পানি, and the boys and girls who encircle him, sing half dancing the chorus– ঘো ঘো রাণি, ঘো ঘো রাণি. It is significant to note, that this very game of Bengal, prevails in the far off Sambalpur tract, and it is this very ঘো ঘো রাণি, conveying no meaning to us, is sung as chorus in the country places of that tract; that the game and the song originated in remote past, is forcibly indicated by this very circumstance. Again, when ঘো ঘো রাণি is sung twice as chorus, the whole portion becomes a লঘুত্রিপদী minus the tag, which may be an improvement upon the song, in the line set forth above.

The Paṇḍits who look for our পয়ার, a respectable origin, make the Sanskrit অনুষ্টুভ, the forbear of our humble পয়ার, though the tune and the form of the one do not agree with those of the other. That our nursery rhyme বিষ্টি পড়ে টাপুর টুপুর, etc., is wholly in accord with our পয়ার, cannot even for a moment be doubted. Though the lines move on keeping time with the note of a tune imbedded in syllabic accent, they contain fourteen letters, and at the end of the first foot of a line consisting of eight letters, we get the requisite cæsura. It will be noticed in the last line of the verse quoted below, that রা of রাগ being lengthened by the stress of an accent, the loss of one letter has been made up for. The verse is :

বিষ্টি পড়ে টাপুর টুপুর নদী এল বান,
শিব ঠাকুরের বিয়ে হবে তিনটি কন্যাদান ;
একটি কন্যা রাঁধেন বাড়েন, একটি কন্যা খান,
আর একটি রাগ ক'রে বাপের বাড়ি যান।

The purpose I have in view, does not allow me to write elaborately on the genesis of our metrical system ; a separate treatise should be devoted to the execution of the work. The nature of our accent, the accentual basis of our metrical system, and the fact that our accent has been retaining its peculiar character since long, are factors which should principally engage our attention. That in respect of our accent, a long continuous current may be observed to have flown through ages, will be clearer when we consider other facts, and the readers will have to form their opinion, by considering the effects of what may be called cumulative evidence.

As to the origin of many Sanskrit metres from popular rhymes, such non-Sanskritic names as তোটক (indicating special emphasis on the third letter—তিরট+ক), দোধক (of equal length with তোটক, leaving out the initial and the final accented syllables ; the accent falls regularly after two intermediate unaccented syllables—*i. e.*, ধক্ or ধাক্কা or 'push' comes after 'দো' or two) লীলা খেল (the word খেল indicates the origin), etc., may be referred to.

I cannot certainly deal with our metrical system at a greater length here, but I cannot at the same time conclude this section of my lecture without referring you to the Hindi and the Oriya modes of reciting poetry, in contrast with our mode. I speak of the mode of recitation only, as it is not possible to analyse here the metrical system of Oriya and Hindi. I doubt not, that you have heard in this city the Oriyas and the up-country men to read aloud their verses. It must be a familiar experience, that from the sound alone from a good distance, a Bengali can know whether an Oriya poem or some Hindi দোঁহা's are being recited. Even where there is no musical chanting, the character of the metres will indicate the characteristic difference. All this is due wholly to different accent systems. As the style of a language is the expression of the thought of the speakers, so is the metrical system in a language, due to the special accent system of the people. The Oriya verse of lines of 9 akṣaras, if read in Bengali fashion, the composition will sound like a disjointed prose piece; so also it will be with such ত্রিপদী lines of Upendra Bhanja, as :

ব্যধি বন্তর বাঞ্ছিত উপচার
বৈন্ধ বিহিলার পরিষে

Similarly if the lines of a Hindi দোঁহা be not read in the Hindi fashion, the music of the lines will fade away. Without pronouncing any definite opinion as to whether the lines quoted below, were composed in old Bengali or Hindi, I may bring to your notice, the basic Hindi character of the metre of the lines; the non-hasanta sound of the final syllable and the long sound of the penultimate, as have to be maintained in rightly reciting the lines, are to be duly noted. The lines are :

কাআ তরুবর পঞ্চবিডাল
চঞ্চল চীএ পইঠো কাল ॥

I do not mean to be exhaustive here; I want however to impress upon you, that we can solve many linguistic problems at least partly, if we take the factor of accent, deeply into our consideration.

SOME FACTORS RELATING TO PHONOLOGY AND ACCENT

LECTURE IX

SECTION 3

Accent traced in Sandhi and Compound Formations

Sandhi.—The phenomenon of euphonic combination or Sandhi should engage our attention next, as by a study of it we can partly ascertain many phonetic and accentual peculiarities. How some stiff Sanskrit rules of Sandhi can be simplified on reference to the original Vedic sound-value of some letters, has been discussed separately, and this discussion has been relegated to an appendix to this lecture. It is true, that unlike what is noticeable in Greek, Chāndasa does not allow any hiatus to exist in a word, but the rigid Sanskrit Sandhi-rules by virtue of which two or more independent words are linked together in an agglutinated unit, do not appear to have obtained in Chāndasa. I need hardly assert, that in a living speech, in which ease and fluency in the matter of articulation of sentences can never be disregarded, and in which words must be uttered in an intelligible manner, Sanskrit rules of Sandhi cannot be strictly enforced. The component parts of Purohita for example, may not be allowed to stand separate, since the newly-formed word, has a distinct signification of its own, but the force of the word Adya, (অদ্য) for example, disappears, if Adyendrasya অদ্যেন্দ্রস্য be substituted for অদ্য ইন্দ্রস্য. We get such a line as বয়ম্ অদ্য

ইন্দরস্য প্র ইষ্টা in the Vedic Padapātha, while the Sanskritic form of the text gives us বয়মত্বেন্দ্রস্য প্রেষ্ঠা, which involves the loss of three syllables required by the metre. I cannot speak here anything regarding what is called স্বরভক্তি as noticed in the Vedic pronunciation of ইন্দর for ইন্দ্র, but the example will fully show, how the rigid Sandhi rules of Sanskrit Grammar make a simple speech, unintelligible. We find in the Vedic verses, as is natural in a living speech, that each foot, nay each hemistich, stands apart, without being united in Sandhi with a succeeding foot or hemistich. We observe only in some rare cases in Sanskrit, that one hemistich is not united with another in a verse, where Sandhi combination is possible; the following is a couplet which illustrates this sort of deviation from the usual rule :

যো ধ্রুবাণি পরিত্যজ্য অধ্রুবাণি নিসেবতে
ধ্রুবানি তস্য নশ্যন্তি অধ্রুবম্ নষ্টমেবহি।

It becomes perfectly clear, that once when the Vedic language became obsolete, various cases of euphonic combination occurring in that language were studied very carefully, and a good number of generalized artificial সন্ধি (Sandhi) rules were framed for their rigid application in what is called the Sanskrit language. This is why the processes noticeable in Chāndasa in such euphonic combinations, as are due to the influence of accent (which is a living factor in a living speech), are not at work in Sanskrit; instances of lengthening the accented vowel, as in বিশ্বামিত্র (বিশ্ব + মিত্র) or অনূপ (অম্বু + আপ) or of dropping the unaccented vowel as in চার্বাক (চারু + বাক্), are not obtainable in Sanskrit.

It is a fact that the rules of Sandhi, as are noticeable in Pāli, are not wholly in agreement with the Vedic rules; that this very deviation shows the living character of that earliest-known Māgadhi Prākṛta, is what we should duly appreciate. How because of the natural accent of the speakers, and owing to the changed value of the sound of some letters, such euphonic combinations occurred in Pāli, as দেবাতি (দেব + ইতি), পন্নরসেরিব (পন্নরসে + ইব), পাদন্তি (পাদং + ইতি), etc., should be a subject of special study. That the Sanskrit Sandhi-system does not support this claim of Sanskrit, that it was naturally evolved out of Chāndasa should be duly noted; we can very clearly see, that the natural Vedic rules of euphonic combination have only been artificially extended in Sanskrit, to cases where combination brings about stiffening of the speech and unintelligibility of meaning.

It is certainly very true, that our Bengali Sandhi system is not worked by the rules of the old time speeches, but we proceed to show that the very principle which governed the phenomenon of euphonic combination, in the speeches of ancient times, governs to-day the Sandhi system of ours. Before I cite examples to substantiate my proposition, I should notice an objection which is raised by some in this direction. On the basis of a superficial and unscientific observation of the fact, that the rules which govern the formation of such combinations as ইত্যাদি, মনোহর, etc., do not prevail in Bengali, some scholars have gone the length of asserting that the natural phenomenon of euphonic combination does not at all exist in Bengali. We have certainly borrowed the words ইত্যাদি and মনোহর in their entirety, and cannot disjoin them in our language; no doubt our ইতি means finish, আদি means original, and ইত্যাদি means etcetera; again there is no such word as মনস্ in Bengali, nor the word হর, if not a name of a man, can have any meaning independently. It is also true that ই and আ do not combine according to Sanskrit rule to form যা, but we have noticed previously, that they coalesce in Bengali quite in another fashion. Non-observance of Sanskrit rules does not however justify us to formulate, that euphonic combination is unknown in Bengali.

In Bengali, we do not and cannot combine different words into one agglutinated whole, for we utter our words one after the other, to convey distinct meaning of them to other ears; but different vowel sounds and allied consonants do combine to form one word. With the অপভ্রংশ word মশা, the Sanskrit word অরি (enemy) being joined in sandhi, we have got one word to mean the distinct article মশারি (mosquito curtain) ; to signify a special sort of আলু (bulb) the adjective গোল and আলু have been joined to form the word গোল আলু; the word কাঁচা as an adjective of কলা does not and cannot change its form, but when the words are combined together to signify the sort of কলা which is used as vegetable, the final আ of the adjective being dropped, the word কাঁচকলা has been formed; we may also get the examples ঘোড়া + গাড়ি = ঘোড়গাড়ি, যোড়া + বাঁধা = যোড়বাঁধা, বোকা + চন্দ্র = বোকচন্দ্র (fool), etc. In such examples as কাঁচ কলা, ঘোড়বাঁধা, etc., we notice the loss of unaccented আ finals of the first component parts of the words; similarly we find the loss of ই of ইচ্ছা in the phrase যাচ্ছেতাই, where the accented যাহা in the form of যা occurs as the first component. We have seen that in the Vedic language, there were elision of the final vowel sounds of the unaccented syllables in their euphonic combination with unaccented syllables, and that is why the final উ of চারু dropped in euphonic combination with accented বাক্, to form the word চার্বাক to signify a man of persuasive speech.

That the lengthening of vowel sound as noticeable in the Vedic words, বিশ্বামিত্র, বৃসা-কপি, etc., is also noticeable in the old Prākṛtas as well as in modern Vernaculars, requires to be pointed out. We may notice, for example, the Pāli idiomatic expression ফলাফল (various sorts of fruits) in such a sentence as ফলাফল স্স অন্তো ন অত্থি, to see unmistakeably that the word has not been formed by the combination of ফল + অফল. This sort of duplication to indicate either variety or etcetera is very much current in Bengali; it is also the rule in Bengali, that in the process of duplication, an আ comes in as a joining link. We must clearly see, that the Bengali words ফলাফল, হিতাহিত, মতামত, চলাচল, etc., do not combine good and bad ideas together; চলাচলের রাস্তা does not signify the path for going and not going. The 'আ' that comes in here as a joining link, indicates emphasis only, when occurs in the formation of compound words; compare the emphasized forms কপাকপ, চটাপট, টপাটপ্, etc., with the ordinary forms কপকপ, চটপট, টপটপ, etc. I feel tempted to notice, that in common parlance it is difficult to many of us to keep the purity of the Sanskrit word দূরবস্থা; because of accent on অবস্থা the word is pronounced usually as দূরাবস্থা.

The natural rule by which one consonant is changed into another, because of the genetic affinity between the consonants, is also at work in Bengali; এক + গঙ্গা = এগ্‌গঙ্গা পাঁচ + জন = পাঁজ্জন, ছোট্ট (ছোট = younger) + দাদা = ছোড়দা, যত + দিন = যদ্দিন are examples. The Sandhi rules of Prākṛta Grammar as are still at work, should be carefully studied by the students in this connection; I point out here a few cases only, where Bengali is in agreement with the old Prākṛtas, in the matter of euphonic combination. From চড়্ + চড়্ we get চচ্চড় and from জগৎ + বন্ধু we get জগবন্ধু; final ৎ is very often dropped in Pāli even though there is no euphonic combination with the initial letter of a succeeding word, for example, কিঞ্চি is the form for কিঞ্চিৎ, and আসী is the representative of the fuller form

আসীৎ. I may remark in conclusion, that the Dravidian method of Sandhi combination, is noticeable in some rare cases only; in Tamil 'ম + কাই' and 'তে + কাই' for example, will be মাঙ্গাই (mango) and তেঙ্গাই (cocoanut) respectively; this growth of nasal sound in Sandhi has only been noticed by me in খোলা + কুচি = খোলাম্ কুচি.

Samāsa—সমাস.—I have spoken above, that change of vowel as well as of consonant takes place in the formation of compounds called samāsa (সমাস); but as many noted scholars are of opinion, that barring a few stray examples, we cannot get samāsa compounds of genuine Bengali words, I must show that compounds or samāsa of all sorts exist in Bengali. I consider this question to be important, for it is to be seen, whether the old mode of thinking which brought about samāsas in particular forms, is still our inheritance or not; it must be borne in mind, that the racial peculiarity in the matter of thinking, governs the style and structure of a language. I cite below the Bengali samāsa forms exactly in that classified order which is maintained in authoritative Sanskrit Grammars.

অব্যয়ীভাব—Adverbial Compounds.—1. In the following examples, অব্যয় words do not occur as in Sanskrit, but the compound forms indicate the sense of the অব্যয়ীভাব সমাস—(*a*) indicating বীপ্সা—গলি গলি, বাড়ি বাড়ি, রাস্তায় রাস্তায়, রোজ রোজ, etc.; (*b*) ক্রম—পরপর, পিছুপিছু, etc.; (*c*) অনতিক্রম—রাতারাত, যত পারি, যা পারি, etc. The following examples may be contrasted which are *not compound forms, viz.*—দেখ্‌তে দেখ্‌তে (quickly), চল্‌তে চল্‌তে (by excessive walking), গাছটি বাড়্‌তে বাড়্‌তে (in the course of growth) শুকিয়ে গেল, ফল পড়্‌তে পড়্‌তে (just on falling) কুড়িয়ে নিল, etc.; in these cases, infinitives being doubled, the sense of repetition has been expressed, but the words do not form Samāsa compounds. (*d*) The following examples indicating "the whole of" are closer in relation with অব্যয়ীভাব forms than with others : মাঠ্‌কে মাঠ, বাজারকে বাজার, ঘর্‌কে ঘর, etc. (*e*) Where to indicate পর্য্যন্ত (up to) 'আ' occurs in Sanskrit, as in আকণ্ঠ, আকর্ণ, etc., only the doubling of the word takes place in Bengali; *e.g.*, 'গলায় গলায়' খাওয়া, 'কানায় কানায়' ভরা, etc., এক নৌকা লোক, ভরপেট, কুঁচ্‌কি কণ্ঠা may be compared with these forms, as indicating the sense of অব্যয়ীভাব।

তৎপুরুষ—Determinative—2.—If the examples grouped under the following sub-heading (1) be regarded as I suggest, as of তৎপুরুষ class (being Determinative, or rather Dependent) wherein the nominative case predominates, we may hold that we have তৎপুরুষ with vengeance in Bengali. I may then classify the তৎপুরুষ forms as কর্ত্তা প্রধান, কর্ম্ম প্রধান and so forth, looking to the sense which the forms convey.

(1) The তৎপুরুষ of nominative prominence, or কর্ত্তা প্রধান তৎপুরুষ :—For this entirely new class of Bengali compounds, my examples are,—দাগলাগা, বাজপড়া, etc. We have to note that such Sanskrit forms as তৈললিপ্ত, বজ্রাহত, etc., are construed as তৃতীয়া তৎপুরুষ ; the form কাদামাখা may be construed as করণপ্রধান তৎপুরুষ, but কাদালাগা cannot be so construed ; we have also to notice that the forms of my example cannot be classed under বহুব্রীহি, for, in বহুব্রীহি forms a person or thing must be indicated irrespective of the meaning of the component parts. This is why I have suggested this new nomenclature for a class of compound words. Mine is a suggestion merely, and not an authoritative statement. Compare all the compound forms occurring in the sentence আমার লাল-পেড়ে তেল-ধুতি খানার এই থানটা বাকুচী-বাড়ীর বাদুড়-চোষা গাছ-পাকা জামের রসের দাগ-লাগা ; the 1st is বহুব্রীহি, the 2nd is তৎপুরুষ of 4th class, the 3rd is ষষ্ঠী তৎপুরুষ, the 4th is তৃতীয়া তৎপুরুষ, the 5th is ৭মী তৎপুরুষ ; and so now the character of দাগ-লাগা may be appreciated.

(2) কর্ম্মপ্রধান তৎপুরুষ (object-indicating) :—মানুষ খেকো (as a tiger), মন ভুলান, ইঁদুর ধরা (as a কল or machine), বৈ পড়া (as in বৈ পড়া বিদ্যা), etc., are examples.

(3) করণ-প্রধান or agency-indicating :—হাত-গড়া, কাপড়-ঘেরা, এক-কম-কুড়ি (signifying ঊণ or less by one) ; at times 'এ' is added to the final letter of the first part of the compound as আরশুলায়-চাটা (আরশুলা-চাটা is another form), মেঘে ভরা (also মেঘ-ভরা), etc. In বাদুড় চোসা, the final letter does not take an 'এ'।

(4) Purpose-indicating or উদ্দেশ্য বাচক :—তেল-ধুতি (cloth worn for besmearing the person with oil), পা-জামা (for পা, *i.e.*, trousers), মরা-কান্না (wailing befitting the occasion of death in the family), বসৎ-বাড়ী (house intended for dwelling), etc.

(5) অপাদান-বাচক, to signify 'away from':—পাল-ছাড়া (straying away from the flock or herd), সৃষ্টি-ছাড়া (different from what is usual), ঘর-পালান ছেলে (a run-away boy), পাহাড়-ঝরা (পাহাড় থেকে) জল, etc.

(6) Relation-indicating or সম্বন্ধ বাচক :—ধর্ম্ম ভয় (the word ভয় does not affect the character of the compound in Bengali), বিয়ে-বাড়ী, মাস-কাবার, বন-বেড়াল, etc.

(7) Locative or স্থান কাল বাচক :—গাছ-পাকা (ripened on the tree), নৌকা-ভরা লোক (*i.e.*, নৌকায়—full up in the boat), ঘর পোষা, etc.

কর্ম্মধারয়—Descriptive—3.—(1) আধফোটা, কালপেঁচা (an inauspicious owl) ; (2) কাঁচা পাকা (ripe *and* unripe), তাজা মরা ; (3) মিশ্-কাল (black *like* মিশি or black tooth powder, here the final ই of মিশি has been dropped), ছেলেবুদ্ধি, কাঁচ-পোকা (looking *like* glass), সোনা-মুগ (a lentil, *like* gold in colour), etc.

দ্বিগু—Numeral compounds—4.—পাঁচ-গজি (as a cloth), তে-হাতি, দু-পিঠে (lit. having two sides), এক চোখো (as a judgment, disclosing partiality).

বহুব্রীহি—Possessive compounds—5.—মা-মরা, হাঁড়িমুখো (long-faced), পাড়া বেড়ানী, বাইশ কর্ম্মা (one who does nothing), etc.

দ্বন্দ্ব—Copulative—6.—মানুষ-গরু, লেপ-কাঁথা, আম-কাঁঠাল, ভাল-মন্দ, উনিশ-বিশ, etc.

Duplicated Words.—The words which are duplicated on account of emphasis, to indicate repetition, or to express the idea of excessiveness, should be noticed and classified here, to distinguish them from the Samāsa compounds. I need hardly remind you that according to the যত্ত rule and by the rule of the ণমুল্‌প্রত্যয়, words are duplicated in Sanskrit to indicate repetition or excess. I refer you to the whole section of the Siddhanta Kaumudi entitled Dvirukta Prakaranam which begins with the rule সর্ব্বস্যদ্বে, wherein reduplication of various sorts has been illustrated.

1. (*a*) The adverbs সোজাসুজি (quite direct), পাশাপাশি (close by the side), মাঝামাঝি (right through the middle), etc. (indicating 'very much'), and হাঁটাহাঁটি, ছুটাছুটি, টানাটানি etc., (indicating 'repetition'), may be classed under one head. Such adverbs as মোটামুটি from মোট (total; taking the whole roughly into consideration) and গোড়াগুড়ি from গোড়া (beginning from the very beginning) come also under this head, as the idea involved in the words is that মোট or গোড়া is taken repeatedly or much into consideration. The vowel changes in this class of duplication must be noted.

(*b*) কাটাকাটি, মারামারি, চুলাচুলি, হাতাহাতি, etc., fall also under this head as a sub-class, as a slightly-differing sense of reciprocity in fight is indicated by them. মুখামুখি (*tete-a tete*), চোখা চোখি (each seeing the other), কোলাকোলি (the act of embracing), etc., are also of this class.

2. Though the idea "very much" is in the following words, they differ from the first class in meaning as well as in form; the words are duplicated without undergoing any change. Thinking too much of, or having anxious solicitude for, or making too much of, will be found to be the idea involved in বাড়ি বাড়ি, দাদা দাদা, and কলিকাতা কলিকাতা, in the following sentences,—আমার মনটা বাড়ি বাড়ি করিতেছে, সে দাদা দাদা করিয়া মরিল, তুমি বড়ই কলিকাতা কলিকাতা কর।

3. When duplication takes place to indicate 'almost like,' or 'similar to,' no change of vowel takes place. The forms কাদা কাদা, জ্বর জ্বর, ঠাণ্ডা ঠাণ্ডা, মানুষ মানুষ, etc., are examples.

4. In the class of duplication noticed below, there is this special peculiarity, that in the process of duplication, the original word without being repeated, is conjoined to a synonym of it. Agglutination of two seemingly different words, should not mislead us to consider the word as a Samāsa compound. The adverbs করেকম্মে, ভেবেচিন্তে, ফেলেছড়ে, বলেকয়ে, মেগেযেচে, etc., are fitting examples. The noun forms ঘরবাড়ি, লোকজন, সোরগোল, মাথামুণ্ডু, গাগতর, etc., are also similarly duplicated. Some duplicated words of this class, may elude detection of their character, as in either the first or the last augmented portion, some obsolete or unfamiliar words appear. I give a few examples. In the word আশেপাশে, the first portion is the Vedic word আশা, which has the same meaning as পাশ of Bengali; the adverb চলেবুলে and the noun form ছেলেপিলে may also be considered; the word পিলা is a Dravidian word for child, and the word বুলা meant walking in old Bengali, and in that sense the word is still in use in Oria; in the word খুঁজে পেতে, the last portion পেতে or পাতা comes very likely from Hindi পাত্তা (*cf.* পাত্তা নেহি মিলা, no trace is obtained); the word পাতি in পাতি পাতি করিয়া খোঁজ, seems to be also of the same origin. Let me adduce a few examples to show, that a word of foreign origin or of classical origin, though really a synonym of a word, is used either as an adjective or an adverb to its synonym, because the real import of the foreign or classical word is lost sight of, or is imperfectly understood; the word গন্ is a corruption or অপভ্রংশ of Pāli গিনি (Sanskrit অগ্নি); this অপভ্রংশ form is found retained in the phrase গন্গনে আগুন. The word or stem হন্ is of Kolarian origin, and

it signifies walking; it is this হন্ which we meet with in our হন্‌হন্ করিয়া ছোটা. These words should not be confused with the words of onomatopoetic origin. In গালি-গোপ্তান, the second Persian word is a synonym of the first. I have heard school—boys saying আকাশ খুব clear পরিষ্কার হয়েছে; as a translation of police investigation we at times meet with তদারকের অনুসন্ধান in our Bengali newspapers. Whatever that may be, let me add a few more examples as may fall under this class. They are: ঘুরেফিরে, ঠেঙ্গিয়ে পিটিয়ে, ডেকে হেঁকে, তেতে পুড়ে, বন জঙ্গল, বন বাদাড়, বেঁচে বর্ত্তে, ভিজে তিতে, ভেঙ্গে চুরে, হাট বাজার, etc.

5. Almost connected with the fourth class is the class I now describe. To give special emphasis to an idea, two words are so joined together, as the second portions may indicate the consequence or completion of the action, indicated by the first portions of the compounds. A few examples are: আণ্ডা বাচ্ছা, উলট্ পালট্, কেঁদে কোকিয়ে, ঘসে মেজে, জ্বলে পুড়ে, টেনে হেঁচ্‌ড়ে, দেখে শুনে, ধুয়ে মুছে, নেয়ে ধুয়ে, নেচে কুঁদে, বুঝে স্থঝে (স্থঝে = to see), মেরে কেটে, রেঁধে বেড়ে, লড়ে ভিড়ে.

6. Such duplications as মানে মানে, প্রাণে প্রাণে should perhaps be classed separately, as they indicate—anyhow saving or protecting মান (honour) and প্রাণ (life).

7. It is difficult to say whether the second portions of the following compounds are meaningless additions, or that they once had some significance, and as such should be grouped under the fifth class. The words are:—কুড়িয়ে বাড়িয়ে, জুড়ে তেড়ে, কাপড় চোপড়. If the last named example is the representative of the প্রাকৃত idiom বত্থ-চিবর, চোপড় may be easily explained.

8. To indicate etcetera or 'the like,' the words are generally duplicated with the loss of the initial letters and by the substitution of ট for the initial letters. কাজ টাজ, ভাত টাত, মাছ টাছ are very familiar examples. When

disgust is sought to be expressed, the initial letter of the duplicated portion is usually changed into ফ, as—এ গরমে কাজ ফাজ করা চলে না, রাত্রে ভাত ফাত খাওয়া দায়, মাছ ফাছে কাজ কি? etc. It is to be noticed, that in some cases, duplication is made not with the ট initial but with some other letters. চাকর বাকর, বাসন কোসন, রকম সকম, etc. are examples; it is rather difficult to enunciate any general rule for these irregular forms. It may be, that in the cases of these exceptions, the augmented portions are but representatives of some obsolete words, and if so, must be grouped under class four. As in পূজা আর্চা the augmented portion is a contracted form of অর্চনা, so there may be many augmented forms, the meaning of which may be traced.

9. Such onomatopoetic words as কচ্, খড়্, পট্, মড়্ are generally duplicated in their use. It is worth noting here, that many words simulate onomatopoetic origin, though they are really but অপভ্রংশ forms; ধব্ধবে is from ধবল (white) or from ধোয়া (washed clean), মিশ্মিশে is from মিশি (black tooth powder), ফুট্ফুটে is from Sanskrit স্ফুট্, ফুরফুরে is from Sanskrit স্ফুর্, ভুরভুর is from ভূরি (much). A special class of onomatopoetic words as ঠঙ্ ঠঙ্, ঝন্ ঝন্, খট্ খট্, etc. is of special interest in the Prākṛta dialects; in olden times the use of such words as well as of Deśī words of all sorts was prohibited by the Sanskrit Grammarians because of their vulgar origin. This is exactly why they are of importance in a history of language. I reproduce in Appendix I, my paper on onomatopoetic words which was published in the Journal of the Royal Asiatic Society in 1905.

APPENDICES TO LECTURES VI TO IX

Appendix I

A study of some Onomatopoetic Deśi Words

(*Reprinted from J.R.A.S. 1905.*)

There can be no doubt, that onomatopœia and interjectional cries played a great part in the formation of our languages. It is true that the 'Bow-wow' theory alone is insufficient to trace the origin of all words; and it is not true, what Professor Noirê would have us believe, that all roots can be traced to some interjectional cries of primitive men. But it is true that a carefully instituted philological analysis can disclose the influence of onomatopœia and interjectional cries in the formation of a very large number of Vedic and Laukika roots.

When by strict, rigid, and thorough-going rules of grammar, an artificial check was placed upon the growth of the Sanskrit language, new words could not be coined except by the fixed rules of grammar, from the definitely established list of roots. How jealously the purity of the literary language was being guarded in the second century B.C., can be known from the Mahābhāṣya of Patañjali. It has been declared sinful in that book, to use words, other than what are strictly Vedic and Laukika.

In the Sanskrit works which have been, with considerable certainty, fixed to a time previous to the second century B.C., no other words than Vedic and Laukika (in the strictest Pāṇini sense) can be met with. Since the Mahābhārata abounds in words not strictly Laukika, may we not venture to say that this is evidence, so far as it goes, that the building up of the poem did not commence till at least a century later than the time of the Mahābhāṣya? Such an orthodox work as the Mahābhārata came eventually to be, could not have departed from the much respected orthodox rules, if time had not then made the rules almost obsolete. What is true of the Mahābhārata, is true also in respect of the Rāmāyaṇa, as we now have it. To my humble thinking, the latter shows signs of lateness to a great extent.

Of words formed by imitating natural sounds and underivable from the fixed stock of Sanskrit roots, kolāhala, kilikilā and the like are only found in the eighteen lengthy Parvas of the Mahābhārata. Halahalā, Gadgada and Humbhā (lowing of the cow) are found used in the Rāmāyana; in the 23rd Chapter of the Âraṇyakāṇḍa, we find exact sounds of birds used as Sanskrit words. "Chīchīkūchīti vāśyanto babhūbustatra sārikā," would have defiled the purity of language in the second century B.C. This very "chīchīkū" we find also in the Harivamśa. These words, as well as the words Khaṭ-khaṭ, Ṭhan-Ṭhan, Jhan-Jhan, and Raṇaraṇaka of still later literature, have been called Deśī words (words of Provincial origin) by Hemchandra. It is known to all that Hemchandra's Deśī Nāmamāla contains such words as were considered not to have been derived from Sanskrit roots. It is true that Hemchandra has declared such a few words to be Deśi, as are really apabhranśa words, but I must also note that some ingenious attempts have been made at a forced affiliation of many real Deśi words to some recognised roots; I do not however consider it worth while to offer any criticism on this point.

When literature grew, the writers felt the want of words, and were forced to borrow many words from the

Prākṛtas. To commence with, it was only sparingly done but when once it was tolerated and approved, the writers introduced the Prakṛta words very largely. This inference receives full corroboration, from the languages of the old inscriptions which have now been chronologically arranged in many books.

The Deśī words of onomatopoetic origin, such as Jhaṅkāra, maḍmaḍa, Paṭ-paṭ, and the like, are nowhere found in the works of Kālidāsa and Bhāravi.* It might be plausibly argued, that the use of such words in dignified Kāvyas was studiously avoided by the poets. But it is worthy of note, that Kālidāsa has not used these words even in the Prakṛta dialogues in his drama, while Mṛcchakaṭikā and Ratnāvalī abound with such expressions. It is also not true, that the use of "Gharghara" for Nirghoṣa and 'Jhaṅkāra' for Aliruta lessen the dignity of the language. These words have been profitably used, to heighten the effect of grand descriptions, by Bhavabhūti in his Uttara-carita and Mālatīmādhava.

The poet Subandhu flourished towards the end of the sixth century, say about a century after the death of Kālidāsa. We find the use of a small number of onomatopoetic words in his Vāsavadattā as nouns only. Three or four such words of this class as are found in Mahābhārata and Rāmāyaṇa are also found used as nouns, -as I have already shown. This is the sort of use made of them (though very sparsely) in the Pañcatantra. Kolāhala is the only word I have met with in the existing Pañcatantra, even though this is not exactly the book which was written in the fifth century.

---

* It should be noted that the word Marmara (and not Maḍmaḍa) is derived from the root Mṛ, and as such cannot be treated as a word of onomatopoetic origin.

In the writings of Bāṇabhaṭṭa, Bhavabhūti, and Sūdraka, these words have been very freely and largely used. Verbs also were made of them, and expressions like Khaṭ-khaṭāyate, Phurphurāyati, and Maḍmaḍāisma are found frequently. The use of these words as verbs commenced only in the seventh century, so far I have been able to ascertain. From the seventh century onward, there is scarcely any Saṇskrit composition, wherein these Deśī words of onomatopoetic origin are not found.

I should like what I have asserted to be tested by reference to the books, the dates of which have been fairly established. If the use of this particular class of Deśī words grew in the manner indicated in this paper, the words will have a special value in determining the chronology of some old books.

APPENDIX II

ব্যাকরণের সন্ধি

[১৩১৮ বঙ্গাব্দের সাহিত্য-পরিষৎ পত্রিকা হইতে পুনর্মুদ্রিত]

একজন লোক নিজের রচনায়, কেমন করিয়া শব্দগুলিকে সন্ধির বন্ধনে বাঁধিয়া লইবে, ইহার শিক্ষার জন্য ব্যাকরণ নয়। যে সকল রচনায় সন্ধি-বন্ধন আছে, সেখানে কি উপায়ে পদবিচ্ছেদ করিয়া মূল শব্দগুলিকে চিনিয়া লইয়া অর্থ করিতে হইবে, তাহার শিক্ষার জন্যই ব্যাকরণের সূত্র। ব্যাকরণ শব্দের অর্থ হইতেই তাহা সূচিত হয়। ব্যাকরণে ব্যুৎপত্তির জ্ঞান হয়,—বিশ্লেষণপ্রণালীর শিক্ষা হয়। পদে পদে সন্ধি যোগ না করিয়া যদি কেহ সংস্কৃত গদ্য রচনা করেন, তবে তাঁহার রচনাকে কেহ দোষযুক্ত বলিতে পারেন না। ব্যাকরণে এমন সূত্র নাই যে সন্ধিযোগ না রাখিলে রচনা অশুদ্ধ হইবে। শব্দের রূপ বা ধাতুর রূপ, স্বতন্ত্র কথা। যে রূপ ধারণ করিলে শব্দের যে অর্থ হয়, কিংবা ক্রিয়াপদে যে কাল বুঝায়, তাহা হইল ভাষার মূল কথা; তাহা না মানিলে কোন পদের বা কোন শব্দের অর্থই হয় না। সন্ধি যোগ করা বা না করা, লেখকের সুবিধার কথা; উহা যে 'পুরুষেচ্ছয়া,' তাহার প্রাচীন উল্লেখ আছে। যেখানে সন্ধি যোগ হয়, সেখানে যে তাহা করিতেই হইবে, এটা হইল অর্বাচীন যুগের সংস্কৃত রচনার একটা অস্বাভাবিক পদ্ধতি।

মানুষের প্রতিদিনের কথা কহিবার ভাষায় সন্ধিবন্ধনের কড়া নিয়ম থাকিতে পারে না; স্বাভাবিক উচ্চারণের সুবিধায় যতটুকু সন্ধির বাঁধন পড়িয়া যায়, ততটুকুই থাকে। বাঙ্গালায় আমরা গোলালু, মশারি প্রভৃতি যেমন বলি, বৈদিক ভাষা বা ছান্দসেও তাহাই দেখিতে পাই। যখন সন্ধিবাঁধনের কড়া নিয়মের যুগে বৈদিক ঋক্‌গুলির পদে পদে সন্ধি জুড়িয়া পুঁথি লেখা চলিতেছিল, তখন 'পদপাঠের' সৃষ্টি। সন্ধি জুড়িলে বৈদিক

ছন্দ এবং স্বর নষ্ট হইয়া যায় বলিয়া, 'পদপাঠে' যেখানে সন্ধি নাই, গোড়ায় সেখানে সন্ধি ছিল না বলিয়া বুঝিতে হইবে। অনেক স্থলে যে সন্ধি করিতে গেলে অক্ষর কমিয়া গিয়া ছন্দ নষ্ট হয়, তাহার অনেক দৃষ্টান্ত আছে। বৈদিক ঋকৃগুলির কেবল পদপাঠ দেখিলেই সকলে উহা বুঝিতে পারিবেন।

ছান্দস হইতেই সংস্কৃত ভাষার উৎপত্তি; কিন্তু হয়ত এই ভাষা খৃষ্টাব্দের প্রথম শতাব্দীর পূর্ব্বে 'সংস্কৃত' নাম পায় নাই; পালি সাহিত্যে অপ্রচলিত Classical ভাষাকে ছান্দস-ই বলা হইয়াছে; বিনয় পিটকের চুল্লবগ্‌গের একটি উল্লেখে উহা সুস্পষ্ট। ১৪০ খৃঃ পূর্ব্বের মহাভাষ্যেও সংস্কৃত শব্দ ভাষা অর্থে পাওয়া যায় না। যখন হইতে ভাষার নাম "সংস্কৃত" পাওয়া যায়, তখন হইতেই উহাতে জটিল রচনার পরিচয় পাই। সন্ধির ঘটা, সমাসের বাহুল্য প্রভৃতি ত আছেই, তাহা ছাড়া অনেক স্থলেই এমন ভয়ঙ্কর দুরন্বয় যে, অনেক টানিয়া হেঁচ্‌ড়াইয়া পদে পদে যোগ করিয়া অর্থ করিতে হয়। ইহাতেই বুঝিতে পারা যায় যে, সংস্কৃত কেবল একটা সাহিত্যের ভাষা হইয়া দাঁড়াইয়াছিল; উহা কথাবার্ত্তার ভাষা ছিল না। যে সময়ে ঐ ভাষাটির নাম হইয়াছিল 'সংস্কৃত,' তাহার বহুপূর্ব্ব হইতেই এদেশে অনেকগুলি 'প্রাকৃত' বা লোকব্যবহারের স্বাভাবিক ভাষা ছিল। সেই সকল স্বাভাবিক ভাষা বা প্রাকৃত ভাষাও ছান্দস হইতে উৎপন্ন হইয়াছিল। লোকব্যবহারের ভাষা যখন পণ্ডিতিধরণে ঘষিয়া মাজিয়া লওয়া হইয়াছিল, এবং ছান্দস বা বৈদিকে অব্যবহৃত অনেক নূতন জিনিষ আমদানি করা হইয়াছিল, তখনই ঐ ভাষার নাম হইয়াছিল সংস্কৃত বা সংস্কার-পূত। যে ভাষা সাধারণ লোক-ব্যবহারে অপ্রচলিত ছিল, তাহা যে ব্যাকরণের নির্দ্দিষ্ট সংখ্যক কড়া নিয়মের মধ্যে আবদ্ধ হইবে, তাহার আর বিচিত্র কি? সাহিত্য, দর্শন, বিজ্ঞান প্রভৃতি সমস্তই সংস্কৃতে রচিত হইত; কিন্তু লোকে কথাবার্ত্তা কহিত আপনাদের দেশপ্রচলিত প্রাকৃত ভাষায়।

সংস্কৃতের সন্ধির সূত্রগুলি হইতে ঐ ভাষার অর্ব্বাচীনতা এবং প্রাচীনতর ভাষাগুলির প্রকৃতি, কিছু কিছু বুঝিতে চেষ্টা করিব।

19

বর্ণমালার মধ্যে স্বরবর্ণ বলিয়া যে শ্রেণীবিভাগ, ওটা হইল ভাষার একটা বিজ্ঞান হইবার সময়কার সৃষ্টি। স্বতন্ত্র ও স্বাধীন অ, আ প্রভৃতির উচ্চারণ ত ছিলই, তাহার পর আবার বর্ণগুলির স্থায়ী উচ্চারণ, আওয়াজ বা স্বরের সহিত ঐ অক্ষরগুলির আওয়াজের সমতা ধরিয়া লইয়া বর্ণগুলির নাম হইল স্বরবর্ণ। 'আ' অকারের দীর্ঘ উচ্চারণ হইলেও, অন্ত দীর্ঘ উচ্চারণের সহিত উহার একটু পার্থক্য আছে। কিন্তু দ্রাবিড়ী উচ্চারণ ধরিলে ই, ঈ-র মতই অ এবং আ বর্ণের উচ্চারণে দীর্ঘতার ভেদই পাওয়া যায়। দক্ষিণপ্রদেশের উচ্চারণের হিসাবে 'আ'কারকে যথার্থই 'অ'কারের একটু দীর্ঘ উচ্চারণ মাত্র পাই। প্রাচীনকালে সেইরূপই ছিল; তবে বৈদিকে কোন কোন স্থলে 'আ'কারের প্রায় হ্রস্ব উচ্চারণ আছে। আর 'অ' বর্ণটি ও স্থলে স্থলে সংবৃত উচ্চারণে প্রায় বাঙ্গালা উচ্চারণের মত ছিল।

ঋ এবং ৯ কিরূপে উচ্চারিত হইত যে উহারা স্বরসংজ্ঞা পাইয়াছিল, তাহা অল্পে বুঝাইয়া লেখা শক্ত। এখনও উত্তর-পশ্চিম সীমান্তে ঋ-র উচ্চারণ প্রায় 'এর' ও প্রাচীন Iranicতে অর্-এ উচ্চারণই ধরা যায়। ঋকারান্ত শব্দের বিকৃতিতে, প্রাচীন কালের প্রাকৃত ভাষায় উ এবং ই উভয়বিধ আওয়াজই ধরিতে পারা যায়; কি কারণে উহা ঘটে, তাহা স্বতন্ত্র প্রবন্ধে লিখিব; বিকৃতির 'উ' দেখিয়া ঋ কারের দ্রবীড়ি উচ্চারণকে ঠিক মনে করা ভুল।

স্বরবর্ণের উচ্চারণভেদে প্লুতসংজ্ঞা নির্দ্দেশ দেখিয়া, মান্দ্রাজ প্রদেশের "এ" "ও" প্রভৃতির দীর্ঘ উচ্চারণের একটা প্রাচীন মূল ছিল বলিয়া স্বীকার করিতে হইবে। পাণিনির ৮।২।১০৬ এবং ৮।২।১০৭ সূত্র হইতে ইহা সুস্পষ্ট হইবে। বৈদিক ছন্দের পাঠে এই প্লুত উচ্চারণ যথেষ্ট আছে, ঐ সকল উচ্চারণ ধরিয়া বিচার করিলে "এ" এবং "ও"কে যুক্তস্বর বলিতে হয়। বৈদিক ব্যাকরণে ঐ, ঔ, চারিমাত্রাবিশিষ্ট (সিদ্ধান্তকৌঃ বৈঃ প্রঃ ৩৬২৫ সূ)।

"এ" যেন অ+ই অথবা আ+ই মিলিত হইয়া উচ্চারিত; উচ্চারণ একটু তাড়াতাড়ি করিতে হয়, নহিলে "ঐ"কারের মত ধ্বনি হয়। ঐরূপ

আবার "ও"কারটি যেন "অ" বা "আ" পরস্থিত "উ"র মিলিত ধ্বনি। অকার কিম্বা আকারের সহিত "এ" যুক্ত হইলে যে উচ্চারণ হয়, তাহা হইল "ঐ"; এবং "ও" যুক্ত হইলে হইল "ঔ"। এই উচ্চারণ যে সন্ধির নিয়মের সঙ্গে মিলিয়া যায়, তাহা পাঠকেরা বেশ দেখিতে পাইতেছেন।

এই উচ্চারণ বা স্বরবর্ণের স্বাভাবিক আওয়াজ হইতেই দেখিতে পাইতেছি যে, পদগুলি উচ্চারণ করিতে গেলে স্বভাবতঃ যাহা ঘটিত, অনেকগুলি স্বরসন্ধির সূত্রে তাহাই বিধিবদ্ধ। যথা—"অকারের পর আকার থাকিলে উভয়ে মিলিয়া আকার হয়; অকারের পর ইকার থাকিলে একার হয়, উকার থাকিলে ওকার হয়; অ কিম্বা আকারের পর এ কিম্বা ও থাকিলে যথাক্রমে ঐ কিম্বা ঔ হয়; ইত্যাদি।" উচ্চারণ যদি প্রাচীনকালের মত থাকিত, তবে এই সন্ধির সূত্রগুলি কাহাকেও মুখস্থ করিতে হইত না। বলিয়া দিলেই হইত যে, ভিন্ন ভিন্ন উচ্চারণ মিলিত হইলে যুক্ত উচ্চারণকেই স্বাতন্ত্র্য বা প্রাধান্য দিতে হইবে।

দুইটি আওয়াজ এক সঙ্গে মিশিলে একটা মিশ্র আওয়াজ হইবেই; সাধারণতঃ শেষের আওয়াজটি প্রথমটিকে ঢাকিয়া ফেলে, অথবা একটু হ্রস্ব বা মন্দীভূত করিয়া দেয়। সন্ধির নিয়মে সর্ব্বত্র তাহাই। এই নিয়মটি সম্বন্ধে দু' একটি কথা পরে বলিতেছি। এখন ঋ-কারের সন্ধির বিচার করি। প্রথমেই বলিয়াছি, যে "ঋ" ও "ঌ" প্রথমে কিরূপে উচ্চারিত হইত, তাহা এখন কোন প্রদেশের উচ্চারণ হইতেই ধরা যায় না। আকারের পর ঋ থাকিলে, আকারটি একটু খর্ব্ব হইয়া "অ" হইয়া গেল, তাহা না হয় বুঝিলাম। কিন্তু মিলিত উচ্চারণটি "অর্" হইল কেন? ইহাতে মনে হয় ঈরাণীর মত ঋ-কারের উচ্চারণ "অর্" ছিল। যদি সহজ "রি" কিম্বা "রু" উচ্চারণ থাকিত, তাহা হইলে শেষের স্থায়ী আওয়াজটি "ই" বা "উ" হইত। স্বতন্ত্র স্বরবর্ণ হইত না। ঋ-কারের স্থানে অনেক স্থলে যেমন "অর্" হয়, তেমনি আবার "ইর্"ও হইয়া থাকে; কিন্তু বৃদ্ধির নিয়মের সূত্রটি বিশ্লেষণ করিলে দেখিতে পাই যে, সন্ধির নিয়মে স্বরগুলির যেরূপ বিকৃতি ঘটে, স্বরের বৃদ্ধিতেও ঠিক তাহাই ঘটে; তখন "ঋ" স্থানে "আর্" দেখিয়া সন্ধির উচ্চারণের

"অর্"ই ঋ-কারের আদিম উচ্চারণ বলিয়া মনে হয়। একে "অর্" ঠিক 'র' নয়, তাহার পরে আবার অন্তঃস্থ বর্ণগুলি যে ব্যাকরণের বৈজ্ঞানিক নিয়মের প্রভাবে সৃষ্ট নূতন বর্ণ মাত্র, তাহাও দেখাইতেছি।

এই প্রসঙ্গে একথাও বলিয়া রাখি, ঋ-কারের অর্ উচ্চারণ ছিল মনে করিয়া লইলে বৈদিক ব্যাকরণের দুই একটি স্থলের ঋ-কারের বিকৃতি স্বাভাবিক নিয়মে ধরিতে পারা যায়; তাহার জন্য সূত্র গড়িতে হয় না। পাণিনির "বিভাষর্জোশ্ছন্দসি" সূত্রের ব্যাখ্যায় পাই যে, বৈদিক ভাষায় যদি ইষ্ঠ, ইমন্, ঈয়স্ প্রত্যয় পরে থাকে, তাহাহইলে "ঋজু"র ঋকার র হইয়া যায় (সিঃ কৌঃ বৈদিক প্রকরণ ৩৫৫৫ সূ)।

অন্তঃস্থ বর্ণগুলি (অর্থাৎ য, র, ল, ব) যে মৌলিক বর্ণ নয়, স্বরমিশ্রণে উৎপন্ন, তাহা দেখাইতেছি। "য"এর উচ্চারণ হইল "ইঅ"; বাঙ্গালা এবং ওড়িয়া ছাড়া এখনো সর্ব্বত্রই ঐ প্রকার উচ্চারণ হইয়া থাকে। আমরা 'য'এর 'জ' উচ্চারণ করি বলিয়া, "ইঅ" উচ্চারণের জন্য 'য'এর নীচে ফোঁটা দিয়া থাকি। "উহ্য" শব্দটিকে আমরা উচ্চারণ করি, "উজ্ঝ," আর অন্য প্রদেশে উহার উচ্চারণ "উ-ই-হ"। ই+অ উচ্চারণ সংযোগে যেমন 'য,' উ+অ উচ্চারণ সংযোগে ঠিক তেমনি অন্তঃস্থ ব। সন্ধির সূত্রগুলিতেও, য এবং ব কেবল উক্ত স্বর সংযোগ, আর কিছু নহে।

যে নিয়ম য এবং ব সম্বন্ধে খাটিতেছে, ঐ নিয়মেই র, ল শাসিত। 'ঋ'র পরে স্বরবর্ণ থাকিলে যখন 'র' হয়, তখন 'র'কারের উৎপত্তি 'য' এবং 'ব'এর মত বলিয়া মনে করা সঙ্গত। এরূপ অবস্থায় ঋ এবং ঌ-কারের প্রাচীন কালের যেরূপ উচ্চারণ ছিল বলিয়া মনে করিয়াছি, তাহা সঙ্গত হইবার সম্ভাবনাই খুব অধিক।

যখন দুইটি স্বর বা আওয়াজ মিলিলে একটা স্বাভাবিক মিশ্র আওয়াজ হয়, তখন শেষের আওয়াজটি বেশী তীব্র হইলে প্রথম আওয়াজটিকে একেবারে ঢাকিয়া ফেলিবে, আর বেশী তীব্র না হইলে প্রথম স্বরটিকে একটুখানি হ্রস্ব বা মন্দীভূত করিয়া দিবে। কারণ দুটি স্বর সমান প্রাধান্য রাখিয়া উচ্চারিত হইতে পারে না। একারের উচ্চারণ অ+ই জাত

কাজেই শে (শ+অই)+অন হইতে শয়ন হইবে ; শেষের ই+অ যোগে 'য়' হইয়াছে। আবার ঐরূপ ঐ অক্ষরটি আ+ই বলিয়া, বিনৈ+অকঃ হইল বিনায়কঃ। অ মাঝে পড়িলে 'য়' উচ্চারিত হইত, দৃষ্টান্তস্বরূপ 'সখ আগচ্ছ' "সখায়াগচ্ছ" এই বিকল্পের রূপ তুইটি লক্ষ্য করিলেই চলিবে। প্রাকৃত ভাষায় কিন্তু এসকল স্থলে 'য়' হয় না, 'অ'ই থাকে। কিন্তু প্রথমের আওয়াজে যদি বেশী জোর দেওয়া যায় (অর্থাৎ যদি তাহাতে Accent থাকে) অর্থাৎ উদাত্ত হয়, তাহা হইলে পরবর্ত্তী স্বরকে তেমনি আবার প্রায় লুপ্ত হইয়া যাওয়া চাই, শেষের স্বর বেশী দুর্ব্বল হইলে প্রথমের Accent-যুক্ত স্বরকে লোপ করিতে পারে না, বরং নিজে অর্দ্ধলুপ্ত হইয়া থাকে। যখন সম্বোধনের পদে, কবে, সখে, গুরো প্রভৃতি উচ্চারণ করা যায়, তখন ঐ শব্দ গুলির স্বরে যে Accent থাকে তাহা বুঝাইতে হইবে না। কাজেই সখে-অর্পয়, প্রভু-অনুগৃহাণ, প্রভৃতিতে যথার্থ সন্ধি না হইয়া কেবল 'অ'কারের অল্প উচ্চারণ রাখা হয় মাত্র। কিন্তু 'আ' 'ই' প্রভৃতি সুস্পষ্ট অথচ তীব্রস্বর পরে থাকিলে প্রথম নির্দ্দিষ্ট নিয়মই ঘটে। শে+অনম্ এবং সখে+ইঁহ প্রভৃতিতে সূত্র-পার্থক্য করিবার প্রয়োজন নাই ; এই নিয়মের মধ্যে ধরিয়া লইলেই চলে। উ+উত্তিষ্ঠ, প্র+ঋজতে, অপ+ঋচ্ছতি, প্র+এজতে প্রভৃতি স্থলে বৈদিক ব্যাকরণে সন্ধি হয় না। পদপাঠে সর্ব্বত্রই ওগুলি স্বতন্ত্র থাকে ; নহিলে ছন্দ পর্য্যন্ত বিগড়াইয়া যায়। কেবল একটা সাধারণ সন্ধির সৃষ্টি করিয়া সকল শব্দকে এক নিয়মে বাঁধিবার অভিপ্রায়েই পরবর্ত্তী যুগে সন্ধির নিয়মের সৃষ্টি হইয়াছে। তবে, এক-স্বর-অব্যয়ে সন্ধি করিলে শব্দ বড় জটিল হইয়া পড়ে বলিয়া বৈদিক বিধিই রক্ষা করিয়া বিশেষ সূত্রে উ+উত্তিষ্ঠ প্রভৃতিকে অযুক্তই রাখা হইয়াছে। এখানে বিশেষ সূত্রই মৌলিক সাধারণ সূত্র।

সন্ধি করিলে যেখানে এক বচন দ্বিবচন বুঝিবার গোল হয়, কিম্বা একটা Accent নষ্ট হইয়া যায়, সেখানেও বৈদিক নিয়ম রক্ষা করিয়া সন্ধি যোগের সূত্র রচনা হয় নাই। তাই এখনো কবি+ইমৌ, অমী+অশ্বাঃ প্রভৃতি গোটাকতক পূর্ব্বকালের মত আছে।

ইহার পর বিসর্গের সন্ধির কথা বলিব। অন্য ব্যঞ্জন-সন্ধি অপেক্ষা সংস্কৃত ভাষাতত্ত্বে ঐটির বেশি প্রয়োজন আছে। কিন্তু বিসর্গের সন্ধির কথা বলিবার পূর্ব্বে কয়েকটি ব্যঞ্জনবর্ণের উচ্চারণের কথা বলিব। যে ভাষা 'সংস্কৃত' নামে আখ্যা পাইয়াছে, উহাতেই বিসর্গের একটা স্বতন্ত্র স্বাধীন উচ্চারণ পাওয়া যায় এবং সে উচ্চারণটি একালে অধিক পরিমাণে 'হ' বর্ণটির উচ্চারণের কাছাকাছি। এই স্বতন্ত্রতা থেকে উহা একটা বর্ণ বলিয়া গণিত হইয়াছে; নহিলে য, র, ল, ব প্রভৃতির মত উহারা বর্ণ সংযোগে জাত 'আওয়াজ' মাত্র। পাণিনি ব্যাকরণে ং ও ঃ (অথবা বিসর্জ্জনীয়) বর্ণমালার মধ্যে স্থান পায় নাই, পরে পাইয়াছে। ং এবং চন্দ্রবিন্দু অনুনাসিকের উচ্চারণ ভেদ মাত্র। যেখানে মিশ্র আওয়াজে অনুনাসিকের খর্ব্ব উচ্চারণ, সেইখানেই সন্ধির সূত্রে ং এবং ँ। সাধারণ নিয়মে বলিতে গেলে স অক্ষরের স্থানবিশেষের উচ্চারণই বিসর্গ। 'র'জাত বিসর্গের কথা পরে বলিব। হয় ত প্রাচীনকালের উচ্চারণ পদ্ধতি আমাদের বাগ্‌যন্ত্রে অলক্ষে লাগিয়াছে বলিয়া, সাধারণ শ্রেণীর লোক কোথাও কোথাও 'দুঃখ' কথাটিকে 'দুস্‌খ' উচ্চারণ করিয়া থাকে। বিসর্গের সাধারণ মূর্ত্ত উচ্চারণ 'স'; শ, ষ, স তিনটির মধ্যে একটা সাধারণ আওয়াজ আছে, যাহার জন্য তিনটিই একনামে পরিচিত হইয়াছে সেই সাধারণ আওয়াজটুকু ভাবিয়া লইতে হয়, লিখিয়া বুঝান যায় না। তালু হইতে উচ্চারণ করিলে 'শ' যেরূপ উচ্চারিত হয়, তাহাতে যে ধ্বনিটি তেলেগু তামিলের 'চ' উচ্চারণের কাছাকাছি যায়, তবে 'শ' উচ্চারণটি আর একটু কঠোর রকমের ফিস্‌-ফিস্ আওয়াজের সহিত যুক্ত। তামিলে 'শ' একটু কোমল করিয়া উচ্চারণ করে বলিয়া 'চ' এবং 'শ'এ কোন প্রভেদ নাই; একই অক্ষর উভয়ের প্রয়োজন নিষ্পন্ন করে। পূর্ব্ববঙ্গের কোন কোন স্থানের চ ও ছ বর্ণের উচ্চারণ প্রায় দ্রবিড়-উচ্চারণের কাছাকাছি। মহারাষ্ট্রের চ ও ছ ও প্রায় তেলেগু তামিলের মত উচ্চারিত। সন্ধির নিয়ম দেখিয়া মনে হয়, পূর্ব্বকালে চ ছ প্রায় দ্রবিড়ি-ধরণে উচ্চারিত হইত, উভয়েরই উচ্চারণ স্থান তালু। ষ টি উত্তর পশ্চিম প্রদেশে খ হইয়া গিয়াছে, আমরাও ক + ষ 'কৃখ' উচ্চারণ করি, আমাদের

ভাষার জননী পালিতেও ঐ উচ্চারণ। প্রাচীনতর উচ্চারণে একটা গম্ভীর ধ্বনি সূচিত হইত। তাহার প্রমাণ দিতেছি। অতি প্রাচীন কালে, 'বৃ,' 'কং' 'ষ' প্রভৃতি দিয়া, যাহাকে 'অনমেটোপইটিক্' শব্দ বলে, তাহা গড়া হইত। যথা ;—বৃহ, বৃংহ, বৃংহতি ; ঘোষ (ঘঃ ঘণ্টা অর্থে+ষ ; ঘণ্টাতে আরও শব্দ যোগ আছে), মেষ ('মে'+ষ বা ধ্বনি) বৃষ, হ্রেষা, হর্ষ, ভাষ, মাহষ, রোষ (রু+ষ) ; কং (বা কণ্)+ষ হইতে কাংস্য, জল শুকাইবার সময়কার শুষ্ ধ্বনি লইতে শুষ্ক ইত্যাদি। সিদ্ধান্ত-কৌমুদীর সঙ্গে মিলিতেছে না দেখিয়া হয় ত কেহ কেহ এ নূতন ব্যাখ্যায় বিরক্ত হইতেছেন। অভিনিবেশ করিলে বিরক্তির কারণ থাকিবে না। তবে আমার এ ব্যাখ্যা লইয়া যদি ললিতকুমার বন্দ্যোপাধ্যায় মহাশয় একটুখানি রঙ্গরসের সৃষ্টি করিতে পারেন, তাহাতে আমি রাজি আছি। অর্ব্বাচীন সংস্কৃতে এবং একালের ভাষায় ভীম শব্দ বুঝাইবার অক্ষর হইল ড। ললিত বাবুর মত লোকেরা বলিতে পারেন যে, সেই জন্যই ভীমের স্ত্রী হিড়িম্বা। বৈদিক প্রয়োগেও 'ড' দ্বারাও ষণ্ড প্রভৃতি কয়েকটি শব্দ পাওয়া যায়। বলিয়া রাখি যে, ঐ শব্দগুলি অতি প্রাচীন বৈদিক শব্দ নয়। আমরা যেমন কথা ডবল করিয়া কড়্ কড়্, হুড়্ হুড়্, ব্যবহার করি, সেরূপে ভাবপ্রকাশের প্রয়োজন হইলে বৈদিক সময়ে কেবল ধ একটু ঘন উচ্চারিত হইত। বলিয়া রাখি যে, ডবল্ না করিয়াও আমরা ড় দিয়া তীব্রতাব্যঞ্জক শব্দ বুঝাই ; যথা—ঝড়, তোড়্ (বেগ অর্থে) দৌড় ('ধা'+ড়), মেঢ়, ভেড় (শেষ দুটি অর্ব্বাচীন সংস্কৃতেও ব্যবহার আছে) ইত্যাদি। প্রাসঙ্গিকরূপে অপ্রাসঙ্গিক কথা বলি নাই। "শব্দ" বুঝাইতে হইলে, আমরা মূর্দ্ধা হইতে উচ্চারিত বর্ণ দিয়া বেশি বুঝাইয়া থাকি। 'ষ' অক্ষরটির উচ্চারণ মূর্দ্ধা হইতে করিলে অনেক পরিমাণে প্রাচীন আওয়াজ পাওয়া যাইবে।

'স' টি মহারাষ্ট্রে সর্ব্বদাই বিশুদ্ধরূপে উচ্চারিত হয় ; ওড়িয়া উচ্চারণও প্রায় ঠিক। "আস্তে" প্রভৃতি শব্দে আমরাও দন্ত্য উচ্চারণ কথঞ্চিৎ ঠিক রাখিয়াছি।

এখন বিসর্গের সন্ধির নিয়মগুলি কয়েকটি শ্রেণীতে বিভাগ করিয়া

ফেলিয়া দেখাইতেছি যে, উচ্চারণের রীতি ধরিয়া লইলে বিনা সূত্রেই বিসর্গ সন্ধির সূত্র অধীত হইতে পারে। সূত্রের সুবিধার জন্য প্রথমতঃ বর্ণমালা হইতে ক খ এবং প ফ দূরে রাখিয়া দিব। বিসর্গের সাধারণ মূর্ত্ত উচ্চারণ 'স্'। প্রথমতঃ ঐ বিসর্গের পর চ, ছ ; ট, ঠ ; ও ত, থ থাকিতে পারে। তিনটি 'স' এর generalised একটা কিছু উচ্চারণ নাই বলিয়া কথাটা লিখিয়া বুঝাইতে কষ্ট হইতেছে। সেই তিন 'স' এর এক অভেদ মৌলিক আত্মাটি, চ, ছ-যুক্ত হইলেই 'শ' হইয়া ফুটিয়া উঠিবে ; ট, ঠ যোগে ষ এবং ত, থ যোগে 'স' হইবে। উপরের বর্ণিত উচ্চারণ থেকেই ইহা সুস্পষ্ট হইবে। সূত্রের প্রয়োজন নাই। (২) বিসর্গের পর শ, ষ, স থাকিতে পারে। এস্থলে সমান শ্রেণীর আওয়াজে মিলিয়া অন্ত সন্ধির মত আওয়াজ ডবল হইবে মাত্র, উহার বিকৃতি হইবে না। বিকল্পে বিসর্গ বজায় থাকার নিয়ম, আওয়াজের হিসাবে অর্থশূন্য। এখন বাকি রহিল ব্যঞ্জনের মধ্যে তৃতীয়, চতুর্থ ও পঞ্চম বর্ণগুলি এবং য র ল ব হ। উহাদিগকে গ হ নাম দিয়া অন্যবিধ শ্রেণী বিভাগে ফেলিতেছি। বিসর্গ 'অ'কারের পর, 'আ'কারের পর, অথবা অন্যান্য স্বরের পর থাকিতে পারে ; এবং বিসর্গের পর 'অ,' অথবা 'আ,' অথবা অন্যস্বর, অথবা ব্যঞ্জনের তৃতীয় চতুর্থ পঞ্চম বর্ণ ও য র ল ব হ (গ-হ) থাকিতে পারে।

(৩) অর্ব্বাচীন সংস্কৃতের পূর্ব্ববর্ত্তী প্রাকৃতে (অর্থাৎ পালিভাষায়) দেখিতে পাই যে, সকল অকারান্ত শব্দই কর্ত্তৃকারকে বা প্রথমার এক বচনে ওকারান্ত হইয়া উচ্চারিত হয় ; যেখানে সংস্কৃতের হিসাবে বিসর্গ থাকিবার কথা এবং না থাকিবার কথা, এ উভয় স্থলেই ঐরূপ উচ্চারণ হয়। নরো, নিব্বুতো, ধম্মো, কম্মো ইত্যাদি। একালের প্রাকৃতগুলির মধ্যে কেবল বাঙ্গালায় প্রাচীন প্রাকৃতের ও-ঘেঁষা উচ্চারণ রক্ষিত আছে। পালি উচ্চারণ বৈদিক সময়ের উচ্চারণের অনুরূপ ছিল বলিয়া মনে করিবার অনেক কারণ আছে। সংস্কৃতের ব্যাকরণের নিয়ম অপেক্ষা, পালির ব্যাকরণের অনেক নিয়ম বা রীতি, বৈদিক ভাষার বেশি নিকট-বর্ত্তী। বৈদিক ভাষার পরবর্ত্তী ব্রাহ্মণযুগের ভাষার সহিত পালির ব্যাকরণের মিল অতিশয় অধিক। সন্ধির নিয়ম হইতে প্রথমে দৃষ্টান্ত

দিতেছি। অথ ঋতু ; বৈ ঋচঃ (বৃহদ্দেবতা ২।১৩ ও ১।১৮) প্রভৃতি স্থলে যেমন সন্ধি নাই, পালিতেও তেমনি। দৃশ্যতে+অস্মাঃ=দৃশ্যতেঽস্মাঃ (বৃঃ-১।১৮), দ্বে+অনুমতেঃ=দ্বেঽনুমতেঃ (বৃ, ৪।৮৮) প্রভৃতিতে পালির মত নিয়ম রহিয়াছে। তাহার পর শব্দরূপে সুদাঃ শব্দ, পালির মত "সুদাস্" রূপেই লেখা পাই (বৃ, ৬।৩৪)। আবার ওই পালির মত বৃহদ্দেবতা গ্রন্থে চতুর্স্ভিঃ স্থলে চতুর্ভিঃ, প্রথম পুরুষের তৃতীয়ার একবচনে অনুশাসতি, অসমাপিকাক্রিয়া বুঝাইতে 'য' স্থানে 'ত্বা' এবং 'ত্বা' স্থলে 'য' ইত্যাদি ইত্যাদি পাইয়া থাকি।

এখন যদি উচ্চারণ ধরিয়া বিচার করা যায়, তাহা হইলে এইমাত্র বলা চলে যে, পালির মত যদি অকারান্ত শব্দের ও-ঘেঁষা উচ্চারণ হইবেই (বিসর্গ পরে থাকাতেই হয় ত সেই প্রকার উচ্চারণের সৃষ্টি) তাহা হইলে সর্ব্বত্রই বিসর্গের উচ্চারণের লোপ, এবং ও-কারের উচ্চারণের প্রাধান্য থাকিবে। 'অ' পরে থাকিলে লুপ্তচিহ্ন রাখিবার ব্যবস্থা আছে, তাহাতে স্পষ্ট বুঝিতে পারা যায় যে, কোন অক্ষরই লোপ পায় না ; কেবল প্রথম পদে যুক্ত উচ্চারণ টুকুরই তীব্রতার প্রাধান্য থাকে। বিসর্গের পর অকার ভিন্ন স্বরবর্ণ থাকিলে প্রথম শব্দটিতে 'ও' আওয়াজ রাখা অসম্ভব ; পূর্ব্বে তাহা অন্য সূত্রের বিচারে বলিয়াছি। তাই সূত্রে কেবল বিসর্গ লোপের ব্যবস্থা আছে। গ-হ ব্যঞ্জন পরে থাকিলেও কেবল ওকার রহিয়া যায়। অর্থাৎ বিশেষ কিছুই হইল না। যেমন ছিল, তেমনি রহিল। ঠিক ঐরূপ আবার আকারের পরে বিসর্গ থাকিলে এবং বিসর্গের পর স্বরবর্ণ এবং গ-হ ব্যঞ্জন থাকিলে কোন সন্ধিই হয় না। বিসর্গের উচ্চারণ ঐ স্থলে বিশেষত্ব পাইয়া ফুটিয়া উঠিতে পথ পায় না ; এই পর্য্যন্ত। তাহা হইলে বিসর্গের একটা সন্ধিই রহিল না, অথচ ঐ সন্ধি মুখস্থ করিতেই যত গোল ঘটে।

ক, খ, প, ফ প্রভৃতি পরে থাকিলেও বৈদিকে কোন সন্ধি হইত না ; তবে যে সময়ে বিসর্গের প্রাধান্য দেওয়া হইয়াছিল, তখন বিসর্গের মূর্ত্ত উচ্চারণ 'স' রাখিতে হইয়াছে মাত্র। সাধারণ সন্ধির নিয়মে উহাই পাই। কাজেই এখানেও কোন সূত্রের প্রয়োজন হইল না। কয়েকটি

বিশেষ দৃষ্টান্ত ছাড়া সর্ব্বত্রই ঐ ষ মূর্দ্ধণ্য। ক, খ, প, ফ পরে থাকিলে কঠোর উচ্চারণই স্বাভাবিক; কিন্তু বিসর্গটি অকারের পরে থাকিলে আওয়াজটি অপেক্ষাকৃত নরম হয় বলিয়া নমস্কার প্রভৃতি শব্দে 'স' উচ্চারিত হয়; অন্য স্থলে মূর্দ্ধন্য ষ হয়।

কিন্তু একটা কথা বুঝিতে পারিতেছি না। কোন একটা বিশেষ রীতিসিদ্ধি (idiomatic use) অনুসারে, অ আ ভিন্ন স্বরবর্ণের পরের বিসর্গের স্থানে প্রাচীন কালে 'র' হইত, দেখিতে পাই। এই নিয়মটি বেদের পদপাঠের প্রতি লক্ষ্য করিলে বৈদিক যুগে ছিল না বলিয়াই মনে হয়। কিন্তু প্রাচীন ব্রাহ্মণ-সাহিত্যের সংস্কৃতে এ সন্ধি আছে। পালিতে আবার এমন অনেক স্থলে সন্ধিতে 'র' আসিয়া উপস্থিত হয়, যেখানে না আছে 'র' না আছে 'র'এর সঙ্গে দূরসম্পর্কযুক্ত অন্য কিছু। তবুও কেন হয়? র পরে থাকিলে বিসর্গ বিকৃতির যে সূত্র আছে, সেইরূপ কার্য্য হইবে বলিয়া আশা করা যাইত; অর্থাৎ বিসর্গের পর একটা কেবল দীর্ঘ উচ্চারণ হইতে পারিত। কেন না ঐস্থলে স্ ও র এর একটা সংযুক্ত কঠোর উচ্চারণ পরিহার করিবার কথা মাত্র। যেমন নীরস, পিতারক্ষ প্রভৃতি হয়, তেমনি যদি নীভয়, নীধন প্রভৃতি হইত, তবে আমাকে মাথা ঘামাইতে হইত না। এখানে রামমাণিক্যের সি, সিজ্, সিম্ মনে পড়িতেছে। যেমনটি চাই, ঠিক তাই ঘটে কৈ? বিসর্গের সন্ধি আদপে নাই বলিয়া খালাসের চেষ্টায় ছিলাম এবং "ভো যদ্রুপতে" এবং "স হসতি" বলিয়া আরো দুটি সূত্র ধ্বংস করিতে পারিতাম; কিন্তু দায়ে ঠেকিয়াছি। একটা অনুমানের কথা বলিব। অনুমান অনুমানমাত্র—সিদ্ধান্ত নহে। নিঃ + ভয় প্রভৃতিতে পালি ভাষায়, আমার আশার অনুরূপ ডবল উচ্চারণ (দীর্ঘের প্রকারভেদ মাত্র) হইত। যথা—নিব্‌ভয়, নিদ্‌ধন ইত্যাদি। পালিতে, অর্থাৎ সেকালের সাধারণ কথোপকথনের ভাষায় রেফ্ লোপ করিলেও দীর্ঘ উচ্চারণ হইত; এখনো বাঙ্গালায় উহা প্রচলিত আছে। যথা—ধর্ম্ম স্থলে ধম্ম, কর্ম্ম স্থলে কম্ম ইত্যাদি। হইতে পারে, যে যখন প্রাকৃতকে ঘষিয়া মাজিয়া সাধু বা সংস্কৃত করা হইয়াছিল, তখন সাধারণ একটা নিয়ম বা সূত্রের মধ্যে

একচেহারার সকলকে ফেলিবার্ উদ্যোগে, "ধর্ম্ম" প্রভৃতির Analogyতে নিব্‌ভয় প্রভৃতিকে নির্ভয় করিয়া নূতন সূত্র গড়া হইয়াছিল। আমার অনুমানটি পণ্ডিতসমাজে যদি দৈবাৎ গ্রাহ্য হয়, তাহা হইলেও একটা খট্‌কা রহিয়া যাইতেছে।

যদি এমন হইত যে, যেগুলি র-জাত বিসর্গ সেইগুলির স্থলেই র হয়, তাহা হইলে সহজ সিদ্ধান্ত হইত। কেন না বৈদিকযুগে র-জাত একটা বিসর্গ নয়; সহজ রকমে র-অক্ষরে হসন্ত উচ্চারণ মাত্র। বৈদিকযুগের বহুপরবর্ত্তী সময়েও পুনর্, প্রাতর্, অন্তর্ প্রভৃতি খাঁজা খাঁজা ব্যবহার হইত; কাজেই সন্ধিতে র জুড়িয়া দিবার সময় বিসর্গের সূত্র ভাবিবার দরকার ছিল না। কিন্তু ব্রাহ্মণযুগের সাহিত্যেই যখন প্রাতর্ প্রভৃতি ছাড়া স-জাত বিসর্গের স্থলে 'র' আগমনের কথা পাই, স্বয়ং পাণিনিকেই যখন বিশেষ সূত্র রচনা করিয়া—অম্নস্, উধস্, অবস্, স্থলে রেফ শুদ্ধ হয়, বলিয়া একটা বিশেষ সূত্র লিখিতে হইয়াছে, তখন আর প্রাকৃত নিয়মের তুড়িতে একটা সূত্রকে উড়াইয়া দিতে পারিলাম না। বিদ্যালয়ের ছাত্রের মুখস্থের জন্য ঐটি জীবিত থাকুক। অন্যগুলির মত একটা উচ্চারণের নিয়মের বশবর্ত্তী করিয়া উহাকে প্রাকৃত আওয়াজ বা শব্দব্রহ্মে বিলীন করিতে পারিলাম না।

HOW CHHĀNDASA IS RELATED TO LATER ARYAN SPEECHES.

LECTURE X

Chhāndasa, *i.e.*, the Vedic language of old, has been spoken of in these lectures, by implication generally, as the source-head from which the Indian Aryan speeches of all times and of all provinces have evolved. I am aware, some noted European names are associated with theories, which run counter to this proposition or assumption ; but as those theories rest wholly upon the authority of noted names, and not on facts which can be handled and discussed, no one can possibly combat them : facts, I have adduced before, I adduce presently in this lecture, and I shall have to adduce in subsequent lectures, should all be considered together, to test the correctness of my proposition. I have stated in some detail, of the influence of the speakers of non-Aryan tongues, to explain various deviations from the norm ; I shall try to show in this, as well as in another subsequent lecture, how in a *prākṛta* or natural way, many Prākṛtas or provincial vernaculars arose from Chhāndasa, and how the ever-progressing Prākṛita speeches went on modifying and being in turn modified by the literary language of curious genesis, which has come to be designated as Sanskrit. It will be seen, how failing to notice the influence of a mixed people, in the matter of formation of the Prākṛta speeches, and how failing to observe the influence, which could not but be exercised by the living vernaculars, upon an artificially set-up literary language, some philologists (Dr. C. C. Ullenbeck, whose words I presently quote, is one of them) have asserted that " the Sanskrit dialect of middle country descends from some other old Indian dialects than the dialect met with in the Vedas." As to this part of our proposition, that the growth of various Prākṛtas has been partly due to diverse ethnic influences, a good deal has already been said, and something more will have to be said later on ; I may however notice here, what Mr. A. H. Keane has observed, regarding the cause of wide diversity existing among the speeches of various groups of Aryan origin (both Asiatic and European), after considering all the groups on a comparative table at p. 412 of his Ethnology. His words are : "The profound disintegration which is shown in this table and which is immeasurably greater than in the Semitic family, is mainly due to the spread of Aryan speech amongst non-Aryan peoples by whom its phonetic system and grammatical structure were diversely modified." That for the very reason, the Chhāndasa speech in its turn, has transformed itself into various dialects in different provinces of Northern India, is what has all along been emphasized.

As in all sober and serious investigations into the causes of phenomena, we have to determine the natural causes and not their supernatural seemings, we have to push on in the matter of our enquiry an intensive study of actual facts, and should not seek to explain things by what might have dropped from the skies—by importing some imaginary patois-speaking hordes from elsewhere. If even the explanation, we offer, prove inadequate, there will not be any justification in setting up the figments of our imagination in the name of theories, to solve our difficulties.

We have to first direct our attention to the character of the language of the Vedas, called Chhāndasa. I use the word Veda in a very restricted sense here ; in this restricted sense the word Veda, indicates the mantra literature, preserved in the four *Saṁhitās, viz.,* the Sāman, the Ṛk, the Atharvan, and the Yajur. The very term Saṁhitā clearly signifies, that the *Mantras* or hymns and prayers as were extant (no matter whether in writing or in the memory of some priestly families) at the date of the compilation, were compiled either exhaustively or by making a selection of them in the books named above. We can very unmistakably see, from the arrangement of the contents of the Saṁhitās, and from what has been said of the Vedas in the old time works relating to them, that different ritual purposes led to the compilation of different Saṁhitās.

It is to be noted however, on the one hand, that the old orthodox works from which the purpose of compiling the Vedic mantras can be gathered, show by their suggestions and discussion regarding the Vedic vocabulary and the Vedic Grammar, that at the date of the compilation of the Saṁhitās, the mantras of varying times (*i.e.,* both old and new) were old and archaic enough to the compilers ; on the other hand, we have to notice, that though many mantras are much removed in time from one another, the language of the Vedic Saṁhitās may be declared to be one and the same. What Whitney has said by comparing the oldest and the latest linguistic forms occurring in the Vedas, may be profitably quoted here, in support of the latter statement ; the scholar writes in his well-known Sanskrit Grammar, that "the language of the অথর্ব্ববেদ though distinctly less antique than that of the Rigveda, is nevertheless truly Vedic. The students should do well to study Professor Macdonnell's excellent work on the Vedic Grammar to learn aright the character of the Chhāndasa speech, and to see clearly how the language even of the oldest Brāhmaṇa literature differs from the Vedic. I can therefore say, that since the compilers of the Vedas got together the then extant hymns and prayers, no matter whether they had been composed at a very early date or at a comparatively recent time, it cannot be asserted with any degree of propriety, that any portion of the contents of a Saṁhitā, is a later addition or interpolation in that Saṁhitā. The language of the mantras, new or old, was old to the compilers, and lateness in the matter of composition, did not or rather could not detract from the religious merit of any mantra. The western scholars, I have stated before, have set forth distinctly, what elements are old and what are new in the Vedic language. The contents of the Vedic Saṁhitās may now be arranged in a rough chronological order on the basis of linguistic evidence. The light furnished by this research, enables us to make this important discovery, that even in the earliest known times, the Aryans of India spoke various dialects of one common speech, and that the *mantras* were composed in a standard central language, which as a *literary language* dominated all the provincial dialects, and at times helped the fusion of those dialects. I use the word 'literary' very advisedly, and propose to explain the significance of it later on. The facts which warrant us in arriving at this conclusion, that even the earliest Vedic mantras point to the currency of many dialects in ancient India, cannot be very fully and fitly discussed here, but as we have to build a good deal on the basis of this proposition, some examples should be adduced to prove its soundness. As of the essential factors which determine a language, the pronouns have a high value, let me put forward here very briefly, the evidence which the personal pronouns tender in this direction.

Prof. A. A. Macdonell has observed with his usual scholarly acuteness in his monumental work on the Vedic Grammar, that the personal pronouns *seem* to be derived from several roots or combinations of roots, as they are specially anomalous in inflexion. An analysis of the pronouns will perhaps justify us in striking a less uncertain sound.*

অস্ (অস্মদ্) and যুস্ (যুস্মদ্) are accepted by all the old grammarians as the basic words for the pronouns of the 1st and 2nd person respectively. I need hardly point out, that the very অস্ and যুস্ occur in many formations in the declension of pronouns of the 1st and 2nd person respectively. It has to be noted that the personal pronouns in the nominative case take অম্ like a suffix (*cf.* ত্ব + অম্ = ত্বম্ and also the অম্ endings in dual and plural), and this অম্ in like manner occurs in the Nominative Singular of the Demonstrative অয়ম্ and the Reflexive স্বয়ং. I do not feel inclined to accept the suggestion that this case-differentiating অম্ came from the Dravidians who affix অম্ to nouns of all classes, though the close proximity of the Dravidians to the Aryans of the earliest time cannot be very reasonably denied. That অস্ and যুস্ are reducible to অঃ and যুঃ in Sanskrit, need not be stated. That the Visarjaniya of অঃ develops the simple aspirate of হ্ in pronunciation, is also very clear. We can see, that denuded of the appendage অম্, অহম্ stands as অহ্. We may note in passing that this অহ্ corresponds with Ich of German, I of English, Io of Italian, or rather Ego of Latin

* I have nothing to do with the theory of Aryan migration, nor with the hypothetical parent tongue of the so-called Indo-Germans, as I have to study the speeches as actually developed on Indian soil. The unscientific theory of the philologists who may be said to be represented by Brugmann, regarding the imaginary old pronouns of a supposed old language, may be left out of consideration, as we are concerned here with the forms of which actual evidence may be collected. The Dodo birds of nasal sonants of an unknowable people may be allowed to remain in the fancy museum of the philologists, for we have to deal with the actual fossils as may be found imbedded here in India.

and Egon of Greek. অহ্ however, does not appear to have been the only form in the Nom. Singular; a pronoun either of simple ম basis or in the form of a মি is strongly supposed to have been a form, in use in a dialect when অহ্ was current in another dialect, for in the first place a মি is found agglutinated with the Parasmaipadi verbs in the first person singular, and in the second place the singular forms মা, মাম্ (মা + অম্), ময়া, মদ্, মে, and ময়ি point to a simple ম base with which etymologically they must be connected. That no ম can be traced either to অহ্ or অম্ is pretty clear. Moreover such a Vedic form as মাবস্তু (like me, *cf.* ত্বাবস্তু like you) shows that মা was treated as a stem, *i.e.*, a word unchanged in form in the process of declension. While considering the early fossils of the pronouns of the 1st person, we have to notice that besides ত্ব, যুস্ is a form of the pronoun of the 2nd person, though the latter form occurs only in dual and plural.

For further fossils let us analyze the interesting dual forms of the personal pronouns. In the language of the early Samhitās, we get বাম্ as the dual form of অম্ and this very বাম্ is the accusative dual of ত্ব or যুস্. The form আবাম is a very late form, occurring not earlier than the time of the ঐতরেয় ব্রাহ্মণ, while the শতপথ ব্রাহ্মণ gives perhaps the earlier form আবম্. We know that বস্ occurs as a plural form of the personal pronoun of the 2nd person and নস্ as a plural form of the personal pronoun of the 1st person. The dual বাম্ appears pretty distinctly as the combination of ব+অ+অম্ to signify 'you and I' together. Perhaps to avoid confusion, আ of অম্ was further prefixed to বাম্ to signify the 1st person, while additional যু was prefixed to signify the second person in creating the forms আবাম্ and যুবাম্. In the plural form বয়ম্, we only notice the lengthening of the penultimate vowel sound with a stress to denote plurality as if by the primitive case-denoting gesture or modulation of voice. This ব্ or rather বস্ and নস্ no doubt occur as plural forms only here in India as well as in other Aryan speeches elsewhere; but we find in India নৌ as a dual and ব in conjunction with অ of অস্ in some dual formations. As নৌ can be detected as a comparatively later time formation, I am strongly inclined to suppose by looking to the use of নস্ and বস্ in the Vedic language, that নস্ of the 1st person and বস্ of the 2nd, were such very early forms in an Aryan dialect as denoted all numbers and cases alike, and their various significations could only be gathered from such accents of the speakers as are allied to primitive case and number-denoting gestures. In this connection I just refer to the personal pronoun of the 1st person in use in Dravidian tongues which has only seemingly the 'ন' stem. I refer to this fact to show that there is no connection or affinity of Aryan ন with the Dravidian ন; I should point out that নী of Tamil and নে of Telegu (as in নেনু or নেমু) which signify 'I,' are based not on ন, but on অ, as the early Dravidian forms show.

We thus see, that অস্, নস্ and a pronoun of ম stem for the pronouns of the 1st person, and ত্ব, বস্, and যুস্ for the pronouns of the 2nd person were once in use in pre-Vedic days. The remarks of Joseph Wright as recorded in his Comparative Grammar of the Greek language, are no doubt correct that many forms of *one single pronoun* may come into existence in one and the same dialect, and that by virtue of different sort of accent on different forms of a pronoun, one form may represent one case and another, the other; but when altogether different forms occur, it is reasonable to hold, that they come from different dialects, since looking to the history of different languages and to human psychology, we have to admit that to express a common or familiar or oft-occurring idea, more than one word does not become current in a dialect. Ethnology discovers to us that the Aryans were not a homogeneous people, but as forming a culture group, they were composed of various ethnic elements; I think what we have discussed confirms the proposition of Ethnology.

Just another fact regarding the lost forms of pronouns. I have spoken of the verbal suffix মি as a fossil of a personal pronoun of the 1st person; let us now inquire into the origin of সি of the second person as in করোসি, and of তি of the 3rd person as in করোতি. As for তি we can trace the origin to তদ্ stem which is virtually but a simple ত, for excepting in the Nominative Singular the stem ত does not lose its identity. Adverting to the cases of মি and তি, it may be naturally supposed, that সি of the 2nd Person Sing. was not an arbitrary symbol at starting, but that সি must have been originally connected with a stem of the personal pronoun of the second person. I am not competent to say if the German form "sich" lends some support to this view. Referring to the history of some Greek suffixes, Joseph Wright has rightly remarked, that though little is known of the origin of numerous suffixes, it may be reasonably supposed that those suffixes had originally an independent meaning and that in some cases they were independent words. A word of caution, however is needed here: some symbols or endings to denote case, or number, or person, as simple আ or ই or এ for instance may be reasonably supposed to have originated from primitive gestures and modulations of voice, and not from words conveying independent meaning. I may add that the Dravidian pronouns অ, ই, এ and উ as well as the Aryan অ of অস্ and যু্ of যুস্ might have originated from mere gestures accompanying sounds in primitive days.

We have not discussed words and forms of various classes, but all the same our brief discussion leads us to hold, that long before the dissemination or dispersion of Aryan speech or speeches in Europe, the Aryans developed a central dominating language, amid a good number of dialects of theirs. This dominating language seems to have attained such a perfection in the dim past, as characterizes a *literary* language,—even though letters or art of writing did not come into existence. I just cite two examples, in addition to what has already been stated, to explain what I mean by the literary character of the pre-Vedic language. Such natural lispings or utterances of children, as have been the roots of words for father and mother in many languages of the world, as Bā, Ābbā, Pā, Āmmā, Mā, etc., are found in well shaped forms in all Aryan speeches, and the forms পিতর্ and মাতর্ framed by a generalized grammatical rule, are found grouped with other relation-indicating words, such as ভ্রাতর্, and দুহিতর্. For the next example, I refer to the tense system; on the evidence of tense system of old Greek as agreeing with those of Vedic, we may hold that the pre-Vedic language attained a high literary character.

I have thrown out suggestions, as to what was in all probability, the position and character of the Aryan language in pre-Vedic days. It goes however without saying that the Chhāndasa language as disclosed by the early Vedic Saṁhitās, is a very rich and well-developed literary speech. It has to be borne in mind, in this connection, that inspite of the unifying influence of a central literary language, the provincial dialects do not all necessarily die out, and they may at times continue to live with full vigour, getting fresh lease of life under some changed conditions. That the Vedic language became in course of time purely hieratic, because of the sacredness of the mantras, and was not, or rather could not therefore be allowed to be changed with the changing conditions of time, can be well established by the evidence of the Vedic Grammarians. Every language is bound to be transformed into a new and a newer form with the progress of time, but if for any reason any particular class of a people seek to keep the obsolescent speech intact, the old speech becomes the special property of the particular class, and ceases to be the language of the people. Moreover, when a people loses its homogeneity, or when class differences occur because of cultural difference, and as a compensating measure a wide mass education through the standard literary language is not adopted, provincial dialects grow with great vigour, and no class, howsoever influential, can keep the literary speech alive. We notice a gap between the language of the Vedas, and that of the Brāhmaṇas, and a wider gap between the language of the Brāhmaṇas and the language which may very fitly be designated as Sanskṛta, to signify its character as dressed up, polished or perfected. That these gaps have to be explained by circumstances broadly indicated above, will be discussed presently.

Our discussion will no doubt be extremely brief for the subject; but all the same we have to take all the salient points into consideration step by step. First of all we have to notice, that Chhāndasa discloses the characteristics of a living language. That the artificial rigid rules of Sandhi or euphonic combination were not in force in Chhāndasa, and that a regular and thoroughgoing accent-system existed in the speech, have been shown in some previous lectures. That we are required to read Sanskrit verses (which are wholly quantitative) by raising or lowering our voice according to the unalterably fixed vowel sounds as long or short, and not according to word accent or phrasal accent, has also been noticed before, to show the artificiality of Sanskrit, from accent point of view.

As it is impossible for a real human speech to be without an accent system of its own, so is it that a living speech must undergo to some extent, what is called phonetic decay. I proceed to show that the phenomenon of phonetic decay, which can be fitly translated in our Vernacular by the term * Apabhraṇśa, is distinctly noticeable in Chhāndasa. Shades of Prakṛta grammarians! What a heterodoxy it is to notice apabhraṇśa in the holy speech of the Riṣis!

Before giving some examples of loss of letters in the Vedic words, we may remark that during the Vedic days (specially the later Vedic days) the speakers did not very much tolerate initial conjunct mutes; that in the Dravidian language Tamil, such a thing is not tolerated as a rule has been distinctly stated in a previous lecture. The examples of loss of vowels and of change of sounds cannot be taken up for discussion, as that task involves detailed exposition of the Vedic morphology. I have already spoken of the reduction of many dentals into cerebrals and of the growth of such forms as বিকট from বিকৃত and প্রকট from প্রকৃত. I give here below, first some examples of loss of consonants, and then some examples relating to general phonetic decay, as the history of the forms for numerals indicates. (1) We get

* *Apabhraṇśa*, in its proposed use requires an explanation. Very arbitrarily, this term which literally means decay or rather phonetic decay, has been made to denote a class of Prākṛta speech of no definitely distinctive character. As all the Prākṛta dialects grew by varying from the norm (no matter what that norm is), and as no standard Prākṛta can really be set up without resorting to an artificial and unscientific method, the term *Apabhraṇśa* cannot be misused to designate a particular class of Prākṛta speech. We cannot forget that all our provincial vernaculars have always been called *Prākṛta* by the Hindu scholars. Consequently the word Apabhraṇśa may be fitly used in its literal sense to indicate phonetic decay.

Kambhana for Skambhana in many passages in the Ṛgveda, though Skambhana is not extinct; (2) Ścandra (brilliant) occurs no doubt in many passages, but candra (brilliant) is generally met with; the word candramas derived from it, is the only form to signify moon; (3) and (4) along with স্তনয়িত্নু, (from স্তন thunder) and স্তায়ু (thief from stena) we get tanayitnu and tāyu; (5) we get the earlier form stṛ as well as the later form tṛ for star; the feminine form স্ত্রী (wife, one who shines in the house) retains the original stem; (6) we notice the loss of initial consonant in তুরীয় (fourth) derived from the word চতুর. Such examples of decay as have been rightly inferred by Prof. Macdonell from the words of cognate languages, are purposely left unnoticed in this lecture.

Numerals.—In the history of the growth of many numeral forms, as discussed hereunder, all such losses will be noticed as are characteristic of downright apabhranṡa words of the Prākṛta grammarians. In the compound cardinals of genuine early formations, we should notice that দ্ব which develops into দ্বা in euphonic combination, indicates two, while দ্বি signifies 'twice' and ত্রয়: and চতুর signify 'three' and 'four' respectively, while ত্রি and চত্বার signify 'three times' and 'four times' respectively; দ্বাদশ (two + ten), ত্রয়োদশ (three + ten) and চতুর্দ্দশ (four + ten) may be contrasted with the forms analysed below. (1) In the formation of the word বিংশ we get দ্বি + দশ; there has first been the loss of initial দ, and then we notice that to compensate for the loss of দ of দশ, a long sound comes in, which is represented by অনুস্বার; that a nasal naturally develops at times in making a sound long, has been fully discussed in the 6th Lecture. As to the decade indicating তি which occurs unchanged as final in বিংশতি, ষষ্ঠি, সপ্ততি etc., and in a changed form in ত্রিংশৎ, চত্বারিংশৎ, and পঞ্চাশৎ, some remarks will presently follow. I may remark by the way, that in the formation of বীসতি in Pali, the loss of অনুস্বার has been made up for by the দীর্ঘ ঈ. (2) In the formation of অশীতি (অষ্ট or অষ্টা + দশ + তি) we notice the loss of the second and the 3rd syllables, and the penultimate is conjoined to the long vowel ঈ. (3) In the formation of ষোড়শ (ষষ্ + দশ) the compensating long ও and the deve'opment of cerebral sound ড় may be explained by সন্ধি rules partly. (4) The history of decade indicating 'তি' is shrouded in mystery. When we compare, for example বিংশতি with Venti of Italian, we may say that the latter form is merely a reduced form of the former, but when we take the history of 'ty'-ending of twenty, for example, our difficulty increases; the word twenty is derived from twain (old masculine form of two) shortened form of twegen, + tig; the last component tig is from Gothic tigjus = ten. Here we see that 'ty' represents the number ten; if we suppose that our তি had such a history to become naturally a decade indicating suffix, we must admit that in the formation of Vedic Compound-Cardinals an additional or unnecessary suffix was added. In Vedic Compound Cardinals Saṣṭi (ষষ্ + তি), Saptati and Navati, 'multiplication by ten' is indicated by 'তি' alone; if these three be really the earliest forms, 'তি' may be regarded as a fossil of a word for ten as might have been current in one dialect of the Aryan language beside দশ of another.

Though our illustrative examples have been a few only, we think we cannot fail to see from the examples of some pronominal forms and from the history of some words, that Chhāndasa was subject to the processes of dialectic regeneration and phonetic decay, processes to which all *living languages* have always been and ever will be subject. I mention over again, that by its regular and thoroughgoing accent system, Chāndasa discloses the character of a living speech.

I have said that we do not know when the Vedic Mantras were compiled as Samhitās. We do not also know what became *the form of the language of the people*, when the Mantras having been an object of special preserving care of the priestly class, a hiyeratic speech had to be necessarily maintained, as Latin was once maintained in Italy, to express religious thoughts with such purity of speech as the gods were supposed to demand. That a long time intervened between the time when the Vedic language was current and the time when a scholastic revival took place can be inferred from lots of statements occurring in the Brāhmaṇas. The fanciful history we get of the Vedic Mantras, the manner in which the Mantras have been explained and grammatical and accentual peculiarities of the Vedic language have been discussed, warrant us in holding that the earliest Brāhmaṇa must be much removed in time from the latest Vedic Mantra. The propositions in the Brāhmaṇic literature, that the Vedic forms should never be deviated from, and the proper accent of the Vedic words, should be carefully studied and learnt, very distinctly show, that for religious purposes a hiyeratic speech was artificially maintained, on the Vedic lines. I am going to adduce many facts in support of my position in the course of this lecture, but the facts noted above justify us in holding tentatively, that when the Samhitās were compiled with the Mantras of varying times, the grammarians of the priestly class studied the language of the holy works with an astonishing scientific accuracy and framed artificial generalized rules to make some heterogeneous elements look like one homogeneous whole. This is why various shades of meaning of many forms merged into a dead unity in the artificial language adopted by the priests in writing on the subject of the Vedas.

As to the true nature of successive changes (I purposely use the word *successive* and not *progressive*) noticeable in the polished literary speech or speeches from the post-Vedic days onward, as differing essentially in character from what may be noticed in a living language in its course through ages, a deal will have to be stated presently; as a preliminary step, I offer my observations, as to why it could be possible for the Brāhmaṇa and the cognate literature produced at different times to present essentially one and the same language. It is a familiar phenomenon, that even to-day our high class Pandits imitate very closely and wonderfully not only the ancient language, but also the style of some ancient works when dealing with them, or when writing something new after those ancient works. For a disquisition, or dissertation on the subject of নীতি or polity for example, scholars of a very late time have been noticed to have adopted the form and style of the old time Sūtras: such a work of a very late time (not earlier than the 6th century A.D.) as the গণেশাথর্বশীর্ষ will be found executed in the style of and partly in the language of the ancient Brāhmaṇas.

I cannot say when the term *laukika* as occurs in Pāṇini's grammar came into use to designate the hiyeratic language of post-Vedic days; in all likelihood it was long after the time of Gautama Buddha, since that sage who was undoubtedly a great *śiṣṭa* person, did not know the term as my reference to the Vinaya Piṭaka (Cullalvagga V. 33. 1) will clearly prove. Two Brāhman disciples of the veritable Śiṣṭa class who avoided speaking the vulgar speech of the time and spoke the speech which was then associated with culture and prosperity in life requested their master that his words or teachings might be allowed to be recorded in the language used by the cultured Brāhmaṇs, *viz.*, the Chāndasa (ছন্দসো আরোপেম are the words in the text) and should not be allowed to be vulgarized by being recorded in the current speech of the people (সকায় নিরুত্তিয়া are the words in the text). The celebrated orthodox commentator of the Vinaya text rightly interprets the polite language by the *Sanskṛta language of the Vedas*, and explains সকনিরুত্তি as মগধবোহারো *i.e.*, the language then current in the Magadha Country. The whole of this important text is given in the foot-note below for reference.*

We have to first notice, that if the polished respectable literary language of the time were known by the name *laukika* as distinguished from the obsolete Chhāndasa, Budha and his learned Brāhmaṇ disciples were sure to use the term laukika, for it was the Classical Laukika of the Brāhmaṇa literature as distinguished from the real Vedic language, which came into vogue in those days as the fit vehicle for all serious thought.

---

* তেন খো পন সময়েন যমেলুতেকুলা নাম ভিক্খু দ্বে ভাতিকা হোন্তি, ব্রাহ্মণজাতিকা কল্যানবাচা কল্যাণ বাক্করণা। তে যেন ভগবা, তেন উপসংকমিংসু ; উপসংকমিত্বা ভগবন্তম্ অভিবাদেত্বা একমন্তম্ নিসীদিংসু ; একমন্তম্ নিসিন্না, খো তে ভিক্খূ ভগবন্তম্ এতদ্ অবোচুম্ : এতরহি ভন্তে ভিক্খূ নানা নামা, নানা গোত্তা নানাজচ্চা নানাকুলা পব্বজিতা ; তে সকায় নিরুত্তিয়া বুদ্ধবচনম্ দূসেন্তি ; হন্দ মযং ভন্তে বুদ্ধবচনম্ ছন্দসো আরোপেমাতি। [Then Buddha says,.........ন ভিক্খবে বুদ্ধবচনম ছন্দসো আরোপেতব্বম্] The commentary has :—ছন্দসো, etc.,... =বেদম্ বিয় সকৃকত ভাসায় etc., সকায় নিরুত্তিয়া=[In the] মগধ বোহারো।

N.B.—It should be noted that though there is mention of ordinary ভিক্খুs to have been recruited from various sections it has not been said that the teaching were being put

We have to consider, in the second place, that if the hieratic language in which holy thoughts relating to the Vedas were being expressed, were regarded as altogether different from Chāndasa, the literature relating to the Vedas, would have much suffered in the estimation of the people. The language in question, we must therefore hold, was worked out on the Chāndasa lines, when Chāndasa became altogether an obsolete speech; this is why, in spite of very close imitation, this language differs from Chāndasa in many essential particulars. I proceed presently to take note of some of the important characteristics of this hieratic language. What I specially emphasize upon here is that in the days of Gautama Budha there was at least in the Magadha country a *living vulgar speech*, called মগধ বোহার by Buddha Ghosha and there was by the side of the dialect (or many other dialects) one literary language which still then claimed the name ছান্দস.

It is now agreed, on all hands, on reference to the rules for লৌকিক in পাণিনি's Grammar, that generally speaking the language of the Brāhmanas can be designated as *laukika*. We do not exactly know when the term laukika, came into use, but we may infer on reference tc the import of the term, that when *secular* literature composed in the hieratic language, forced itself to the recognition of the orthodox class, the term laukika, as distinguished from Chāndasa became the name of the fashionable literary language. We do not also know

---

in *various speeches*; for, in the first place we get the instrumental singular of নিরুত্তি and in the second place we do not get 'সকায় সকায়' to indicate as usual 'everybody's own'; as the commentator gives only মগধবোহারো for the নিরুত্তির dialect in question, the word সকায় should be carefully judged for its proper significance.

when the term সংস্কৃত was brought into use as a substitute for লৌকিক, but it is an undoubted fact that the grammatical rules for লৌকিক as occur in পাণিনি as well as in the মহাভাষ্য of the 2nd Century B.C., are essentially the rules of standard Sanskrit Grammar of later days. We find that what is called লৌকিক at one time and সংস্কৃত at another, is closely related etymologically with the Chāndasa language; at the same time it must be observed, that even in early times, the Classical Sanskrit or the Laukika language of Panini so very materially differed from the Vedic or Chāndasa speech, that a fresh set of rules had to be framed to give the Classical Sanskrit a well-defined individuality. We should not here fail to notice that those orthodox Grammarians who gave to লৌকিক the name সংস্কৃত, were perfectly aware of the character of the language as a polished, dressed-up and perfected speech. The Vedic has all along been, from Panini, downwards, the object of veneration, as an ideal language and consequently the polish or perfection referred to above, could not be given to the Vedic for the formation of a laukika in the sinful days; that a polish was given to the vulgar speeches or dialects of natural growth will be abundantly clear from the remarks of the Grammarians themselves.

In the grammatical work of Panini (which will never fail to extort a high tribute of wonder and respect) and in its learned commentories, we meet with this definite statement that the forgotten things of the Chāndasa speech should be diligently resuscitated while things occurring in the popular speeches should be studiously eschewed to save one's soul from being contaminated by sin. It has been stated under a sūtra, that the enemies of the cultured Aryas met with defeat and discomfiture for having uttered their barbarous apabhraṇsa word হেলয়; we get also one statement of emphatic expression that to know the Vedic words is to acquire religious merit, while to know the popular or vulgar speech is to commit sin. Writes the author of the Mahābhāṣya যথৈবহি শব্দ জ্ঞানে (meanngi Vedic words) ধর্ম্মঃ এবং অপশব্দ জ্ঞানেঽপ্যধর্ম্মঃ, অথবা ভূয়ানধর্ম্মং প্রাপ্নোতি etc, etc.

In his tirades against the popular speeches, Patanjali gives us materials to find out that many provincial dialecs were current during his time. That the pure Vedic words were very limited in number while the vile words were very many, has been thus expressed ভূয়াংসোঽপশব্দা অল্পীয়াংসঃ শব্দাঃ একৈকস্যহি শব্দস্য বহবোপভ্রংশাঃ ; তদ্‌যথা গৌরিত্যস্য শব্দস্ত গাবী গোনী গোতা গোপোতলিকেত্যেবমাদয়ো বহবোঽপভ্রংশাঃ।

We meet with গোণী and its plural গোণা in the standard Prākṛta called পালি, and meet also sparingly with the form গাবী in a প্রাকৃত dialect which though despised by the sages assumed the form গাভী in the classical Sanskrit itself at a later time. We can very well see that in the second century B.C., many Prākṛta dialects flourished in N. India. No doubt for the evidence of this fact we have other definite records but I make the sage পতঞ্জলি to give evidence on the point, to serve a special purpose I have in view. I have to show that the sages and শিষ্ট's made an infructuous attempt to rule the dialects which were rolling on all around like the waves of the sea by taking a boat of literary language on the waves, not seeing that the boat itself was bound to be tossed about and the waves were not to be dominated. It is interesting that the sage Patanjali knew other forms of Prākṛta than what we learn not only in the Bhudhistic works but also in the Aśoka inscriptions. It has been mentioned that for the usual standard word of গন্ origin হম্মতি was in use in সৌরাষ্ট্রে and রংহতি in the North-Western India. We may note that রঙ্গুছি (is crawling) is the Oriya form which has, come on somehow or other, as a further অপভ্রংশ of রংহতি, and 'রংহ' by itself came into use in later Sanskrit in a secondary or tertiary sense; again though 'হম্ম' of হম্মতি is not now in use either in Surat or in any part of Western or Northern India, the direct descendant হম্ম (to crawl) on all fours may be unmistakably identified with our Bengali হামা as in হামা দেওয়া.

The existence of various provincial Prākṛta dialects by the side of the old *laukika* or classical Sanskrit is not denied by the scholars; but some want us to accept the proposition that the Classical Sanskrit evolved naturally from the Vedic speech and the Prākṛta dialects were formed by corrupting the Sanskrit language. The facts which are principally adduced in support of the proposition are: (1) All the past-indicating forms, *viz.*, লিট্‌ লঙ্‌ and লুঙ্‌ are in use in Sanskrit while there is principally but one generalised past form of finite verbs in the Prākṛtas old and new. (2) The dual form unknown in the Prākṛtas is fully maintained in Sanskrit. (3) The Prākṛtas of a very late date are more Sanskritic than the earlier ones and as such these late time Prākṛtas cannot be said to have descended from the older Prākṛtas. I proceed to examine all these points which stand against my proposition.

The variety of Past Forms—It is true that all the systems of past tense are set forth in the Sanskrit Grammars, old and new, but is it true that in their use in literature the time systems represent their value correctly? Can it be denied, as was pointed out long ago by Whitney, that in the *Brāhmaṇas*, the distinction of tense value between perfect and imperfect is almost altogether lost, as in the later Sanskrit language? It is given, no doubt in the Grammatical works, that the perfect is to be used in the narration of facts not witnessed by the narrator, but Whitney has rightly remarked that there is no evidence of its being either exclusively or distinctively so employed in the literature. That in the Vedas, the case is quite different, may be seen on reference to Macdonell's Vedic Grammar. It is to be noted that all the varieties of the Aorist, as occur in the Vedas, have been bound together in the Post-Vedic times, and have been made into one system. In the Classical Sanskrit, the Aorist forms are only preterites and are freely exchangable with imperfects and perfects. Whitney remarks, after collecting examples, that the aorist of the Classical Sanskrit is simply a preterite, equivalent to the imperfect and perfect, and frequently co-ordinated with them. It is a significant thing to note that adverting to a particular use of the Aorist in the Vedas (though that use is not exclusive in the Vedas) a definite generalized rule was framed for the use of the Aorist as is disclosed by the Brāhmaṇa literature; the use of Aorist as a tense of narration is very closely observed in the language of the Brāhmaṇas, the Upanishads and the Sūtras of early time. I have already remarked that to create a hieratic language on the Vedic lines, generalized rules were framed and thereby the naturally developed heterogenuous elements were reduced to a state of homogeneity. Indiscriminate use of the past systems distinctly shows that the past systems in their variety were only maintained in grammar to make the hieratic language look respectable when in reality, the classical language had no natural link to bind itself with the Vedic language. It has to be specially and particularly noted that লিট্, লঙ্ and লুঙ্ forms do not only exist in the early পালি forms but their use in Pali, unlike what we have noted just now in the Brāhmaṇa literature is much after the Vedic use: the supposed irregularities in the Vedic speech, have been artificially avoided in the Brāhmaṇa literature by framing some generalized rules. Again the simplified past system of the later Prākṛtas, shows what naturally came into use in the country in the

প্রাকৃত speech, in contrast with the unmeaning retention of various obsolete systems in Classical Sanskrit, in its unnatural attempt to get away from the natural state of things. It is notorious that the Ramayana, and the Mahabharata in all its parts, abound with examples of indiscriminate use of various past forms in one and the same sense; it is not in the late time literature alone that we get বৈবস্বত মনুর্নাম......আসীৎ, etc., along with বভূব রাজা কিলকার্ত্তবীর্য্যঃ but we get আসীৎ রাজা নলোনাম, etc., by the side of পুরা বভূব, etc. ......in the মহাভারত.

We notice that for the mode of expression "I have done" or "It has been done," participle forms came into use in the Prākṛta and even long before the time of পতঞ্জলি, the form was being freely used to indicate that sense in the Classical language; it could not but be so, as the writers of the Classical language, possessed the very mind and thought of the speakers of the vulgar tongue. To assert that the use of finite verbs in their special past form, where participle form was in current use, should not be regarded obsolete, the author of the মহাভাষ্য has cited some examples which are very often quoted. The examples show that for তেৰ, চক্ৰ, পেচ, the forms তীর্ণাঃ, কৃতবন্তঃ and পক্কবন্তঃ were in use. However much the শিষ্ট people kept themselves aloof, they could not possibly create a narrow little world of theirs but had to hold conversation at least with their wives, who could not but speak the vulgar tongue, being always in close touch with the neighbours; howsoever easy it might be for the sons of the শিষ্টs to learn their শিষ্ট speech, they could not lisp in Classical Sanskrit, when in the arms of their nurses. The influence of the real language of the people could never be kept off by setting up a barrier-wall of culture.

Pronunciation.—Not only in the matter of the use of tenses, but in other matters as well, the শিষ্টs imported

23

the peculiarities of the vulgar speeches in their holy literature; being men of the society, the শিক্ষs imbibed the altered pronunciation of the common people, and thus unawares deviated from the Vedic norm: we notice in the very ব্রাহ্মণs how in some cases the বিসর্জ্জনীয় has been disregarded, ন has been reduced to ণ, and ঋ has been reduced to ই. That in the matter of general accent, the শিক্ষs do not disclose a regular accent system but only uphold the Vedic recent for the words of the Vedic mantras alone, by a study of the Vedic accents, cannot be illustrated in this brief review.

Dual.—A dual in addition to a plural was no doubt a commonly accepted form in the pre-Vedic days, for the classical Aryan languages of Europe disclose some almost effete dual forms. To express two together as a pair, is a familiar mode of thought exhibited by all peoples all over the world, but to retain a regular dual system, does not appear to be a normal inclination in man, in any part of the globe. I am inclined to think, that the formation of dual, was in the case of some people, the first step towards expressing a general plural number; but when a regular plural was reached, the earlier form in this grade of evolution, either died out or was retained only for very occasional use. It is not unlikely, that dual was a regular plural form in the dialect of one section of the culture group of the Aryans, and at the fusion of dialects in the growth of one generalized common speech, the non-regular plural (*i.e.*, the dual) forms stuck to the language as dual, but for practical purposes, the dual was only restricted in use, in expressing the special thought relating to a pair. That in the Vedic language, the dual has this sort of restricted use, cannot be very much doubted. What has been observed by the Vedic scholars in this matter, has been fitly expressed by Whitney in the following words; "The dual is (with only very rare and sporadic exceptions) used strictly in all cases, where two objects are logically indicated, whether directly or by combination of two individuals. Dr. Bloomfield has very rightly observed, that while the employment of the dual is generally strict in the truly post-Vedic language, the plural is often used instead of the dual of natural pairs in the archaic parts of the Ṛgveda. It is because of natural disinclination, that the dual system was not maintained in the European languages of Aryan origin, and it was owing to this naturalness of thought, that a regular dual system was falling into disuse in the living Vedic speech; the dual system could not survive into the Prākṛtas, because the Aryan people of India ceased to have the sort of thought in their mind, which either generates or cherishes such a system in addition to plural system. We may consequently assert, that the co-existence of the dual forms with the plural forms, and the mainteinance of the dual forms, not as worn-out unnecessary survivals, but as forms having meaning and use, point to a fixed literary character or rather to an unnatural artificial character of the post-Vedic language as well as of the classical Sanskrit. In their zeal to perpetuate the purity of the Vedic speech, the शिष्टs out-Heroded Herod, in maintaining a rigid dual system.

Why the Prākṛtas of rather a very late date, are more Sanskritic than their early predecessors, should now be explained. Had it not been for the religious activities of the Buddhists and the Jains, what we can know of some old time Prākṛtas, would have been out of our reach. For reasons I shall state in a subsequent lecture, these Prākṛtas were standardized, and became the sacred language of some religious sects; even though new Prākṛta speeches came actually into being, the sectarian religious works were composed during those later times, in the earlier obsolete Prākṛtas. Consequently, a general continuity of the Prākṛta speeches in their transformation through ages, cannot very easily be traced in literature. Properly speaking, no general secular literature existed in the provincial dialects, to give models of language to the Prākṛta-speaking people of successive generations. The people continued to speak in their Prākṛta speeches, but serious literature was always being composed by the learned in Sanskrit. When, therefore any good or elevated thought had to be expressed in a public document for universal use, in any Prākṛta dialect, a great want was felt in getting adequate terms in the current speech of the people. Sanskrit words were therefore laid under contribution, from the current literary works. This is why during the early literary activities in all our Vernaculars, we notice the influence of Sanskrit upon the Vernaculars. We should not, at the same time, fail to notice, that the Prākṛta or vernacular-speaking people of all times, have maintained the non-Sanskritic structure of their speech. It is by Grammar principally, and not by Vocabulary, that the character of a speech is to be judged; if we do so, we will find that the genetic affinities between the Prākṛtas of early and late times, will be clearly noticeable. As the subject will be specially delineated in another lecture, no further remarks need be added here.

That the classical Sanskrit has been through all times greatly influenced by the Prakrtas, has been shown by a few examples only; a further consideration of the subject is necessary. The শিষ্টs who could not but belong to the dialect-speaking people, could not but use the Prākṛta forms (though unawares) in their Sanskrit composition. I adduce below some examples to show how this was done. I cannot however resist the temptation of quoting here the words of Dr. Skeat, which are applicable to the শিষ্টs of all countries and times: "The speaker of the 'standard' language is frequently tempted to consider himself as the dialect-speaker's superior, unless he has already acquired some elementary knowledge of the value of the science of language, or has sufficient common sense to be desirous of learning to understand that which for the moment lies beyond him."

First of all I notice, that as after framing some artificial general rules, the শিষ্টs were forced to explain away some naturally developed Vedic words, by setting them down as cases of আর্ষ license, so in respect of some Prākṛta or Deśi words assimilated by them unawares in the Sanskrit language, the śiṣṭas invented the *nipātana* rule, considering perhaps what was but a natural growth, to be due to vagaries or freaks of nature.

That there was a scholastic revival in building up Sanskrit, and that the popular dialects (which could not but have been the property of the শিষ্টs) had to be polished from time to time, to make sanskṛita of them, will be partly demonstrated by the following examples. The examples are given in an alphabetical order and not in what may be called chronological order; the remarks against them will however show in some cases, when they were introduced from the Prākṛtas into the holy speech.

(1) অধঃ means no doubt the lower part as adjective or adverb. It is interesting to note, that in the popular speech, অধর্ the first component of the compound word অধরোষ্ঠ came to designate the lower lip; this অধর was taken into the classical Sanskrit without any question.

(2) উপর.—In Vedic denotes lower; but by false analogy of other words connected with the উপসর্গ 'উ' it was made by the শিষ্টs, themselves to convey exactly the opposite meaning.

(3) একাং-ন.—How in the early Brāhmaṇa language this round-about and clumsy expression took the place of Vedic নব (nine, pronounced as ন-উ-অ) of the cardinal compounds নবদশ (nineteen) নববিংশতি (twenty-nine) and so forth to নবনবতি (ninety-nine), is not clear. The earliest Prākṛta has উন which may be formed by metathysis from ন-উ-অ; it is not likely that একাং-ন was reduced to উন. I think উন being un-orthodox, the new expression was coined, when নব fell into disuse, and উন was wrongly supposed to be something like একাং-ন because of its final ন.

(4) কর্ম্মার.—in Vedic it means the smith; কম্মার is the natural Prākṛta form of it, from which the vernacular কামার has come out. The purists, in ignorance of Vedic form polished the prākṛta form in analogy of other words, by adding কার indicating doing to কর্ম্ম, to form কর্ম্মকার.

(5) The word গ্না signified a married lady and a goddess in the early speech, and so who was not a গ্না, *i.e.*, who was not lady-like was ন-গ্না; thus মহানগ্নী came to signify a বিশ্যা (viśya) or courtesan. The shamelessness of a courtesan gave the significance naked to the word. So by its derivation neither গ্না nor নগ্না was a feminine form of any masculine word; but not knowing the character of the word, the word নগ্ন was created as the original masculine form, even in the Brāhmaṇa literature. I must also note, that from the original meaning of the word গ্না, a married woman, the word নগ্না also came into use to signify an unmarried girl; in this meaning of the word the age of the girl could not be and cannot be read. The Vedic rule having come down by tradition, it was prescribed in the ideal form of marriage, that one who was not married to another, was to be taken as wife. The commentators, in the teeth of the fact that the ceremonials recorded in the Gṛhyasutras, relate to the marriage of girls of mature age,

interpret the word নগ্না as a girl walking about without covering her shame. The Philologists should take care not to equate nude with নগ্ন because of the lateness of its formation.

(6) দম্পতি.—In Vedic means master of the house (দম house + পতি). Exactly when দম (*i.e.*, গৃহ) coming to signify গৃহিনী, the meaning changed in a popular dialect, is not known; দম্পতি with its Prākṛta variant জম্পতি (*cf.*, জসপুর for দশপুর, বৈজনাথ for বৈদ্যনাথ, etc.) came no doubt into use in Sanskrit, as the false Sanskrit derivation shows. In ignorance of Vedic form, the Prākṛta forms were explained and reconciled in Grammar by a false rule, which gives us জায়া + পতি = জম্পতি and দম্পতি. That the phonetic change of দ into জ is noticeable in the Vedic itself, may be illustrated by one example: we get জ্যোতি as a changed form of দ্যুতি in the Vedic; জ্যোতিস্ however became in the Vedic a new stem to signify a meaning different from but allied to দ্যুতি.

(7) নাপিত.—The word is unknown in the Vedic speech; the word for it was বপ্তা (vaptā). The barber on some ceremonial occasions had the duty of cleansing the body of a man and so he was called in the Māgadhi Prākṛta or Pāli a নহাপিত; this নহাপিত is the causative form of নাহা derived from the root স্না. The purists in the analogy of other words, made নহাপিত a নাপিত, and thought they are not using a vulgar word in the place of the orthodox Vedic word. The word occurs in the Brāhmaṇa language.

(8) ভগবান.—When a generalised rule relating to বৎ-প্রত্যয় was framed in Sanskrit, and Pāli words with বা final were thought by a false analogy to be the words of বৎ origin, the word ভগবা was reduced to ভগবান্; then again to meet a difficulty the Vedic vocative form ভগব had to be declared as an ārṣa license.

(9) মাতুল.—No word for maternal uncle is traceable in the Vedic; Macdonell very rightly infers that this word

was presumably a dialectic form which made its way into Sanskrit. In Sūtra literature, it is মাতুল which was no doubt taken from the popular speech. The popular word was wrongly sought to be derived from a Vedic stem, and as such মাতুল was imagined to be a variant of মাতুর, and then the curious word মাতুর্ভ্রাতা was coined as the supposed original word in the Maitrāyaṇi Saṃhitā.

(10) মন্মথ.—I have shown in a previous lecture that this purely Prākṛta word was adopted on account of long use in the Classical Sanskrit, but failing to derive it properly from মনস্ of Sanskrit (which was only মন in Prākṛta), a rule of exception was invented for its justification.

(11) বিধবা.—In the Vedic speech বিধু means 'alone' and বিধু with the feminine suffix আ became বিধবা (a widow); there was no ধব in the Vedic speech to dominate this বিধবা and we get a Vidova in Italian, for example without any masculine form for it. As বি (vi) was wrongly thought to be the initial উপসর্গ, বিধবা was derived as a woman who lost her never existent ধব ; ধব is a pseudo-Sanskrit word. (12) বিশ্যা, a courtesan, signified in derivation a woman who was accessible to the Vis or the Aryan people in general. When the corrupt Prākṛta form Vissā was purified, an imaginary origin of the word was sought in the dress, etc , of the displayer of beauty, and hence Veśya (from Veśa), was used as the correct form. (13) শুতুদ্রী of Vedic use was made a শতদ্রু by imagining a hundred streamlets for the river.

(14) সরল—signifies 'a species of pine tree' as well as 'straight.' The original Vedic for the class of the pine tree is শরল (the tree which is straight like a শর) ; the word সরল occurs in the Brāhmaṇa literature after the pronunciation of the common people.

It is notorious that the Classical Sanskrit has swelled with words of Prākṛta and Deśi origin ; as these words are interesting for many reasons, I give a small number of them in an appendix to help the students to study the matter separately.

I cannot possibly dilate upon the subject any further. We may very well hold, that the non-existence of dual and the currency of a simplified past system in the Prākṛtas, argue in favour of the natural growth of the Prākṛtas. That the early Prākṛta or Pāli, retains many archaic Vedic forms, as are unknown in Sanskrit, is admitted by all scholars ; this point of structural unity of early Pāli with the Vedic, will be very briefly noticed in the subsequent lecture. I now proceed to notice a fact, which will show (though perhaps faintly) that a continuity of the Vedic was maintained through many Prākṛta dialects, which have now died out without leaving any literary evidence of their existence.

It is a striking phenomenon, that we have stored up many words in our vernacular which are met with in the oldest known Vedic speech only, and which were not in use in Sanskrit, which is wrongly regarded as a direct and pure offspring of the Vedic language. I do not claim to be exhaustive, but I should think that the list I append here, is not a very short one. (1) অঙ্কী and অঙ্কুশী correspond in meaning exactly with আঁকুশী—in ignorance of the origin, the wrong derivation আ+কর্ষ has been imagined. The word অঙ্কুশ is a separate word altogether. (2) The Vedic word অমলা is used by us in the form আমলা ; আমলক became a pedant word even in the days of the early উপনিষদs and the word আমলকী derived from it, is used in our high flown language. (3) আণ্ডা is an egg as well as a fœtus in the womb. The Sanskrit form অণ্ড is a later form derived from আণ্ডা. Considering it a Prākṛta word, the শিষ্টs dropped the final আ, as non-feminine forms with আ final could not be adopted.

(4) আদার—The pungent juice of it became once the substitute for সোমরস. Our আদা is closer to the early word in form; the Sanskrit word আর্দ্রক is only a pedantic form. (5) আশা—means side in the Vedic speech; in that sense we use the word in the phrase আশে পাশে. The word is in use in Sanskrit in a secondary meaning indicating direction. (6) এনা—means like this; from this comes our now poetic word হেন. (7) ওদতী to be wet with dew; ওদা signifying wet was in general use in old Bengali, and is still in use in the district of Bankura and in Orissa in that sense. (8) কুদী and কুডী jujube; the Bengali form is কুল and the Oriya form is কুলী. (9) কুশর a sort of reed; this word is in use in Eastern as well as in Northern Bengal to mean sugarcane; in this very sense the word is in use in Eastern Māgadhi and in Oriya of the district of Sambalpur, while in the intervening tracts of Bengal the word আখ from ইক্ষু is in use; the form is আখু in Orissa proper. The word কশার as in কশার বন to indicate cluster of reeds, is however in use in Central Bengal. (10) We get in the Ṛgveda the interjection বট্ (truly) and বত (alas); our বটে (truly) comes from the earlier Bengali form বট as in "কে বট হে." It is not correct that this word comes from বর্ত্ত to stay or exist; the Western Bhojpuri বট from বর্ত্ত is not in use in Eastern Māgadhi, nor there is any verb in Bengali or Oriya which is even remotely connected with বট. (11) ভর্ভরা, a Vedic interjection, which signifies confusion of thought; ভেবড়ে যাওয়া conveys exactly the same meaning. (12) বয়া, the aerial root of a tree. The aerial root of the Peepul tree (বট) is called বয়া in many parts of Bengal. (13) বশা, a calf almost mature enough to become a cow; in this very sense the word is in use in the district of Sambalpur, where it is pronounced as বছা. The word is in use in the Bengali-speaking district of Purulia. (14) বাশী occurs also in Pāli

and our বাশ is exactly the instrument which is used by the carpenters. (15) শিম্বল—its synonym শাল্মলী is in use in Sanskrit, while our শিমুল comes directly from শিম্বল through the medium of Pāli. (16) স্কম্ভ (not স্তম্ভ which is a separate word, and from which we have got থাম a pillar) has its অপভ্রংশ form খাম্বা or থাম in Bengali; it signifies a prop and so is closely related to স্তম্ভ in meaning.

I speak of a few other words in this connection, though to illustrate a different phenomenon. The words গাত্র (limb), দাত্র (knife), etc., of the Vedic, were formed with the suffix ত্র, and as such the words গা and দা, as original words, may be supposed to have existed in an once-existing dialect. Coming through Sanskrit, 'গাত্র' has been reduced to গতর্ in some vernaculars, but গা and দা seem to have come to us like the words just set forth in the above list, through some provincial dialects, of which no trace can now be obtained. As not altogether irrelevant, I cite the history of another word here. The word 'কপাল' indicating skull or skull-bone, though of pure Vedic origin, was regarded as unfit to be uttered by the holy people (at least in Patanjali's time), on account of its gruesome association; the euphemistic term ভগাল was recommended for substitution. We know, however, that the fate of কপাল was not doomed in Sanskrit, but it is curious that this euphemistic word ভগাল had the ill-luck of earning for itself the very unpleasant idea, which it was intended to dispel; the slightly-changed form of ভগাল as ভাগাড় denotes in Bengali, the place where dead animals are allowed to rot and the bones of the animals bleach in the sun.

From the cumulative evidence it is rather clear that the literary Vedic speech stood in a close relationship with many provincial dialects, some of which at least continued through all ages, to live to be transformed into later vernaculars, and that the Classical Sanskrit, on the other hand, came into existence as an artificial language.

We have shown to a certain extent, that Laukika or Sanskrit was sought at first to be kept in close unity with the Vedic, but as a matter of fact this language could not maintain any continuity with the Vedic, and with the progress of time, it went on drawing largely upon the Prākṛta dialects. Facts have also been adduced, to show or rather to suggest, why most of the important links in the chain of evolution of the Prākṛta dialects, leading up to our modern vernaculars, are missing or rather irrevocably perished.

APPENDIX.

Only a few Sanskrit or rather pseudo-Sanskrit words are listed below, just to show the influence of Prākṛtas of all times, upon the language which is said to have kept itself aloof from the Prākṛtas.

(1) কৌপীন—from কু+পরিধান or পিধান. The vernacular word কাপড় and the provincial Oriya word কপ্টা are derived from it. In the Sanskrit of a very late time, this কপট was made into কর্পট.

(2) কেলি—from ক্রীড় came out of two Prākṛta words, কিল and খেল; কেলি is from কিল and খেল, as in খেলন, খেলৎ, etc., remains unchanged.

(3) খর্পর—from কপাল (skull) we get কপ্ড়ি and its variant খপ্ড়ি; from খপড়ি we get খুলি as মাতার খুলি, as well as খাপ্রা; either খপ্ড়ি or খাপ্রা has been sanskritized into খর্পর.

N.B.—খুলি as of মাতার খুলি, should not be confounded with খোলা which is a synonym of খাপ্রা; from কোষ we have got both খোসা as well as খোলা; from কোষ we have got খোল besides খোলা. This খোল again is not identical either with খোল derived from খণ to excavate, or with খোল to loosen, derived from স্খল.

(4) গেহ—from গৃহ requires no comment.

(5) ঘর্ম্ম—from গ্রীষ্ম came out গিম্হ, and this গিম্হ gave birth to ঘম্ম; ঘম্ম was sanskritized into ঘর্ম্ম in the analogy of ধর্ম্ম, কর্ম্ম, etc.

(6) চটুল—from চতুর. Very likely from চতুর (clever) we also got চউর and this word came to signify a clever thief, and thus the Sanskrit words

চোর and চোর were formed. Prof. D. R. Bhandarkar thinks that the Sanskrit word চোর comes from the tribal name চোল or চোড়.

(7) ক্ষুরিত—from ক্ষরিত.

(8) জটা—from যুক্ত; a matted lock of hair not being easily separable into component parts.

(9) ঝটিকা—from ঝড়; so also other words of ঝ initial.

(10) All words with ট, ঠ, ড, ঢ initials.

(11) তড়িৎ—from ত্বর indicating quickness. From the very word ত্বর, তাড় was formed as an independent root (*cf.*, তাড়ন, তাড়য়ামাস, etc.).

(12) দুর্ব্বা—Sanskritic form of দুব্ব or দুব্বো which is an অপভ্রংশ of দর্ভ.

(13) ধান্য—a pseudo-respectable form of ধান; ধানা (fried paddy = লাজা) was adopted in Sanskrit without change.

(14) নাটক—from নৃত্ to dance.

(15) পটহ—from প্রহত comes পহত or পহট and then by metathysis.

(16) পীড়, পীড়ন—comes from পিষ্ট of the root পিষ্.

(17) Excepting a few words such as ফল, ফাল (plough-share) and ফেন almost all words having ফ initial; even the word ফল is suspected to be of Dravidian origin.

(18) ভট্ট—from ভর্ত্তা.

(19) মড়ক—from মৃ; used in the sense of plague.

(20) মাম and মাতুল—already referred to and discussed.

(21) রণ্ডা—a pure দেশী word.

(22) লুণ্ঠন—from লুট, originally that which is lost by theft, *i.e.*, which becomes লুপ্ত.

(23) বঙ্কিম—from বক্র we got first বঙ্ক in Pāli.

(24) বল্মীক—from বম্র, বম্র and বম্ম being one and the same the word was formed by metathysis.

(25) বাট—from বর্ত্ম.

(26) শপ্—a new root to indicate curse; original form অভিশম্পাত=অভি+শং+পাত—that which befalls by destroying শং signifying কল্যাণ; this shows that শপ is a corrupt form of অভিশম্পাত.

(27) শেল—from শিলা; stone implement originally.

(28) অট—(walking or wandering about) from the Vedic root অত (compare অতিথি).

(29) উড্ড or উড্ডীন from উত্থ.

LECTURE XI

Pāli and other old Prākṛtas.

Prākṛta defined.—Sanskrit as a hieratic language, occupies naturally a position of very high honour. It is no wonder therefore, that our old Prākṛta grammarians regarded it in their fancy, to be the very speech, in its original purity, which the gods and holy men spoke at the very dawn of human creation. Some Prākṛta grammarians have formulated (no doubt very wrongly) that Sanskrit is in the state of প্রকৃতি or natural purity, while, the provincial dialects alone disclosed বিকৃতি or corruption of the original প্রকৃতি, by deviating from the norm of Sanskrit. This is how these grammarians have sought to explain the term Prākṛta, though the word প্রকৃতি cannot be shown to have been in use at any time, to signify a speech, holy or unholy. Prakṛti no doubt signifies nature, but in its secondary signification as 'subjects' or 'common people' or 'people in general,' the word is in very common use in our literature of all times. Prākṛta, in its signification as a speech, seems therefore to be associated with prakṛti or the common people. No matter what the derivation may be, it is undoubted, that the term Prākṛta has always denoted the current speech of the people in general, in contradistinction with the cultivated literary speech of the learned. It is significant that our provincial vernaculars of to-day, are called by the orthodox Pandits as so many Prākṛta speeches. No one can fail to notice, that the early poets of Bengal as well as of Orissa have designated the language of their effusions as Prākṛta. It is therefore admitted in a manner on all hands, that

Prākṛta is the speech, in which the babies commence to lisp and which the people very naturally learn untaught. The oriental scholars of Europe however, make a sharp distinction now between the modern vernaculars and the obsolete Prākṛtas, to secure some definiteness in the matter of classification. In this classification, the scholars have followed those Prākṛta grammarians, who have appropriated the name *prākṛta* for an artificial standard literary speech, and have given the term অপভ্রংশ, to the vernacular speeches of their time; I should notice in this connection, that Apabhranśa as reported by the grammarians is also an unreal apabhranśa speech. That the term apabhranśa should now only be used to denote phonetic decay, has been my suggestion in the foregoing lecture. We have to again notice with reference to the use of the term prākṛta by the modern scholars, that where a prākṛta ends and a vernacular begins, is not at all easy to determine and demarcate; it will not help us in the matter of classification, nay it will create anomaly and confusion, if the obsolete forms of our present day vernaculars be all designated as prākṛtas. If the term prākṛta be applied to signify those remote forbears of the modern vernaculars of Northern India, as may not be quite directly traced to be such forbears, a workable definition may be obtained. Practically speaking, this definition does not militate against the current definition of the scholars. I need hardly point out, that by the phrase 'remote forbear' in this definition, I do not refer either to Chhāndasa, which is the source-head of all our Aryan speeches, or to Classical Sanskrit, which has made from time to time some contributions to the Aryan Vernaculars.

Pāli defined.—Pāli, I have all along designated as an early Māgadhi prākṛta, on the authority of Buddha Ghoṣa, who has called it 'Magadha Bohāra.' The capital town of the Magadha country, we know from the phonetic representation of it in Greek as Palibothra, was once called পালিপুত্রো or পালিপুত্তো; the name Pāli, as a place name, is still in existence in Behar. I think that the people of Ceylon gave the name Pāli to the prākṛta speech in question, as the Buddhist canonical works were obtained by them in the Pāliputto country. Now that we see, that the word Pāṭaliputra could be, or rather was in reality reduced to the form Pāliputto, the objection that the term Pāli cannot come out of Pāṭali, will not be seriously urged. It will certainly be admitted, that the meanings given to the word Pāli by the Siṁhalese, are wholly unknown in the literature of India; once the Siṁhalese gave the name Pāli to the language of the canonical works, the secondary or tertiary meaning of the term could easily come into use in Ceylon.

Since Pāli has never been in use in India, as a term to denote either Prākṛta in general or any special Prākṛta in particular, Prākṛta should be the legitimate name for the language in question; if the Prākṛta of the Tripiṭakas be given a special name, the students of the Prākṛta speeches will be led into the wrong notion, that in the matter of origin and general character, Pāli differs widely and essentially from the other Prākṛtas. To use the word Pāli to signify "Buddhistic Prākṛta," is equally misleading; for the prākṛta in question was not during its currency, the speech of the Buddhists alone. In their canonical works the Buddhists have preserved a class of Prākṛta and the Jainas another; we are not on that account justified to designate those Prākṛtas by the names of those religious sects. I should also notice here another suggestion regarding the origin of the term Pāli: it is urged by some, on the strength of the supposition, that the speeches of the common people were not much in current in urban tracts, that the word Pāli may be a decayed form of the non-Aryan term Palli (পল্লী=village). Certainly phonology does not offer any difficulty in the matter of this etymology, but facts of history do not support this proposition. In the first place, it cannot be proved that the people of the rural tracts differed widely from the people of the urban tracts, in the matter of speech. In the second place, the word Pāli cannot be proved to have ever been in use in India, to denote a speech, and consequently it will not be correct to suppose that the people of Ceylon coined the term, by making historical investigation regarding the rural origin of the speech of their canonical works. I must however mention here, a hitherto unnoticed fact, which may be urged with some force in support of the theory. To speak in praise of the speech in which the গাথাশপ্তশতি has been composed, the author has designated the language by the name 'পাড়অ' in the 2nd verse of the work. The commentator has explained the term 'পাড়অ' by প্রাকৃত very correctly, but he has not given us the derivation of the word. The word looks like an apabhranśa of the word পল্লী, since পাড়া of modern vernaculars can easily be derived from পল্লী. But as this solitary use of a comparatively later time cannot be connected with a cognate word of idiomatic use of earlier times, Pāli, as an Indian name for a প্রাকৃত, cannot be accepted. Again it is difficult to say. how far the word পাড়অ for প্রাকৃত is a genuine অপভ্রংশ form of a particular time; that we meet with fanciful corruptions of Sanskrit terms in the literary prākṛtas, will be specially discussed afterwards. পাউঅ, and পাউদ are two terms for প্রাকৃত which occur in the কর্পূরমঞ্জরী; in this case it is rather certain that the terms were coined to maintain the character of the prākṛtas as given in some Prākṛta Grammars. I do not propose to do away with the term

Pāli, which denotes a particular class of Prākṛta of the olden time, but I discuss the question to remove the wrong notions which this term, as well as the term prākṛta may generate, regarding the origin, position, and value of the obsolete speeches of India.

The Character of Pāli.—I have tried to show in the previous lecture, that if we look into the evidence furnished by a comparative study of the early and later forms of Vedic speech, and if again we compare the Vedic speech as a whole, with Classical Sanskrit, we are led to the conclusion, that the old Grammarians seized on the salient features of the Vedic speech, and moulded them into one harmonious whole, to create a hieratic language. I have moreover setforth some facts, which make it probable, that even when Chhāndasa continued to be a living literary language, some provincial vernaculars (though derived originally from Chhāndasa) co-existed with Chhāndasa as closely related dialects. One fact indeed can never be doubted, that when the priestly class was busy in reviving, or in maintaining the purity of the Chhāndasa speech, the Aryan people in general spoke one form or another of the Aryan speech, which must be designated as Prākṛta. How far Pāli is removed from a Prākṛta speech, which co-existed with, or succeeded immediately to the latest phase of the Chhāndasa speech, is perhaps impossible to determine now, but that the early Pāli may be regarded to be closely allied to Chhāndasa, is admitted by all scholars.

I have pointed out in the previous lecture, that by unmeaning retention of the dual forms and of the tense systems of Chhāndasa, Classical Sanskrit reveals its own artificial character, while the structure of the Pāli language, discloses a natural modification or change of the early Aryan language. To show that how in some other points, Pāli retains to some extent the morphological structure of the Vedic speech, I refer here to some scholarly remarks of V. Fausboll, as appear in his preface to "Sutta Nipāta" (S. B. E., Vol. IX). He has shown with reference to the oldest portions of the Sutta Nipāta, that those richer forms of Vedic language which we find wanting in the Classical Sanskrit, were in use in the oldest Pāli. The great scholar has pointed out, that we meet with in Pāli, "the fuller Vedic forms of nouns and verbs in the plural, the shorter Vedic plurals, and the instrumental singular of nouns, Vedic infinitives, and many other Vedic forms and words."

The position of Sanskrit as a literary language, in its relation with Chhāndasa on the one side, and with the Prākṛta speeches on the other, has been discussed in several lectures from various view points. The relation of Pāli however, with several provincial Prākṛtas of the Post-Mauriyan times, is not easy to determine. I discuss some facts which show how this investigation is involved in difficulties: (1) Pāli was retained and used as a literary language by the Buddhists when it actually became an obsolete speech; (2) Sanskrit, though an artificial literary language ceased, at one time, to be a purely hieratic speech, and having become the vehicle of thought of all men, dealing with different branches of knowledge, it exercised such an influence in the country, that the living speeches which succeeded Pali, could not become respectable enough to leave literary monuments for us; (3) To ensure intelligibility in all provinces of India, the Prākṛta books (very limited in number), were composed in such an unreal generalized form, as does not help us to reconstruct the living speeches of old days. I notice the significance of all the points briefly below.

Pāli, a literary speech.—We clearly see, why Gotama Buddha insisted upon getting his teachings recorded in the vernacular of his time. What he aimed at however, was not secured, when without following the spirit of his words, his disciples stuck to the speech of his time in their literary composition, when the speech in question became obsolete, and as such uninteresting and repulsive to the non-Buddhistic people. Even to the ordinary Buddhistic people of mundane thoughts and worldly aspirations, this literature which was severely religious, could not be attractive; despite their deep veneration for their *Śāstra*, the people in general, who as a matter of course wanted to enjoy life, left the dull works of holy character to the care and custody of a small number of religious teachers. The language of the Aśoka inscriptions and references to (অপশব্দ) *apaśabdas* by Patanjali, distinctly show that the Pāli speech of Buddha's time was being changed with the progress of time, and various provincial dialects came into existence in the 2nd Century B.C.; yet it is a fact, that the author of the Milinda panha tried his best to write in the language of the Buddhistic canonical works. Changes effected by time are distinctly noticeable in the Pāli canonical works themselves, even though a general standard was set up for the language. No doubt the old Pāli of Buddha's days was being transformed into new and newer dialects, but the old-time Pāli failed to become a living heritage with the speakers of the newly-transformed speeches. In that the literary Sanskrit in its broader and more catholic character was being enriched every day by the composition of interesting and entertaining secular literature of various genre, the influence of Sanskrit became more potent and abiding, upon the laymen of letters all throughout the country. True it is that the author of Sanskrit works, who lived, moved and had their being in the living atmosphere of the Prākṛta speeches of their days, introduced various Prākṛta forms in Sanskrit, but the speakers of the Prākṛta tongues, could not but draw upon Sanskrit for want of a living literary tradition of the Prākṛtas, when they sought from time to time to enrich their dialects.

It became impossible in those days to write in any particular vernacular of the province which might be intelligible to the people of all the provinces. The Buddhistic writers, who wanted to adhere to the Prākṛta speech, but found Pāli could not be made intelligible even in the Magadha country, mixed up Sanskrit forms with some অপভ্রংশ forms common to many provinces, and thereby created a curious hybrid language, which has acquired the designation, the Gāthā language. It was to ensure universal intelligibility that an artificial literary Prākṛta was set up, and it is the artificial Prākṛta, which is generally met with, in the old Prākṛta works. These Prākṛta works do not give us the real vernaculars of the past time, and so we cannot directly trace the evolution of our modern vernaculars through the speeches preserved in those works.

It is perfectly certain that the language of the Aśoka inscriptions is not artificial; but one thing strikes us very much, that there are many words in these inscriptions, which are more Sanskritic in form than the words occurring in Buddhistic canonical works. I am strongly inclined to think, that some words in the inscriptions were made purposely Sanskritic to make the edicts thoroughly intelligible at places far away from Magadha. If we compare the Pāli language of Buddha's days, as preserved in the canonical works, with the contemporary classical Sanskrit of the Brāhmaṇa literature, we may notice, that the latter artificial language cannot be said to be only the literary form of the former; but the classical Sanskrit of the 3rd Century B. C., can be easily set down as the literary form of the language of the inscriptions. Mr. F. W. Thomas very rightly observes, in his paper published in the J. R. A. S. 1904 (p. 461), that "It is not too much to say that in modern English both spoken and written, we find greater deviations from the norm, than what may be observed between classical Sanskrit and the language of the edicts of Aśoka." The learned orientalist has further asserted, that if the text of the Pāli inscriptions of Aśoka's time and the literal translation of those texts in Sanskrit were placed side by side, one would find only such differences in pronunciation, etc., as always exist between the literary and spoken forms of the same dialect. I need not halt to explain this phenomenon, for I have already stated, how with the progress of time, Sanskrit was being modified by Prākṛta, and how Prākṛta was being influenced by Sanskrit.

How, stage by stage the Māgadhi language underwent successive changes for one thousand years after the time of Aśoka, cannot be very easily determined, for reasons already suggested; I may however add this observation, that it will be very unsafe to judge the Māgadhi language by the language of the inscriptions of later times, since it appears, that at one time it became a fashion, even in far off Southern India, to use the Māgadhi language in inscriptions. I am not concerned with the question of introduction of Māgadhi language into Peninsular India, nor have I to trace the influence of it on the languages of Western India. How the Māgadhi language was shaped in the province of Magadha itself, and how and in what form it got into Bengal, are questions which should be relevantly discussed. How the old Māgadhi Prākṛta or Pāli is related to what is called the Jaina Prākṛta, is a subject of very high importance for inquiry; it is also necessary to discuss the character of the speech which has been called Māgadhi by the Prākṛta

Grammarians ; but before I take up these questions for discussion, I proceed to examine if we can trace the blood of old Pāli itself (unstrained through the transformed Prākṛtas of subsequent times) in the veins of our Bengali language. It may be repeated here, what has been shown before, that the province of Magadha-cum-gauḍa always overflowed itself into Bengal, till the end of the 10th Century A.D.

I have noted in previous lectures, that in the matter of accent, there is much agreement between Pāli and Bengali. I doubt not this will be admitted to be a factor of much importance in a language. We should also remember in this connection, Mr. Pischell's weighty observation, that Vedic accent and stress survived in Pāli. The importance of the matter urges me to repeat one or two facts in this connection over again.

That because of the old time accent on the first syllables, the words অৎথি (অস্তি), প্পসন্ন, (প্রসন্ন), বক্‌খ (বক্ষ), etc., have been reduced to আছি (not অছি as in Oriya and Maithili), পের্‌সন্ন (not পর্‌সন্‌ of other provinces), বুক্‌ pronounced as বূক্‌ (not বুকু as in Oriya), etc., in Bengali, can be clearly seen ; that the pronunciation of ধম্মো, কম্মো, etc., of the old days has only been retained in Bengal, and that the forms ধরম্‌, করম্‌, etc., have only been recently borrowed in a class of artificial poetry, cannot be denied. However, I give below a list of words which have come to Bengali perhaps direct from Pāli, for they are not met with in the Prākṛtas of later days.

(1) অট্‌ঠি = আঁটি, stone of a fruit,—we do not get either আঁটি or any word derived from অস্থি in use in other dialects to indicate this meaning. (2) অথচ and অপিচ,—these words signify 'and' or 'still more' in Sanskrit ; the meaning 'nevertheless' as they signify in Pāli, is only found in Bengali in the use of অথচ. In Oriya, this word, with its

Pāli or Bengali meaning, has only very recently been borrowed. (3) অ-ফাসুক (seems to be *Desi* word and not an Apabhraṁśa) means indisposition or illness, Bengali অসুক বিসুক or simple অসুক does not seem to be derived from সুখ, happiness, for the idea of illness is not expressed with reference to the feeling of happiness; I think ফাসুক is the originator of the Bengali word. (4) ইতি—stands at the end of a speech, or section to denote " this is what it is "; this use of ইতি at the end of a composition, became once a mere form in Bengali, and subsequently from its position in a sentence, it acquired the meaning " the end "—in which sense, it is now in use. This ইতি does not occur in other dialects; in Oriya for example, the word indicating " finish " or " the end," as occurs at the end of an epistle is শুভ. (5) উন্হ ('hot,' উষ্ণ), উন্হন (the act of heating), [উম্ or rather ওম্ signifies warmth in Bengali] Bengali উনন্ (oven) comes from it though উদ্ধন is the word we get in Pāli for oven. (6) উপাহন (by metathysis from উপানহ্ shoe; the নহ ending again represents earlier নদ্ধ), the Oriya form is পন্হাই, which was in use in old Bengali. (7) ওর signifies 'this side,' but ওরপার signifies both the banks of a river and also the far-off bank of a river; only in old Bengali, we get this word in such a phrase as ওরনাই indicating কুলনাই, *i.e.*, the other bank—cannot be reached, *i.e.*, endless. (8) কুৎথ=old Bengali কুথ, modern কোথা where. (9) কবল (as in Sanskrit) a mouthful to be swallowed; only in Bengali, there is the Apabhraṁśa form of it in use which is খাবল. (10) কসট (from সকট=bad, vile, by metathysis) indicates a thing of bad or insipid taste; Bengali কসাটে, of insipid taste is from this word; the word কষায় of Sanskrit is of comparatively later date, and so it is a Sanskritization of a Pāli word; the readers should not confound this with Sanskrit কষ্ which exists in the word কষণ signifying unripe (distinguish this also from

কষ্, to touch or to injure); from কষ্, unripe, we get the Oriya word কসি, unripe, and this old form কসি unripe is in use in Bengali, in the shape of কচি. (11) গোণা (cows in plural)—in this form, the word travelled to Ceylon from old Bengal, our গরু is from গ-উ, where উ has been changed to রু. (12) ঘত or ঘ্রত (ghee). It is curious that following the traditional spelling, the rude villagers of Bengal still write ঘ্রত and not ঘৃত, when they make an attempt at dignified spelling. (13) চুল exactly signifying hair, as in Bengali; this word is found at one or two places in the Jataka stories, bearing evidently marks of lateness. (14) চঙ্গোট, a bamboo basket=Bengali চাঙ্গাড়ি and Oriya চাঙ্গোড়ি. (15) চাটি—a pot or a vessel, is found exactly in this sense in Oriya; that it was in use in old Bengali can be detected in the modern Bengali phrase চাটি বাটি as in চাটি বাটি তুলে চলে যাওয়া (to leave a place by carrying away all pots and pans). (16) ছবি—(a skin disease; the Oriya form ছোই signifying the same meaning is similar to Pāli, as the final ই is equivalent to the final vi (বি) of the Pāli word; the Bengali word derived from it is ছলি. (17) জাগু (rice gruel—originally barley-gruel জবাগু) equal to Bengali জাউ. (18) জহ excessive, is in use in Oriya and was in use in old Bengali; its real origin is from হা to leave, which gives rise to the form জহাতি—'something in excess that had to be thrown away' was the idea at the root. (19) দহ, a pool, is from দই, which is formed by metathysis from হ্রদ; we use the word দহ as in Pāli but the Oriya form is দই. (20) দুম from Sanskrit দ্রুম; in many parts of Bengal, little pieces of wood or say the internode portion of sugarcane is called ডু-ম or ডুমা. (21) নেলা (pure, innocent or inoffensive); Buddhaghosa gives the derivation of it in his commentary on the Dīgha Nikāya—'এলা' বুচ্চতি দোসো; ন অস্সা এলনৃতি নেলা; a goodnatured innocent man is always regarded as a fool or an insane, and so we get the word in our Bengali phrase নেলা কেপা to indicate a fellow without common sense and so also the word নেলা by itself conveys the same meaning in the Oriya speech of Sambalpur. (22) পাচন-ষট্‌ঠি Bengali পাচন-বাড়ি. (23) নিবেসন (from Sanskrit নি+বেশ্ম house) the vulgar people ask of the নিবেশ of a man to inquire where he hails from or where he lives, but wrongly considering the form to be incorrect, we have substituted নিবাস for it. (24) পলি-পথ a muddy road ; the first portion of the compound পলি indicating mud is in use in Bengali in the case of sediment thrown by streams of water. (25) পেক্‌খুণ, the feather of a peacock ; our word পেকম্ as in পেকম্ ধরা, blandishing the wings by a peacock, comes from the word. (26) মহল্লিক signifies old ; hence the word conveyed the meaning 'wise' in later times ; in Orissa, the state councillors were called 'mallikas' and one particular State, once governed by eight malliks, still bears the name আটমল্লিক ; this word as surname is in use in Bengal and Orissa. (27) লঞ্চ bribe ; the Oriya word লাঞ্চ still bears the same meaning, but I do not know if it was in use in Bengal ; my information, that it is in use in Purulia, has not been confirmed. (28) বণ্ট (from বৃন্ত), a peduncle = Bengali বোঁটা. (29) বিচিকিচ্ছা doubt or rather an impious doubt regarding the truths of religion ; hence what is bad or undesirable ; Bengali বিজিকিচ্ছি is equivalent to it in form and in secondary meaning. (30) সুশান (from শ্মশান) = Bengali শশান,—because of this derivation, no nasal sound is attached to the first 'শ.' (31) হরণী is the passage that is made in the river for a boat by removing the sand ; the passage was perhaps chalked out by dragging the boat itself ; in this meaning the word is used in the district of Sambalpur and that very use was current in old Bengali. (32) হেট্‌টা under, beneath ; Bengali হেঁট, as in মাথা হেঁট করা, comes from it.

We have to look very carefully into the deep significance of what has been illustrated above. Even though we fail to get definite literary evidence of successive changes which Pāli underwent on the soil of its birth in the course of a thousand years or more, we cannot but admit, that change did occur, and the older forms faded imperceptibly into new and newer forms. On reference to the Jaina Prākṛta and to the Prākṛtas either noticed in the Prākṛta Grammars or preserved in some works of poetry and drama, we may notice, that the old Pāli forms and Pāli pronunciation were very much changed in later times ; yet it is a fact that the method of Pāli pronunciation and many Pāli words and phrases, unknown to the later Prākṛtas (with which Bengali must have been directly c nnected), stick to Bengali. This shews very unmistakably, that a genuine genetic bond of affinity exist between Pāli and Bengali; the people who had originally Pāli for their language, could only retain the obsolete things as so many survivals, in course of successive transformation of their speech. We are at times led to form wrong notions regarding the origin of Bengali, by looking to the non-Prākṛtic or rather the Sanskritic form of many Bengali expressions ; we forget that for reasons stated more than once before, there has been purposeful sanskritization of Bengali as well as of other vernaculars from time to time. Owing to intermittent Sanskrit renaissance, a very large number of Bengali words are now so dressed up, that their real pedigree cannot be easily determined ; that our তৎসম words, চ্যুত, মধু, হৃদয়, etc., were once চুক, মহু, হিঅঅ, etc., may be easily seen,. on reference to some common expressions as ভুলচুক, মৌচাক, and হিয়া. I have stated before, that it is because of this sort of sanskritization, that the Prākṛtas are more in অপভ্রংশ form than the modern vernaculars. We should notice moreover that in the outlying tracts of Bengal, many words and grammatical forms of Pāli and of later Prākṛtas are still retained; in the district of Rungpur, for example, the word ইসি for ঋষি, দুতীয় for দ্বিতীয়, পধান for প্রধান, etc., and such a grammatical form as the formation of nominative by 'এ' are in full use. It is also noticeable that many archaic forms which were in use in Prākṛta, and are now in use in Rungpur, are in general agreement with the Oriya words; কোট্ঠে, where (Oriya কেঁউঠি, Marathi কোঠে), এট্ঠে, here (Oriya এইঠি), মাউসি (for মাসি), পিউসি (for পিসি), শাশু (for শাশুড়ি), চাঁদিয়া (bald headed), টেংনা (for টেংরা fish), are some examples.

In spite of the prevalence of Pāli words and Pāli forms in Bengali, some are doubtful if Bengali actually originated from Pāli and its later successors, as looking into the morphological structure of the above speeches, they find পালি, a highly inflexional language, and Bengali as mainly agglutinative, like the Dravidian speeches. We must now all learn that reversion from inflectional to agglutinating has been observed in many European and Indian languages. How by the mere process of phonetic decay, an inflectional or agglutinating speech may be reduced to what is called monosyllabic or isolating, has also been very scientifically demonstrated in the case of the Chinese language. The old theory of gradation from isolating to inflectional has been found utterly untenable. To account for the agglutinating character of our speech, we need not import a Dravidian influence, though in other matters such an influence upon the Bengali language cannot be denied, or rather has been fully admitted. We should bear in mind that all the modern Sanskritic speeches of the Gauḍian group are mainly agglutinating. Certainly, no one can possibly deny the potent factor of non-Aryan influence in the matter of the formation of provincial dialects, but it will be too much to assert that the contact with the savage races alone had, on the Aryans, the effect of breaking down their rigid inflectional system, and of causing the Aryans to substitute, for case-endings in nouns and verbs, distinct particles and auxiliaries.

Origin of a class of long-winded সমাস *compounds.*—Let us take account of one simple case which illustrates how a tendency to agglutinate words arose, and a class of long-winded samāsa compounds came into being in Sanskrit composition. It will be observed in the Prākṛta prose, that nouns or objectives in apposition in a sentence are not usually linked together by conjunctions. This style of composition was no doubt after the general style of ordinary conversation, in which not only the copulative but the disjunctive conjunction as well is at times dispensed with. Let me illustrate by example this conversation style, as still obtains in Bengal.

Q—বাজারে কি কি কিন্‌লে ?

A.—আম কিনেছি, কাঁঠাল কিনেছি, দুধ কিনেছি।

Q.—তোমরা সকলে ভাল আছ ?

A.—আমি ভাল আছি, বাবার শরীর মন্দ নয়, [here তবে—but—is seldom used] মার একটু অসুখ।

The authors who had the Prākṛtas of their time for their real speech, did not like to put in such a conjunctive conjunction as চ in their elegant Sanskrit composition, as that would not make the sentence sweet-sounding to their ears, trained to regard the Prākṛta method as sweet and agreeable; to compensate for the loss of চ, long samāsa chains were forged which in their natural sonorousness heightened the effect of the style.

Jaina Prākṛta.—I have stated that the links which bind Pāli with modern vernaculars are almost missing; the Prākṛta, which we meet with in the Jaina works, is in my opinion, a real link in the chain. I should not proceed seriously to controvert such a queer opinion that the

Jaina Prākṛta is Mahārāṣṭri; I shall show presently that not only the term Mahārāṣṭri, but other terms as well as have been used by the Prākṛta grammarians to classify the Prākṛta speeches, are misleading. This Jaina Prākṛta discloses many characteristics of a real speech, and it is almost doubtless that it was once a vernacular in the land of Mahābīr's birth, but when did this language flourish, has not been satisfactorily determined. The very fact that many forms occurring in this speech, cannot be explained by the rules formulated by Vararuchi, urges us to believe, that unlike the Prākṛtas of the grammarians and the dramatists, which were no real spoken vernaculars, but were essentially literary fictions founded on the vernaculars, the language in question, was once a living speech in some parts of the province of Behar. This speech is no doubt highly important; but it is regrettable, that in proportion to its importance, the material available at present is rather scanty. It must be mentioned however, that minds of scholars are not free from doubt, as to the thorough correctness of the Prākṛta texts of the Jaina canonical works, hitherto published. The Jaina scriptures, which have been critically edited, are only a few in number; it has been rightly observed by Dr. Barnett that this language "is a rich mine for the seekers of philological treasures." The learned author remarks, that as long as the whole of the Jaina scriptures have not been critically edited, many dark pages of the history of the ancient and modern Indian languages and literature will not be illumined. Dr. Barnett says that "neither the political nor the literary nor the religious history of India, can ever be written until an exact study has been made" of the Jaina scriptures composed in this Māgadhi Prākṛta. What has been opined with reference to the history of India in general, is specially and particularly true regarding the history of Bengal in all its aspects. We generally speak of the Buddhistic influence in Bengal, but it will be very soon recognized that the influence of the Jainas in this country, has been of far greater importance and consequence. This is not the subject which I can deal with here, but I doubt not that our Bengali scholars will direct their serious attention to this matter of great moment.

As far as it has been ascertained, even the oldest portion of the Jaina scriptures did not come into existence, in the form in which it is now obtained, earlier than the last half of the 5th century A.D.; consequently, to be on the safe side, we may hold that the language which the Jaina canonical works present, is the Eastern Māgadhi Prākṛta of a time, not later than the 6th century A.D. Be they Jaina inscriptions or not the Khaṇḍagiri Inscriptions of Khāravel give us the Māgadhi language of the second century B.C. But as this language differs only slightly from Canonical Pāli, and as it differs on the other hand, very greatly from the Jaina Prākṛta, this inscription language cannot be considered to be a link in the chain of evolution of this so-called Jaina Prākṛta. As the time of the Kuśana kings has not yet been satisfactorily established, it is difficult to assign dates to the Mathurā inscriptions of the Jainas, which have been preserved by being transcribed in Sir A. Cunningham's Archæological Survey Reports (*vide ibid*, Vols. III and XX). It is curious that the language of the Mathurā inscriptions does not much differ from the language of the second century B.C.; but as the texts of the Mathurā inscriptions contain only a small number of sentences, we should refrain from offering any remarks regarding the character of the language of the texts. This is however very clear and definite, that the language of the

Jaina canonical works differs very widely from the aforesaid inscription language either of the second century B.C. or of the second century A.D. Looking to all these circumstances, we are inclined to think that, the canonical works of the Jainas disclose the speech, which was current in some Eastern parts of Behar, some time between the third and the 6th century A.D. In the Mathurā inscriptions of Kuśana time, we get, for example, the same nominative case endings as we meet with in the Aśoka inscriptions and Khāravela inscriptions, but the nominative case ending in the canonical works under review is এ (e); Mahāvīra Bardhamāna is always Mahāvīre Bardhamāne. A critical consideration of this প্রাকৃত should be a subject for separate study. We may notice here only those points which are in agreement with Bengali. (1) We know that অ and য় have the same sound value in Bengali; even in Oriya 'য' is pronouced as ই-অ; in the Jaina Prākṛta, 'অ' which is the particle to signify 'and' (=ও of Bengali) and which appears exactly in the form of অ in the 'সেতুবন্ধ' and the 'গৌড়বহো' occurs indiscriminately as 'অ' or 'য়'; this shows the sound value of 'য' in the Māgadhi. In Bengali it is a peculiarity that when য is the initial letter, it is sounded as 'জ' and is uttered as 'অ' when it is a medial; we find, for instance in the Aṇuttarovavāiya Ḍasāo, that 'জ' is the initial of the word জালি (a name), while 'য' occurs as medial in spelling the name উপযালি. (2) The letter ঐ discloses the Bengali pronunciation, as ঐরাবত has been very often spelt as অইরাবত. It is no doubt true that in all Prākṛtas, ঐ occurs as অই but as ঐ is also at times met with, as for instance in the Khāravela inscriptions, as 'ঐল,' this point has been noted here. (3) The form for দ্বিতীয় is at times দুচ্চ and at times দুত্ত; in the pronunciation of some words in Eastern Bengal, as well as in Jessore, we detect the use of the early form of হুত্ত, for example the ceremony of consummation of marriage is called হুত্তু-ব্বিয়ে, the loss of one 'ত' of the final ত্ত of the word হুত্ত is indicated by the doubling of ব of ব্বিয়ে; as to হুচ্ছ, the Bengali form দোজ as in দোজবর may be noted. (4) It is exactly চোদ্দ (and not চউদ্দ) that occurs in this Prākṛta to denote fourteen; this form of pronunciation is wholly peculiar to Bengali. (5) I have just noted above that the nominative case ending is এ, it may be noticed, that in the provincialism of Rungpur, this case-ending is strictly maintained, and in the standard Bengali this case-denoting suffix has not been done away with. স became সো in Pāli and this সো occurs in the form of সে as is current in Bengali and Oriya. (6) The Vedic adverb কত্তি (how much) is not wholly extinct in this প্রাকৃত, but we get also the additional form কয়, which is just equivalent to কত and is in use in Bengali. (7) To denote 'which' or 'what' (though not 'who' as in Bengali), we meet with 'কে'; কি for কিম্ occurs with the adjunct অ as কিঅ. (8) I notice here one case-forming particle which is of much interest and importance. Not knowing the origin of our instrumental case-ending দিয়া, an imaginary দ্বারা was brought in by some Pandits as its originator. We get the particle 'দে' in this speech which is exactly equivalent to our obsolete 'দি' (still in use in Rungpur) and modern 'দিয়া.' This দে also occurs in the form of ডে; the passage which stands as জালি······বিমান পথডে (দে) উদ্ধম দূরম বিবস্থিত্বা বিজয়ে বিমানে দেবওয়ে উববন্নে, means that Jāli, after *passing through* the bimānapatha went to the higher world, etc. The pandits, who accuse the old Bengali poets for using the word 'বিমান,' deviating from its Sanskrit meaning, should take note of the Prākṛta use of it in this text. (9) The আছ ending of a verb, to signify past tense (or more properly present perfect) may be noted in such a form as 'কিচ্ছা' (did or has done); 'স'

as additional ending does not appear, but if this is added, the modern Bengali present perfect form is fully obtained; there is another form for the present perfect which takes 'ই' (as হোই) and not 'ছ' as the ending. 'কিচ্ছা' also became 'করিয়চ্ছা' later on and both 'করিয়চ্ছা' and 'হোই' stand as 'করিয়াছিল,' and 'হইল' in modern Bengali.

I just notice three words which clear up the history of those Bengali words which are regarded as, Deśī. (10) 'কল' as the word for peas has been mentioned along with the name of lentils 'মুগ' and 'মাস'; our modern word is 'মটর,' but we have not lost the word as the pod of it is still called কড়াইসুঁটি; in North Bengal, in East Bengal, as well as in Jessore, the name 'কলই' for peas is still in use. (11) 'করিল্ল' signifies the sprout or shoot of a plant; 'কোঁড়া' or 'কোঁড়ক' (as বাঁশের কোঁড়ক) is now in use; in the District of Sambalpur, the bamboo sprout, which is used as vegetable is called কর্ডি, or কড্ডি or কর্লি. (12) The origin of the word is unknown, but it is curious to note that the word 'কড়িপত্ত' signifies 'foot' in this Prākṛta, while 'কর-পত্ত' signifies the 'hand' or 'the palm of the hand'; I am inclined to think that 'কড়ে-আঙ্গুল' originally signified toe in Bengali, but now only a particular toe is meant by it; the Dravidian করিকল্ or bad foot shows that কল্ which is easily transformed into কড indicates foot. It is very interesting that not only in Jaina Prākṛta but in Jaina Sanskrit works also several Prākṛta words occur which in their old meaning and almost in their old form, are in use in Bengali only. For example (13):—কিল কিত দ্বার (in Jaina Sanskrit form) = খিড়কি দুআর (Jaina Prākṛta form) signifies exactly "Back door" as in Bengali, খিড়্কি দুআর. (14) উজ্ঝিকা (both in Jaina Sanskrit and Prākṛta) = House-maid and specially the kitchen maid who throws away the offal or other উজ্ঝিত matter; the first syllable উ and the otiose ক final, having been dropped, the word is in use in

Bengali only as ঝি to denote maid servant. This form should not be confounded with ঝি or ঝিউড়ি derived from ধি (দুহিতা = ধিতা = ধি = ঝি). (15) The Bengali word হের, to see (now in poetic use only; fully in use in Assam), occurs even in Jaina Sanskrit in the form হেরয়িত্বা, on seeing.

I think a short interesting article may be written on the peculiarity or rather the speciality of the names of men and women of Bengal. It is no doubt a speciality in Bengal that though the real portion of the name of a man does not require any additional word, such words, as চন্দ্র, নাথ, etc., are added to the names, but it is not on account of this alone, that the Bengali names indicate the nationality of the men bearing the names to the people of other provinces. 'নাথ' as an addition to the names of the Jain Tirthankars and চন্দ্র as a part of the old Māgadhi names, as well as the names themselves bear a sort of provincial peculiarity; and this may be illustrated in a separate paper as I have suggested. Though we cannot judge the nationality of men of old times by the form of their names alone, the peculiarity of Bengali names may be studied to see if men, having such names ভুস্কু, কাহ্নু, can be supposed to have flourished in Bengal. I note here a few old time Māgadhi names of women which are popular in Bengal; they are 'মুত্তা' (মুক্তা) পুট্টিমা (পুষ্টিমতি); সামা, সোনা, খেমা, and চাঁপা; the second name পুট্টিমা is current in Bengal alone in the shape of 'পুঁটি.' অভয়চন্দ্র, আদিনাথ, তারকনাথ, পরেশনাথ, (and not পারশ), etc., are some special male names of Bengal. We have got such a name ষষ্ঠী but such তিথি names for men and women as দুতিয়া (m), দশমী (f), একাদশিয়া (m) and ওঁয়াসী (fem.) are unknown in Bengal. Such names as বইজনাথ, বাজি (contraction of সত্যবাদী), বিষ্‌কেসন্‌, ধনুর্জ্জয়, চমরু, চক্রধর, হনুমন্ত, বিভীষণ, etc., are never met with in Bengal.

LECTURE XII

THE LITERARY PRĀKṚTAS

Mr. Stenkonow very rightly holds that the Prākṛta speeches, we meet with in the dramas of olden days, or in which the poetical works like the সেতুবন্ধ and the গৌড়বহো were composed, were not really spoken vernaculars, but were rather essentially literary fictions founded on the vernaculars. It was no doubt unavoidable in the very nature of things, that the authors of the class of literature, indicated above, had to use many words and grammatical forms, as were really current in the living vernaculars of their time, but it is difficult now to differentiate the real from the unreal elements, as occur in their works.

The Prākṛta grammarians of old did not think very much to preserve for us the provincial vernaculars of their time, but were concerned in the main, to frame some rules (with reference to some actual phenomena, no doubt) by which Sanskrit could be reduced to the Prākṛtas of their classification. These rules were useful alike to the authors and the readers, in dealing with not only the literary Prākṛtas, but also the অপভ্রংশ forms of partially artificial character. Again, the rules were needed not merely to standardise the provincial Prākṛta or অপভ্রংশ forms, by referring them to their Sanskrit originals, but also to serve a curiously queer purpose: the তৎসম words which were *in actual use in the vernaculars* and those which had to be used as loan words, to express new ideas, had to be reduced to *imaginary Prākṛta forms*, as in their queer sense of propriety, in the matter of diction, the authors could not allow the তৎসম words to be mixed up with the অপভ্রংশ words. Even to-day the use of our highly expressive দেশী and অপভ্রংশ words in the company of popular তৎসম words, are not countenanced by some Pandits, for in their opinion a 'শব-পোড়া' or 'মড়াদাহ' speech may be created thereby. Mr. Beams has rightly shown in his work on the comparative grammar of our vernaculars, that though of the word রাত্রি, for example, রাত্তির, রাতি and রাত have been the real অপভ্রংশ forms with the peoples of all provinces, the unreal form রাই occurs in the Prākṛta works. No doubt the Prākṛta literature abounds with genuine অপভ্রংশ forms, but it is difficult to determine now, when and where those forms came into use: for instance, as derived from আত্মন, first অত্তন and then অপ্পন appear to have come into use, but exactly when and where we do not know.

I take the following words from the Gauḍa Baho Kābya, edited by the late renowned scholar Sankar Pandurang Pandit, which will show what an anomaly the Prākṛta authors created by reducing different words into one and the same form. The words are—'ওআর' from অবতার, অপচার and অপকার; গঅ from গজ, গদ, and গত, কঅ from কৃত and কচ, মঅ from মৃত, মৃগ, মদ, মত and মগ্ন, বাঅ from বাত, বাদ, বাক and বাজ. We may also notice that though the word অতি (very much) has retained its pristine purity from the Vedic times to the present day, it has been reduced to অই (as in অইদীহ=অতিদীর্ঘ) in the কর্পূরমঞ্জরী.

I adduce here one example from the Setubandha, to show how by reducing different words artificially to one and the same form, a verse in যমক has been composed almost in the form of a riddle; the verse 47 of the 9th Canto stands as:

রম্মঅন্দরা অচ্ছঅং রম্মঅন্দরা অচ্ছঅম্।
সগ্‌গ গ্‌গহণি সামগ্‌গঅং সগগগ্‌গহণি সামগ্‌গঅম্॥

The Sanskrit form of the verse will be :

রম্য রাগচ্ছদং রম্যকন্দরাবৃক্ষকম্ ।
সর্গগ্রহনিঃ শ্যামাগ্রকং স্বর্গগ্রহণী সামগ্র্যম্ ॥

As many old Aryan words have been reduced to unreal forms in the প্রাকৃত, it will be interesting to notice the following words, more than 50 in number, as have not undergone any decay or অপভ্রংশ in Bengal from remotest antiquity till now ; the words here grouped together are such as are used and understood by even the uneducated people in rural areas in Bengal. Some of these words have no doubt changed their original meaning, but have not changed their form. The words marked with asterisks were not in use in the early Vedic time, but have been in use in Sanskrit, since a very remote time. The words are :

অতি, অলঙ্কার, অহংকার, আকাশ, আচার, আনন্দ, ইচ্ছা, উপর, কপাল, কাল, খুর,* গন্ধ, গুরু, গোল, ঘন, ঘাস, ঘোর, চিন্তা, চির (as in চিরদিন), ছাগ্‌ল,* জল,* জাল, তাল,* তিল, দণ্ড, দূর, দোষ, ধন, নল, নাম, পর, পণ্ড, পাপ, পার, ফল, ফাল, বুদ্ধি, ভাগ, ভার, ভাব, মন্দ, মাঘ, মানুস, মাস, মূল, মেঘ, রস, লোক, বন, বল, শীত, সার, সুখ, হার ।

It is difficult to say what linguistic value should be attached to the old time classification of the literary Prākṛtas. Looking to such names of the Prākṛtas as Māgadhi, Sauraseni and Mahārāṣṭri as occur in some works on poetics and dramaturgy, one is naturally inclined to hold, that there were good grounds for classifying the Prākṛtas by their respective provincial names, but these Prākṛtas now survive in such an artificial form that the elements of real, provincial speech in them elude our grasp. Moreover, the characteristic peculiarities of Mahārāṣṭri, for instance, as have been noted in the aforesaid works, are not what can be shown to bear genetic affinities with the modern vernaculars of the Mahārāṣṭra country.

If really the Mahārāṣṭri প্রাকৃত was based upon a living vernacular, we must say, that either the old ethnic element has disappeared from the Mahārāṣṭra country, or that by virtue of a serious revolution, a new ethnic element of dominating nature has come into the composition of the people of the country. I am aware that one or two scholars have tried to show on the strength of a few examples of word-forms, that the modern Mārāṭhi can be affiliated to the old Prākṛta of the same name. Referring to this unscientific procedure, I can simply say, that if the scholars under review, choose to collect an equally good number of words from the literary Māgadhi Prākṛta, they will find that they may equate them as well with some words of the modern Mārāṭhi speech. It will be interesting to the aforesaid scholars to note this anomaly, that many so-called Mārāṭhi and Sauraseni forms of old are conspicuous by their absence alike in Mārāṭhi and W. Hindi, and by their presence in Bengali and Oriya, which are directly connected with old Māgadhi (as has been demonstrated before) and are not at all connected either with Mahārāṣṭri or Sauraseni. Here are a few illustrative examples :

(1) অচ্চত্তুদ—অপভ্রংশ of this very so-called Sauraseni form became current in Bengal and Orissa; Oriya still retains the early form অচ্চাভুআ and in old Bengali we get it as আচাভুআ. (২) কওারেই (Mahārāṣṭri) = Carving stone, etc., into statues. This form unknown in the literary Māgadhi of the artificial classification, is in existence in Oriya; we get the অপভ্রংশ of it as কণ্ডেই to signify a doll. (3) The Mahārāṣṭri form কহম্ and not the Sauraseni form কধম্ as derived from কথম্ is traceable in Hindi and Oriya. (4) কোড্ড (Mahārāṣṭri) = strong desire; its অপভ্রংশ কোট্, signifying strong persistent desire, is in use in Bengali only. (5) খিড়ক্কি দুআর (Mahārāṣṭri) = back-door; খিড়্কির

হুআর, to signify the very meaning, is in use in Bengali only. On reference to Jaina Sanskrit, we get the form 'কিলকিত হুআর'; this shows that the literary Mārāṭhi of old classification must have borrowed the term from Māgadhi. (6) From তিষ্ঠতি comes the Sauraseni form চিট্ঠদি, and the Mahārāṣṭri form of it is ঠাই; ছিড়া of Oriya and দাঁড়া of Bengali are connected with the first form, while the second form is in use in Bengali, as an undeclinable adverb in such a phrase as দু ঘণ্টা ঠায়ে দাঁড়িয়ে আছে; note also that the form ঠিঅ from স্থিত is similar to ঠাই, and the current Oriya form is ঠিআ to indicate standing. (7) থোর (Mahārāṣṭri) from স্থূল = large; in use in old Oriya only as in থোর হস্ত, to signify the trunk of the elephant. (8) দেউ—as the Mahārāṣṭri form of দদাতু—is in Oriya and in old Bengali; the modern Bengali form is with an otiose ক as দেউক or দিক. (9) ধাড়ী or ধাটী (Mahārāṣṭri) = assault; in this meaning the word is met with in old Oriya only. (10) ফরক্কিদ (Mahārāṣṭri) = that which swings (স্ফারীকৃত); ফরি is in use in Oriya to signify the end of the পাগড়ী (head-dress), that swings about. The plume of a bird is still called ফড় or ফোড়্ in some parts of Eastern Bengal, but it is from the foreign word পর = plume. (11) মেল্ল্ (Mahārāṣṭri) = to loosen, to scatter; to loosen the rope of a boat, for example, is expressed in Oriya by নাও মেলি দেবা; to spread or to scatter for drying a thing is মেলে দেওয়া in Bengali; *cf.* also মেলানি of old Bengali and modern Oriya, which signifies parting or farewell; we may note the name of the ceremonial dinner given at parting which is called মেলানি ভাত in Bengal. (12) বাঅ, which is the Mahārāṣṭri form of বাত is often met with in the poetic literature of Bengal; *e.g.*, 'তুই আয় রে মলয় বাঅ' (বায়).

One or two grammatical forms of the standard literary Prākṛta may be noticed in this connection to further illustrate the case. (1) It is very well known that in the Prākṛtas, no distinction is made in the use of the কৃৎ suffixes ত্বা and য, and both the suffixes are found reduced to one simple form 'অ'; thus we get for example করিঅ andবিণিজ্জিঅ for কৃত্বা and বিণির্জিত্য respectively. It is in Bengali that we get the forms করিয়া, প্রকাশিয়া, etc., exactly corresponding to the standard প্রাকৃত forms, and these forms or rather this form cannot be met with either in Marathi or in Hindi. It may be noted that the contracted Bengali form করি or প্রকাশি for করিয়া or প্রকাশিয়া, is in use in Oriya. (2) The case-denoting suffix ই of the so-called Mahārāṣṭri Prākṛta, as occurs extensively in the Setu Bandha for example, is in use in Bengali in its later form এ; in our modern literary Bengali this' এ' is written as 'য়'; for example ইচ্ছাই = ইচ্ছয়া (because of the desire or by the desire) corresponds to old Bengali ইচ্ছা—এ or modern Bengali ইচ্ছায়; to express the sense conveyed by the form, either সে or মে has to be added to ইচ্ছা in Hindi which is supposed to be derived from Sauraseni; how the modern Marathi form differs from this form need not be mentioned. What these seeming anomalies mean or tend to prove, will be discussed presently. I may notice however, that Oriya, the origin of which must undoubtedly be traced to an old Māgadhi speech, had developed in it some forms akin to modern Marathi, centuries before Orissa came in contact with the Marathas : for example, the Oriya forms করিণ (by doing) and এহুঁ (from here) are closely allied to the Marathi forms করুণ and এথুন্ respectively.

As to the name মহারাষ্ট্রী for the standard প্রাকৃত, a word need be added. We do not exactly know when the noted work নাট্য শাস্ত্র which is fathered upon ভরতমুনি, was composed, or rather compiled; but we can confidently pronounce that the bulk of the book including the Chapter XVII came into being long before the time of the Prākṛta Prakāśa of Vararuchi. In Vararuchi's work,

Mahārāṣṭri is the প্রাকৃত par excellence, while Sauraseni occupies the second place. In the Nātya Śāstra of Bharata Muni however, the name Mahārāṣṭri for a Prākṛta is wholly unknown, and it is Sauraseni which has been accorded the rank of honour. Be the composition in prose or in poetry, the language of a drama should be শৌরসেনী according to the dictum of the Nātya Śāstra; the direction is 'শৌরসেনং সমাশ্রিত্য ভাষা কার্য্যা তু নাটকে.'

Even the country name মহারাষ্ট্র was unknown in the days of নাট্যশাস্ত্র, since in noticing a provincial linguistic peculiarity of the Mahārāṣṭra country, as well as of some tracts adjoining to that country, only a general geographical description occurs in the 60th verse which runs as :

স্থরাষ্ট্রাবন্তি দেশেষু বেত্রবত্যুত্তরেষু চ
যে দেশাস্তেষু কুর্বীত চকার বহুলামিহ।

If the statements and illustrations of the নাট্যশাস্ত্র be compared with those of later works on Dramaturgy, we can clearly see that the high class artificial প্রাকৃত which is closely allied to Sanskrit, has been called শৌরসেনী in the নাট্যশাস্ত্র and মহারাষ্ট্রী in the later works. It appears that the artificially got-up standard Prākṛta obtained the name শৌরসেনী in the নাট্যশাস্ত্র, as perhaps the seat of Northern culture was transferred in the days of the Nātya Sāstra, from Magadha to the country watered by the Jumna; it seems that for similar reasons, the standard Prākṛta, acquired the name Mahārāṣṭri, in the days of Vararuchi. It is highly probable, that the name of the standard Prākṛta indicates culture-centre, and does not signify any provincial language or dialect. That the standard প্রাকৃত was the Prākṛta, of no particular province, but was in reality a language fabricated by reducing Sanskrit to

Prākṛta forms, can be detected very easily, on referring to the poetic composition in the standard Prākṛta language. For example, the Prākṛta verses are found composed in such works as শকুন্তলা, রত্নাবলী, etc., in such an artistic manner, that if for the প্রাকৃত words their Sanskrit equivalents are substituted, the verses correctly maintain their meters.

The rules laid down in the first part of Chapter XVII of the Nātya Śāstra relating to the use of provincial peculiarities in the speeches of the actors of different rank and position, very distinctly mention that the standard Prākṛta of the drama has only to be nominally modified to suggest provincial peculiarities to the audience. The peculiarities or rather the points of deviation from the standard Sauraseni have been noted as follows: (1) The speech of all people of the Eastern Gangetic valley is to be made full of এ-sound:[1] গঙ্গা সাগর মধ্যে তু যে দেশাঃ সংপ্রকীর্ত্তিতা ; একার বহুলাং তেষু ভাষাং তজ্ঞঃ প্রযোজয়েৎ. (2) ন is said to be the characteristic peculiarity of all peoples of the tract extending through the Vindhyas to the sea-coast;[2] (3) 'উ' is said to be the peculiarity in North-West India,[3] and (4) 'চ' is noted to be the characteristic of the speech of the peoples of Surāṣṭra and its neighbourhood as has been mentioned above.[4] Regarding the aboriginal

---

[1] This is perhaps on reference to the nominative-denoting এ.

[2] The tract seems to be of the Hinduized Dravidians using ম or ন at the end of nouns; the বিভাষা speaking tribes including Oḍras, were certainly excluded.

[3] In later times the apabhraṁśa-speaking Ābhīras are given this characteristic; but the Ābhīras are বিভাষা speaking here. উ is rather the Maithili characteristic in later প্রাকৃত. To reduce some vowels to উ sound in names as in কালু, নরু, বীরু, হরু, etc., has been usual in Bengal, since long.

[4] In modern Marathi, genitive-indicating suffix is চ; but this could not possibly have been the characteristic here referred to.

tribes (Barbaras), it has been said that they have not to speak their own speeches but that a few শবর peculiarities have to be introduced by them. It is highly interesting to note by the way, that in the list of non-aryan peoples or hordes, we get the আভীরs in the company of ওড্রs, শবরs, চণ্ডালs and so forth ; these আভীরs have been mentioned by Hem Chandra of the 12th century as wh lly অপভ্রংশ-speaking people.

The directions in the works on Dramaturgy that the domestic servants and artisans should speak the Māgadhi speeeh, may be interpreted perhaps by the fact, that from the 6th century onward, the people of various industrial occupations flowed from Magadha into other parts of the country. It will not be correct to hold, with reference to the statements in the works which are later in date than the Nātya Sāstra, that actual Māgadhi speech had to be spoken by dramatic characters representing the industrial or labouring classes. That the dramas had not really to be made polyglot in character, but only some suggestions had to be offered to the audience regarding the various provincialities of the *Dramatis Personae* can be clearly gathered from the rules occurring in the নাট্যশাস্ত্র; however to make the matter convincing an analogous phenomenon which occurs in our widely popular and very familiar Jātrā-Gān, may be noticed here. In this Jātrā-Gān, a person enacting the part of a door-keeper or a porter speaks Bengali slightly incorrectly, in the manner in which the Behāris at times speak Bengali, merely for this reason that the Behāris usually come to Bengal to do the work indicated above; the clown usually imitates Eastern Bengal provincialism by only substituting হ for শ all throughout. Here the door-keeper does not speak Behāri, and the clown does not care to imitate correctly the provincialism of our Eastern districts; the actors, by their linguistic suggestions only work up the imagination of the audience regarding the special situation in the plot. That this is exactly what took place in ancient times in the matter of representation of provincial speeches on the stage, can be very clearly inferred not only from the rules given in the works on dramaturgy but also by the analysis of the language of the plays.

It may very reasonably be urged that the early time Prākṛta works which contain many দেশী words and no portion of the text of which can be easily rendered into Sanskrit, by only substituting corresponding Sanskrit words for the Prākṛta words, should be considered to represent some ancient living vernaculars. গাথাসপ্তশতী which is regarded by some as the earliest known Prākṛta work, is the only book I know, which answers to some extent the description given above, but questions relating to its time, authorship and place of origin, are not free from difficulties. From the reference to it by বাণভট্ট, it appears that the book once bore the title জাতিকোষ and according to general tradition, it was composed under the auspices of some Andhra rulers at Paiṭhān or প্রতিষ্ঠাণপুর. The present book does not appear to be that old work, for in the first place, it is an anthology containing the poems composed by various poets, as admitted in the colophon portions of the work at the end of each section ; in the second place the verses occurring even in one and the same section are very loosely connected together without there being any unity of thought or purpose ; in the third place, many verses bear evident marks of lateness, all of which cannot be fully discussed here. I note here however, one point which will show that this book of anthology cannot be said to have been composed in the 2nd century A.D. We know that রাধা as the principal heroine among the গোপীs, around whom all other গোপীs are but satellites, does not appear in any secular literature or পুরাণ, which is of a date earlier than the 8th century or at best the 7th century A. D., but this রাধা is met with in the 89th verse of the first section of this book; moreover the relationship that রাধা is a 'মামি,' of her lover, is also found in the 93rd verse. It must be admitted however in respect of many words used in this book, that they are not artificial reductions of Sanskrit words; a few of these words are noted here: (1) রেহই (akin to vernacular রহ) = রাজতে, (2) লডহ (read in one manuscript as পডহ akin to পোড়া of Bengali and Oriya) = বিদগ্ধ, (3) ছিত্ত (to touch as well as *to sprinkle*; in the first sense it is equal to ছিব্ব = স্পৃষ্ট, but in the second sense it is akin to ছিটা of Bengali), (4) পাব = প্রাপ্নুহি (the final ব (v) being pronounced as 'ও' as usual it becomes wholly akin to vernacular পাও of the Imp. Mood), (5) বুড্ড (বুড়া or বোড়া and its variant ডুবা or ডোবা current in many vernaculars) = মজ্জ, (6) থো-অ (or থোক) = স্তোক (compare our adverb থোকে in such a phrase সবগুলি জিনিস থোকে কিনিলাম).

As it is uncertain when and where all the poems of the book were composed, nothing definitely can be said of the language of it. I must notice, that at the time of the collection of the manuscripts one copy of this গাথাশপ্তশতী with a Bengali commentary was obtained at শান্তিপুর in the নদীয়া District; how old that manuscript was, is not on record.

As it appears that the authors of the প্রাকৃত books used the অপভ্রংশ forms of various provinces in one and the same work, in order to make their composition universally intelligible, we fail to localize the literary প্রাকৃতs; under the circumstances, we can refer to all the প্রাকৃত works to trace the history of our অপভ্রংশ forms, no matter in which vernacular those অপভ্রংশ words now occur. I shall have occasion presently to adduce some undeniable evidence of the fact that the authors of many প্রাকৃত works used indiscriminately the অপভ্রংশ forms of various provinces in the same composition.

We see that the class of literary Prākṛta, we have reviewed in this lecture, does not give us such definite material, as may enable us to determine the character of the Māgadhi speech with which we are mainly concerned in tracing the history of the Bengali language. We may note however, that in enumerating various styles (রীতি) of composition রাজশেখর substitutes the term মাগধী for the usual term Gauḍi in the introductory portion of his কর্পূরমঞ্জরী; this indicates, what has been asserted previously. that Bengal did not get the name Gauḍa before the 10th century. How the early Māgadhi speech Pali, and the Jaina Prākṛta are related to Bengali, has been discussed in the previous lecture; that these old Prākṛtas in their later transformation, have not been properly represented in the dramatic literature of old, need not be any further discussed. We may now take up for consideration some Prākṛta effusions of a comparatively recent date, which now survive only in fragments, and are found embodied in the Prākṛta Paingala. This work on the Prākṛta metrical system has been very ably edited by Dr. Chandramohan Ghose, B.A., M.B., and I take all my examples from that edition of the work. The learned editor has very rightly held that this work did not come into its present form earlier than the latter half of the 14th century A.D., and that it cannot be later than the early decades of the 16th century. I need hardly point out that all the Aryan Vernaculars of India which are literary languages to-day, became well-developed literary languages, previous to the 14th century. Many effusions appearing as illustrations in the Prākṛta Paingala, which can be easily detected on account of historical allusions, to have been composed in the 12th or in the 13th century, must be admitted to have been artificially composed in Prākṛta, at a time when full-fledged vernaculars, could be made by the authors their vehicles of thought. That even Oriya acquired its distinctive characteristics in the 12th century A.D., by being fully differentiated from Bengali and Bihari, can be proved by the text of the Rock inscription which has been preserved in the Khameśwari temple at Sonepur ; a portion of this inscription runs as : যে হরই তাহার মুণ্ডরে ব্রহ্মতাল রুদ্র তাল পড়ই.

As the literary fragments which will be quoted presently very liberally, came into existence when the maintenance of artificial long and short sounds of vowels became very difficult with the authors on account of their settled pronunciation and the prevalence of provincial pronunciation in the vernacular composition, many metrical irregularities may be noticed in them ; the author of the Prākṛta Paingala has been forced to formulate a rule as to where the long vowel is to be treated short. The rule reads : জই (যদি) দীহো (দীর্ঘ) বিঅ (অপি or ও) বণ্ণ (বর্ণ) লহু (লঘু) জীহা (জিহ্বা) পটই (পড়িতে হয়), হোই (হয়) সোবি (সেও) লহু। বণ্ণ বি তুরিঅ (ত্বরিত) পটিও (পঠিত), দো তিনি বি এক জাণেহু।
The rule purports to indicate, that if a varṇa is দীর্ঘ or long in form, but it is usual to read it লঘু or short, it is to be read as লঘু; again, if the usage of the language requires it, two or three letters should be read together in quick succession to form one syllable, for a word of two or three letters may be required to be treated as one syllable. The verse illustrative of the rule is :

অরেরে, বাহহি কাহ্ন! নাব ছোটি ; ডগমগ কুগতি ন দেহি।
তই ইংথি নই-হি সন্তার দেই, জো চাহহি সো লেহি।

The directions in respect of the verse are that the first রে of অরেরে, and বা of বাহহি are to be treated short, while হি of বাহহি is to be read (no doubt on account of emphasis) long ; again, ডগমগ is to be read as ডগ্‌মগ্‌, and though the first two syllables of সন্তার are long, only the first syllable স has to be read long ; then it is stated that জো of the 4th line is to be read হ্রস্ব for the evident reason that a stress or emphasis on চাহহি renders the initial syllable short in the metre. That the irregularities have been due to the usual vernacular pronunciation of the words, can be well illustrated by the example of a Bengali তোটক, in which only unawares, the Bengali author has made the last two syllables of সাঁতারে (*i.e.*, তা and রে) short ; the lines are :

কত কাল পরে, বল ভারতরে
দুখ সাগর সাঁতারে পার হবে।

In respect of the language of the above-quoted প্রাকৃত verse, a few remarks may be offered. The metre is no doubt Hindi ; but there are many forms which are foreign to Western Hindi, and which prevailed only in a comparatively recent time in Eastern Māgadhi, which is undeniably very closely allied to Bengali. তুই for thou is Eastern Māgadhi ; this very form was in use in old Bengali and it is now current in Assamese. The Māgadhi form ইৎথি became a special property of Bengali amid the speeches of the Eastern Gauḍi group ; the ablative case-denoting suffix থি as occurs here, has transformed itself in modern Bengali into 'থে' which appears as 'থেকে' with an otiose ক. The form দেই is wholly equivalent to our old Bengali form, and this very form is still current in Oriya ; the modern Bengali form দিয়া only slightly varies from it. The locative denoting হি as in নই-হি is also peculiar to Eastern Māgadhi. We can therefore very easily say that the language of the verse represents the Māgadhi speech which was current at a time not far removed from the date of birth of the Eastern modern vernaculars.

I proceed now to give some examples to show that the authors of several verses wrote in Prākṛta, at a time when modern vernaculars became respectable literary languages.

I shall quote generally those verses which have been composed in that Māgadhi which is very much allied to Bengali, or which may be reasonably supposed to be proto-Bengali. I use this word of caution here, that some examples will disclose the fact that some authors in collecting obsolete প্রাকৃত words could not discriminate between different provincial forms, and as such mixed up the forms of different languages in one and the same poem. The first example given below is of a poem which was composed to describe the expedition of হমীর of admittedly recent time.

ঘর লগ্‌গই অগ্‌গি, জলই ধহ ধহ;
দিগ-মগ ণহ-পহ অণল ভরে।
সব দিস পসরি, পাইক লুলই ধনি,
থণ হর জঘণ দিআব করে।
ভঅ লুক্কিঅ থক্কিঅ বইরি তরুণি জন
ভইরব ভেরিঅ শদ্দ পলে।
মহি লোট্টই পিট্টই, রিউসির টুট্টই,
জক্খণ বীর হমীর চলে। *

It should first be noted that this metre of প্রাকৃত which was taken up by the author is more allied to Bengali metre than to any other. The dropping of the locative sign

---

* A few remarks as to the correct reading are needed

L. 1. লগ্গিঅ of MS. B for লগ্‌গই seems better.

L. 2. কই as the initial word in the published text requires that for the sake of metre two syllables of the text should be deleted; in the second place proper construction with কই requires a negative particle in the line to signify—nothing could be visible anywhere because of the conflagration; as such, either the reading of MS. F is to be partly accepted or কই has to be omitted; I omit কই to avoid all complications.

L. 3 The reading দিস of MS. A is adopted.

L. 4. জঘণ of MS. B, C & E substituted for জহণ; ফুহাব of MS. F to signify 'to hanker for' is evidently a better reading.

এ in ঘর (=ঘরে), দিগ-মগ (=দিক্-মার্গে), ণহ-পহ (=নভ-পথে), etc., is due to the metre in which long sound with এ cannot be tolerated. ভরে (ভরিল or ভরিয়াছিল), করে (করিয়াছিল), পলে (পলাইয়াছিল), and চলে (চলিয়াছিল) are interesting past forms ; the older past forms আসী, করী, ধরী, etc., should be compared with these forms, and it is to be noted, that in t ie 3rd person 'এ' came into use for 'ঈ.' It is significant that the past form here illustrated, is in use in modern Bengali, as we may note the use in such a sentence as সে আমাকে আগে মারে, তাই আমি মারি ; again, when negative sense is indicated, this past form is specially idiomatic in Bengali, for example, সে করে নাই, আমি মারি নাই are more idiomatic than সে করিয়াছিল না, or আমি মারিয়াছিলাম না, as at times noticed in Eastern Bengal speech. It is highly interesting that the commentators of the verse, have failed to understand the meaning of the word ধনি which means woman in the text; that the soldiers were seeking for women is clear from what subsequent lines distinctly indicate ; Hem Chandra gives the right meaning of the word in his দেশী নামমালা, but the word is in use in B-ngal alone. ভঅলুক্কিঅ থক্কিঅ is equivalent to Bengali ভয়ে লুকাইয়া থাকিয়া which is exactly the meaning of the phrase. The women, it has been stated, did flee afterwards from their hiding places on hearing the fearful sound of ভেরী ; so we see that ভেরিঅ is in the possessive case. Thus it is doubtless that the language of the text is not only Eastern Māgadhi, but is proto-Bengali.

The following verse shows that the Oriya form কাইঁ has been used in the midst of that Māgadhi language which did not develop the special provincial Oriya form on the soil of Magadha. It is also noticeable, that the term ছইল or ছইলি, which means coquette and is in use in Oriya now, occurs in the verse; the word স্বৈরিণী was, we know, reduced to ছৈরিণী or ছৈনিনী on one side, and to ছৈনিলি or ছিনারি on the other; the form ছিনার which occurs in Hem Chandra's দেশী নামমালা under a misconception, has been the form in Hindi, as well as in Bengali. I have to add, that the metre of the following verse was never adopted in Oriya, and the term ধনি for a woman has been the special property of Bengal.

রে ধনি, মত্ত মতংগঅ গামিনি,
খঞ্জন লোঅণি চন্দমুহি,
চঞ্চল জোব্বন জাত ন জানহি ?
ছইল, সমপ্পহি কাইঁ নহি ?

The next verse I quote, contains grammatical forms which were undoubtedly formed on the soil of Bengal, when Bengali was wholly differentiated alike from Māgadhi and Oriya.

নব মঞ্জরি সজ্জিঅ চূঅহগাছেং;
পরিফুল্লিঅ কেসুলঅ বন আছে ;
জই এৎথি দিগন্তর জাইহি কন্তা,
কিঅ মম্মহ নৎথি কিনৎথি বসন্তা ?

The reading লিজ্জিঅ for সজ্জিঅ (সজ্জিত) does not alter the speech, for we get the form লিজ্জ in such an old Bengali শুভঙ্করী formula as কাঠায় কুড়্বা কাঠা লিজ্জে. চূঅহ (চ্যূতের for আমের) seems unnecessary prākṛtization, since it is আম and not চ্যূত which has ever been in use in all the Northern Indian Vernaculars. It is true, that for emphatic expression of possessive, 'হ' was generally used in Prākṛta for the possessive-denoting অ, which being boneless had subsequently to be reduced to 'র.' The forms গাছে and আছে are purely Bengali; from গচ্ছ we got গাছ because of our accent on the first syllable, while on account of the accent on the last syllable গ-ছ and গছ came into use in Oriya and Maithili respectively; for similar reasons it is not অছি

but আছে (in the 3rd person) which has been the Bengali form derived from অৎথি. We notice again, that it is not জব্ but জই (যদি) which is the form here, as met with in Bengali, Oriya and Assamese. That এৎথি is proto-Bengali, has already been remarked. The আ final of কান্ত and বসন্ত is peculiar to many nominative (as well as objective) formations in old Bengali. The হি suffix in the subjunctive mood, indicating futurity, is a speciality in the later মাগধী প্রাকৃত.

That the following verse was composed in Bengal has partly been admitted by a commentator :

ওগ্গর ভত্তা রম্ভঅ পত্তা,
গাইক ঘিত্তা দুধ্ধ সজুত্তা,
মইলী মচ্ছা নালিচ গচ্ছা,
দিজ্জই কন্তা খা পুন বন্তা।

It is significant that the non-Bengali commentators have failed to explain ওগ্গর ভত্তা; ওগ্রা ভাত is a familiar thing with us in Bengal and it must be therefore provincial in formation. We notice that to denote possessive case there is the old অ in রম্ভঅ as well as the later ক in গাইক ; possessive with ক-ending is in use in Hindi now. মইলী fish is মৌরলা which is a delicacy in Bengal, and নালিতা which signifies the leaves of jute plant may be found still in use in Bengal.

The poem I next quote reminds us of Jayadeva ; there are many lines in some other poems occurring in the প্রাকৃত পৈঙ্গল which are almost word for word equivalent to some lines of Jayadeva's গীতগোবিন্দ : for example, মুনিজন মানস হংস is met with in the প্রাকৃত পৈঙ্গল.

জিনি কংস বিনাসিঅ কিত্তি পআসিঅ
মুট্ঠি-অরিট্ঠি বিনাশ্ করে
গিরি হৎথ ধরে ;

জমলজ্জুন ভঞ্জিঅ পঅভর গঞ্জিঅ
কালিঅ কুল সংহার করে,
জস ভুঅন ভরে ;
চাণূর বিহণ্ডিঅ নিপকুল মণ্ডিঅ
রাহামুহ মহু পান করে,
জিমি ভমর বরে ;
সো তুম্হ নরাঅণ বিপ্প পরাঅণ,
চিত্তহ চিন্তিঅ দেউ বরা,
ভব-ভীই হরা ।

'জিনি' (who—honorific) is wholly and purely Bengali. Some foreign commentators unfamiliar with Bengali have read it জিন as a variant of Sanskrit যেন and have made বিনাসিঅ (বিনাসিয়া), পআসিঅ (প্রকাশিয়া), etc., বিনাসিত, প্রকাশিত, etc.; no doubt 'অ' stands equally for ত, for য় (of modern vernaculars), and for the প্রত্যয় 'ত্বা' or 'য়,' but the construction 'যেন বিনাশিত' etc., fails, because the passive voice cannot be thought of in the sentence ending with the finite verb করে; again, it will be noticed that 'জিনি' is related to 'সো' which occurs in the beginning of the 7th line. I must remark by the way, that old Bengali did not inherit জেন or জিন (by whom) as is supposed by some; in দোহাকোষ edited by the renowned scholar Haraprasad Sastry, very wrongly a 'ন' has been added to তশে (in thirst) to indicate instrumentality (দোহাকোষ, p. 115); the ন in question has been wrongly taken over to the end of তশে, while really it is the initial letter of the next following word, which has been reduced to ভজ্জল signifying rain water; that the meaning of the decapitated word is rain water, has been admitted by the commentator, but he has not seen that it is নভজ্জল which yields the proper meaning. Why the form সো occurs for সে, in the poem above quoted has been stated before in a general remark. In জিমি ভমর বরে (যেমন ভ্রমর

বর়) the case-denoting suffix এ of the Eastern Māgadhi Prākṛta, has to be noted. That the form দেউ is in use in Oriya, and was in use in Bengali, and that it does not differ from দেউক and later দিউক, need not be discussed. The অ ending of চিন্তিঅ is certainly equivalent to 'ত.'

I dare say we have got enough material to examine the various forms of মাগধী speech which transformed itself into Bengali. We do not exactly know, when the effusions quoted above adorned the Prākṛta literature, but we can see very clearly, by comparing the language of the poems with our modern language, that the forms which occur in the poems are genuine predecessors of our modern forms. I do not mean to say that the passages, I have quoted from the Prākṛta Paingala, should alone be referred to in tracing the history of our modern forms, and that the other literary Prākṛtas dealt with in this lecture, should be left altogether out of view because of their artificial character. I have no doubt tried to show, that the old classification of the literary প্রাকৃতs by some names indicating provincial origin of the speeches, is highly misleading, but it must be remembered that inspite of their provincial names, the artificially got up প্রাকৃতs contain forms and idioms of the dialects of the provinces, which their names do not indicate; as such we must look into the treasures of all the literary প্রাকৃতs, to get the মাগধী elements of our quest.

We have noticed this significant peculiarity in our investigation, that from the remotest time our literary languages have been different from the real living speeches of the people. The standard literary speech is bound to differ from the vulgar speech in every country, but the sort of gap which we notice in India, between the literary and the popular, is of such width and character, as is generally unknown in Europe. I cannot take up to discuss those social and other conditions of India, by virtue of which the people of this country were never stirred up to do those adventurous deeds, which all nations of Europe have always been forced to undertake. For various reasons, the Indian peoples of all social conditions, did never combine together to attain an object of common aspiration; the high class literary men of ample leisure and decent competence have always created a literature in India, which the common people settled in industrious or agricultural life, could never take any interest in. There was never such a thing as mass education, for hardly the common people felt any necessity to make themselves literate. I cannot discuss this subject of great historical moment in these lectures, but this special peculiarity of Indian civilisation should always be remembered, to account for the character and qualities of our literature.

It concerns more the history of literature than the history of language, to deal with the questions why the literary men of old, took at all to writing in the Prākṛtas, when they were conversant with Sanskrit, and how for erotic composition the authors were principally drawn to the Prākṛtas; but in tracing the history of a language, we cannot afford to forget facts as they stand, and must take due note of them. We should also bear in mind, that the special Indian tendency, I have spoken of, in giving the peculiar character to literary speeches, is still our heritage; if we overlook this fact, we are sure to fail to estimate properly the value of our modern literary idioms and syntactical structure.

LECTURE XIII

Some Hints on the Right Method of Investigation.

In this lecture I propose to survey briefly the whole field traversed up to now, to offer some suggestions or practical hints as to what should be the right method of investigation. To get together the broken parts, scattered all about, and then to put them in order, to effect a reconstruction, is a hard work. It becomes harder still when some broken parts survive in fragments only, and when again, some fragments elude recognition in having been polished off and fitted into a new structure. Hard though the task has been, I have tried with my best effort to collect, examine, and classify such facts relating to the history of our vernacular, as I could lay my hands upon. I am perfectly aware that the facts I have collected and classified, cannot all be interrelated with equal success, though in the main they all point to the conclusion I have arrived at, or rather I have suggested. As facts, their value cannot be overrated, but I have to admit that they are a bit shadowy here and a little definite there, amorphous here and partly crystallized there, in broken fragments here and in their entirety there. However, I hope they will readily render themselves useful in the constructive hands of the trained scholars.

I have sketched out, though in shadowy outlines, the course of the stream of our language that stretches forth itself from the Vedic source-head to the Gauḍa-Magadha valley, by receiving numerous affluents at several points from various directions. That the main current of this very stream inundates Bengal, has only been partly demonstrated in the previous lectures; for the full demonstration of it, the next lecture which will be the last, has been reserved. By keeping up the metaphor, I may say that the limpid stream of this river running parallel to the artificial channel of Classical Sanskrit, from a dim past to the second century B. C., is distinctly noticeable. If the Jaina inscriptions unearthed at Muttra, be of the second century A. D., we may unhesitatingly say that the Māgadhi speech of the second century B. C. did not undergo a very severe change in its course of progress for full three centuries, but the chronology of the Kushana time remains still unsettled. From this time forth to the end of the 5th century A. D., we can get no definite trace of this stream. During the 6th and the 7th centuries we find the Māgadhi speech in the Jaina scriptures considerably altered and modified; we learn from the records of Huen Tsiang that at this time the speech of Magadha prevailed over all the different provinces of Bengal, namely, over Rāḍha or Karṇa Suvarṇa, over Kie-chu-ho-khilo or Berhampur cum Nadīyā, over Northern Bengal, consisting of Puṇḍrabardhan and Barinda, and over Samataṭa, consisting of a portion of 24 Parganās, of Jessore and of a considerable portion of Eastern Bengal. How this speech was subsequently modified both in Behar and Bengal till the displacement of the Pāla rule in Behar by the western invaders, can only be guessed from some literary fragments which have been noticed in the previous lecture.

I have stated in a previous lecture that when the rulers of Western and Central India conquered Magadha-cum-Gauḍa of old, the civilization of Magadha found a safe shelter in the extensive country of Bengal, while the people who were left in Behar or Gauḍa-Magadha country, had to adopt in due course of time, not only many forms of newly imported speeches, but also the food and the dress of the powerful new-comers. The people who took kindly to the habits of life which the Buddhist householders had brought into vogue, did not care either for a head-dress or for a garment which was not wholly white. The Dravidians, among whom these people came to live, had not then or have not now any head-gear, but were fond however of coloured pieces of cloth for their garment. The flowing white dress of the Bengali male people is now coming into fashion in other provinces also, but the Bengalis and Oriyas are only found to use no head-dress at all. I mention these facts with the object of showing, how deep and abiding, how intense and extensive, has been the influence of Magadha culture in Bengal. We may, I daresay, be fully justified to assert, what has been asserted before, that we in Bengal represent to-day the old Behar, more than the modern Beharis do in Behar. Our language is essentially Māgadhi; and trace it as far back as we may, it cannot be found to have been originated from the Classical Sanskrit language, to which we only owe a debt of many loan words only, to express high thoughts in the Vernacular.

The Behari speeches of to-day contain elements foreign to the old Māgadhi; we have to be consequently very careful in taking up Behari forms in elucidating the history of our Bengali forms. What light the speeches of Assam and Orissa may throw on the history of our Bengali forms, should also be duly gauged to avoid much misconception. I cannot halt to discuss fully the history relating to the origin of Assamese and of Oriya, but a few words relating to the topic need be added.

The very geographical situation of Assam clearly shows, that Aryan culture could not possibly reach that country, without passing through Magadha and

Northern Bengal. Huen Tsiang records in the 7th century A. D., that the then short-statured people of Assam, who had no faith in Buddha and who were worshippers of Devas, spoke a dialect which was a little different from Māgadhi. The difference that existed in those days between the speeches of Bengal and Assam, was no doubt due to what the Chinese traveller has suggested in a short sentence: in the first place, the then short-statured people of Assam differed ethnically from the people of Bengal, and in the second place, because of non-adherence to the Buddhistic faith on the part of the people of Assam, the culture of Magadha could not flow freely into that country. That in later times religious differences disappeared, and for some time during the rule of the so-called Pāla Rajas, Assam came directly under the influence of Bengal, are too well known to be repeated here. We may notice, that in many particulars Assamese agrees with the provincial dialect of Rangpur, which retains nothing but the old Bengali forms; we shall also see from examples which will be adduced in the next lecture, that many grammatical forms of old Bengal which were once abbreviated on the soil of Bengal itself, are current in Assamese. Another fact need be pointed out. We shall presently see that the main stream of Oriya language flowed into Orissa, through Bengal. It is a striking phenomenon that there are some linguistic peculiarities, wherein Oriya agrees with Assamese, and differs from Bengali. This phenomenon can only be explained by this, that Bengal as a progressive country has altered the early forms, while the archaic forms have been retained in Orissa and Assam. We can safely hold, that the Māgadhi language, as was once fashioned and modified on the soil of Bengal, got into Assam to take a fresh root there to develop into a new language under the influence of a language altogether foreign to the Aryan speech. That the script of modern Bengal, which can be proved to have taken its modern shape and form on the soil of Bengal at a comparatively recent time, is current in Assam, should not also be forgotten. There are instances, how many scholars by forgetting this fact have pronounced very wrongly the language of some old books to be Assamese, on the ground that the language discloses many forms which are now current in Assamese.

How after the complete disintegration of the old Kaliṅga Empire, a province bearing the name Orissa was constituted, and how a new Aryan speech, now called Oriya, came into being, cannot be detailed here. It will suffice to say, that when Huen Tsiang visited the land in the 7th century A.D., the people of Kaliṅga with their Dravidian speech were found confined within the confines of the Andhra country, and Orissa was struggling into a new life, with new ethnic elements and a new speech; the Utkala people, in the north were not aryanized at that time, and the people in the District of Puri (Kongada) were only learning Northern Indian speech and script under the influence of the successors of Raja Narendra Gupta of Karṇa Suvarṇa in Bengal. We learn also from some old works on Dramaturgy that the Oḍras and their congeners the Śabaras, used only some Aryan words in their non-Aryan speeches in the 6th century A.D., and their speeches were then called বিভাষা on that account. How because of the supremacy of the Kośala Guptas for about three centuries, a Māgadhi speech took deep root in Orissa, has been narrated briefly in the 4th lecture. The Northern boundary-line of Orissa runs from the North-East corner of the District of Balasore to the North-West corner of the Feudatory State of Gangpur, along the Southern limits of Bengali-speaking and Hindi-speaking tracts; how therefore two different varieties of the Māgadhi speech could come together to form the Oriya speech, may be easily imagined. We should be very careful therefore in referring to the archaic forms of Oriya, to trace the history of our words. The reason why Oriya abounds with archaic forms, may be stated in the words of Mr. Beams: "Oriya is the most neglected member of the group [of the Aryan languages], and retains some very archaic forms. The repulsive and difficult character in which it is written, the rugged and mountainous nature of the greater part of Orissa, and its comparative isolation from the world at large, have combined to retard its development." It is not the place where I can show that many letters of the Oriya script owe their origin distinctly and definitely to their corresponding Bengali forms—brought into use on the soil of Bengal at a comparatively recent time; ঘ, ছ, ট and ঋ are some of these letters; these letters only seemingly differ from the Bengali letters because they are written in a mode wholly peculiar to Orissa; that this mode of writing has made the Oriya letters unattractive to the foreigners, may be known from the following remark of Mr. Beams as appears in his Comparative Grammar of the Aryan Vernaculars: "The Bengali is the most elegant and easiest to write of all the Indian alphabets, Oriya, is of all Indian characters the ugliest, clumsiest and most cumbrous"—(Vol. I, p. 62).

We can very well assert on the strength of the facts adduced in this as well as in some other lectures, that the Eastern Māgadhi vernaculars were very much alike and did not much differ from one another, when they first came into being by being differentiated in different provinces; consequently we may refer to many archaic forms, retained alike by Oriya and Assamese, to trace the history of our words. Written vernacular literature of this very early period has not been hitherto discovered, and old songs, proverbs, adages and saws as have come down to us, have lost their old linguistic character in the course of being transmitted orally from generation to generation. 10th century A.D. is the approximate time when Oriya was fully differentiated as a provincial vernacular, but of this time we do not get even any literary fragment composed in a genuine vernacular. In the name of the Bengali language of the 10th century A.D., a recently published volume of verses has attracted our attention; it is quite fitting that the language of this collection should be examined here. The book I have to notice in quest of the old Bengali language, is a collection of three doctrinal works recently published by the Bengal 'Sāhitya Pariṣat' under one general title—'বৌদ্ধগান ও দোহা'; the noted Scholar Mahamahopadhyay Haraprasad Shastri brought the doctrinal works from Nepal, and it is he who has edited them in the aforesaid collection. It has been prominently inscribed on the very title page, that the contents of the collection preserve for us the language of Bengal as was current thousand years ago. What Pandit Shastri says, commands my respectful attention, but I fear that it is difficult to support the claim of antiquity that has been preferred for the hieratic effusions in question. I have to remark here that I do not take any account of the ডাকার্ণব portion of the collection, as it is not in Bengali, but composed in corrupt Sanskrit,—interspersed with some Prākṛta slokas.

These doctrinal works, we learn, were translated into Tibetan, but when, we do not know. The fact that some scholars of Tibet are known to have been active during some centuries in collecting various books in India, does not prove when these works were collected; it could be previous to this period of special activity, or it could be subsequent to it. Looking to the metrical system and the grammatical forms, some verses may be declared to be composed in Hindi. Generally the language of many effusions is such a jumble of various words and grammatical forms of various provinces and of various times, that we can hardly say that the writings represent any particular dialect. I do not think anybody will proceed seriously to determine the language of the following hybrid sentence, which I compose to illustrate my case, *viz.* :—মালাবাড়্তে (I think—Mārhātti) কো ই এক শক্স্ (somebody—Hindi) মোক কহি ছিল (told me—Asamese) যে এই ঘরে (that in this house—Bengali) পূর্ব্বরে (previously—Oriya) মিয়াদ্ (one—Mundāri) বিরাম্মণন্ (Brahman, Nominative—Tāmil) গলাডু (lived—Telegu). Why this strange phenomenon occurs in this book is partly explained by the name of the language 'সন্ধ্যা ভাষা.' The male অবধূত's and the female 'বিয়ালি's came together very likely in a colony of theirs, and there composed the secret tenets, etc., of their cult for their disciples in such a manner, that when the songs would be sung or muttered, the uninitiated might not understand either the language or the purport of them. Though the language is mainly Hindi, the authors allowed words and forms of many dialects to flow freely into their composition. No doubt, to us now, the veil is very thin, and we can see the whole thing through and through. The collection is highly important to the philologists and the Anthropologists. We are not concerned here with the doctrine, but can say that such a sentence of the book as "রুখের তেন্তুলি কুম্ভিরে খাঅ" reminds us of the Bāul song—

উঠন্ ঠন্ ঠন্, করে রে ভাই, ঘরে জলের ঢেউ ;
নৈরামনির নিরঞ্জনে পায়না খুঁজে কেউ।

some tracts still wear as underlinen, and as such may be called নীবী in the Vedic sense; কনাৎ is in use to signify a piece of cloth or a tent. (See নেঙ্গট below.)

(3) কানা (edge) being wrongly supposed to be derived from কর্ণ, it is spelt usually with ণ, but the word comes really from স্কন্ধ, for we see, that not only in the District of Jessore, and Eastern Bengal Districts, but also in the Districts of Nadya and Berhampore as well, the word কাঁধা is in use. No doubt the line, 'মেরেছ কলসীর কানা' has become widely popular even within the area indicated above, but in common parlance the form is always কাঁধা and not কানা.

(4) কিরে (oath); the Hindi form as well as the form used in Sambalpuri Oriya is কিরিআ. The history of it is highly interesting. The method of taking an oath by what is called সচ্চ কিরিআ (সত্য ক্রিয়া) is certainly familiar with the Pāli scholars; it has been illustrated by a good number of examples by E. W. Burlingame in the J. R. A. S., 1917, pp. 429-67. That কিরিআ or কিরে comes from সচ্চ-কিরিআ is doubtless. In this connection, I may refer the students to the method of warding off curses and also of taking oath by touching the hair, as was once universal all over the globe and is now also in vogue among many rude tribes of India as well as of other countries of the world; it is because of this custom that the word মাইরি (Dravidian—মাইর্-hair) is still a term for assiveration; মাইকি is the form in use in Orissa and in Nepal.

(5) খাড়া—The origin of it may be easily traced on reference to Oriya ছিড়া derived from স্থিত as discussed before.

(6) গাড়ু—This word as well as ঘড়া, ঘটি, etc., must be traced to ঘট.

(7) ঘাট—That the pseudo-Sanskrit form ঘট্ট should be ignored, need not be asserted. Certainly the word ঘাটি

(mountain pass) comes from গিরি-সঙ্কট, since সংঘাটি, to signify the meaning, occurs in Prākṛta, but the word ঘাট is not associated, in idea with ঘাটি. (See হাট below)

(8) চাহ—In Aśoka inscriptions, we meet with 'চাগ' from which Bühler derives the word, but no Aryan root has been suggested for চাগ; it is certainly not Dravidian.

(9) চিনি—The supposition of Carey's Pandits that the word comes from the name চিন (China) is absurd. As চীর্ণ means divided, or split, I think the term চিনি for sugar is from চীর্ণিত গুড়.

(10) ছেলে—The earlier Bengali form of it is ছাওয়াল or ছাবাল. Certainly the word ছা or ছাঁ or ছানা comes from শাব or শাবক; in Eastern Bengal, the word ছাও, exactly corresponding to শাব is still in use. The Oriya word ছুআ is applied to human young ones also, in the Sambalpur tract; it is difficult, however, to form ছাওয়াল or ছাবাল by adding ল to either ছাও or ছুআ, since the ল suffix as diminutive-indicating (*i.e.*, indicating affection) is not met with in Bengali. Very likely the word বাল (child) was added to ছা, or that the ল suffix signifying the very idea indicated above was once in use, for ছাও, ছুআ, and ছাওয়াল are very closely related. Sir R. G. Bhandarkar's supposition that the word comes from চেলা (disciple) cannot but be rejected; চেলা comes from চেট (originally চেড়, *cf.*, চেড়ী a female attendant of the Rākṣasas); neither the idea of a disciple nor of a servant can be associated with the term for an infant darling; moreover, there is a phonetic difficulty, since the original derivative is not ছেলে but is ছাবাল. The word ছাবাল could perhaps be reduced to ছাওআলিয়া and then to ছালিয়া and again to ছেলিয়া to become ছেলে.

(11) ছোঁড়া—comes distinctly from ছোট which is a decayed form of ক্ষুদ্র=খুল্ল=খাট. The Nepalese form is ছোরো (properly ছোর; final ও is nominative-indicating);

the Hindi form ছোক্‌রা with ক in the middle is only a variant.

(12) ঝুনা as in ঝুনা নারিকেল is generally treated as দেশী, but it suggested to me once, that it may be a derivative of জীর্ণ, as জুন্‌হা (old) is in use in some provinces, but as we get ঝুনী in Prākṛta as derived from ধ্বনি, it does not appear unlikely that the term ঝুনা was applied to that cocoanut, which produces a splashing sound when shaken.

(13) ঝাল—seems to be derived from ধার or ধারা (sharp cutting edge), as pungency is indicated by the term. Oriya meaning of the word is 'perspiration'; ধার or ধারা, a stream, is also closely associated with the idea; our ঝোল (Oriya ঝুল) which signifies broth, seems connected with ধার; *cf.* ঝরা, ঝরণা, etc. The word ঢাল, to pour, seems also to be derived from ধার.

(14) টল্লা—no doubt টল is in Sanskrit, but there it is a dignified প্রাকৃত word. It may be derived from চল, but very likely the original word is স্খল.

(15) টুকু or টুক—there cannot be any doubt that it is to be derived from স্তোক; from the very word স্তোক we have also got থোক, as I have shown before. One Prākṛta variant of স্তোক is থিক or থিঅ, as we meet with in the গাথা শপ্তশতী; so we think the Oriya word টিকিএ also comes from the word স্তোক (for the origin of টি see next lecture).

(16) ঠেং (slang—a leg, Hindi টাং) is an অপভ্রংশ form of জঙ্ঘা; the word জং indicates জঙ্ঘা as well as 'bone' in Eastern Hindi or Lariā; the meaning *bone*, comes perhaps from Muṇḍāri জং = bone which is not connected with জঙ্ঘা. The word জাং for thigh is in use (I am told) in the District of Berhampur.

(17) ডাল (branch)—comes from Prākṛta দালু a branch, derived from দারু.

(18) তোলা to pluck is not from উত্তোলন but from ত্রুট; টলিবা or টুলিবা is the Oriya form and তোড়না is the Hindi

form ; to raise up is not the idea associated with it ; তোড়া (a nose-gay) is also a cognate word.

(19) তোলো (a big earthen pot) comes from স্থণ্ডিল ; the primary অপভ্রংশ form তন্দুল a big cooking pot, is in use in Hindi.

(20) নেওটা (affectionately attached) and নাই (indulgence) are derived from Prākṛta নেহ S. স্নেহ.

(21) নেকড়া—a torn piece of cloth ; it is difficult to derive it from লেঙ্গট or লেঙ্গটি or নেংটি, which is, no doubt an apology for a piece of cloth to cover nakedness ; I cannot uphold that নগ্ন is the word from which লেঙ্গট is derived. How the words লুগা (Oriya), and লুগ্ড়া (Hindi) may be connected with লুঙ্গি I do not know ; but লেঙ্গট is not connected with it. I think the apology for a cloth worn by a নিগন্ঠি (নিগ্‌গন্থ জৈন) was called a নিগন্ঠি which may be equated with নেংটি, নেঙ্গট, লেঙ্গট, etc.

(22) পাগল (insane)—this word seems to have a curious history : পুগ্‌গল (a man) is a term which the Buddhists appropriated and Buddhist mendicants not caring for the world very likely won the name পাগল as derived from পুগ্‌গল ; hence the modern meaning.

(23) পাহাড়—Hill—the term পথন for stone as derived from পাষাণ is well known ; to the Buddhists পাষণ্ড was he, who did not care for the Buddhist religion, being impervious like a stone ; the derivation given by বুদ্ধ ঘোষ as পাসং ডেন্‌তিইতি, has to be rejected. It is from পাখণ্ড that পাহাড় seems to have originated, being a heap of পাথন্ or পাহন্ .

(24) পুতুল (Pseudo-Sans-form পুত্তল or পুত্তলি) must be traced to পুত্রক used to signify a doll. *Cf.* Kalidas' description of উমা's play by the phrase কৃত্রিম পুত্রকৈশ্চ.

(25) ফেল-ফেল as in ফেল ফেল করিয়া চাওয়া, to look vacantly and innocently. From অবলোকন we get বলোকন or rather বলোক ; this বলোক in the shape of ভুলুক (to peep in)

is in use in E. Bengal, and the form ভেল to look vacantly is in use in the west of Burdwan, as we may notice in the expression টুক্‌টুক ভেল্‌চে (he is looking vacantly) ; ফেল ফেল, most likely comes from ভেল.

(26) বেআড়া—The Persian prefix 'বে' (corresponding to Vedic বি) as in বে-আক্কেল, বে-কসুর, বে-মউকা (Beng. বেমক্কা), etc., and which is in use with many Bengali words, such as বে-গোছাল (untidy), বে-চপ্পা (ill-shaped), বে-দাঁড়া (irregular), etc., is wrongly supposed to be the prefix in বে-আড়া ; this word is identical with বিঅড় derived from বিকট as met with in the Gauḍa Bahō. In this connection, I may mention that the word বেভুল used at times in non-urban tracts is not a hybrid formation, but is really the original form of ভুল, since the word ভুল comes from বিহ্বল.

(27) ভণ্ড—like the word পাগল this word has a curious history : the Buddhist religious men of high order were addressed by the term ভদন্ত which was, as we know, reduced to ভঅন্দ ; it is the history of a satire, that ভঅন্দ in the form of ভণ্ড signifies a hypocrite.

(28) ভাসা (floating)—The word is wrongly treated by some as Sanskrit, for we can notice such a curious form as ভাসমান. The original Sanskrit word বৃষি was reduced, to ভিসী (a raft) in Pali ; from the idea, that which floats, comes the word ভাসা to signify the meaning. The word ভেলা seems to be connected with the word. I need not perhaps point out that the original Prākṛta form of উড়ুপ is উলুম্প which is derived from উৎ+প্লব্.

(29) মটুক, মকুট or মুকুট—The last word is the pseudo-Sanskritic form of মকুট which was formed from the first word by a metathysis. The word মটুক signifying a head-gear comes from মস্তক ; *cf.* মট্‌কা the top of a thatched house.

(30) মেকুর—this name for a cat is not current either in Western Bengal or in Central Bengal, but that it was

once so current, appears from a line of a nursery rhyme which runs as মেকুর মেকুর, কটা ছানা. Sir R. G. Bhandarkar gives us two অপভ্রংশ forms of মার্জ্জার in use in different parts of Western India, which are মজার and মেজুর ; that from মেজুর the form মেকুর may easily come out, need not be asserted.

(31) হাঁটা—as the verb হিণ্ড occurs mostly in Jaina Sanskrit, it has become difficult to many to derive হাঁটা from হিণ্ড (to trudge).

(32) হাঁড়ি—from the genuine Sanskrit word ভাজন comes the pseudo-Sanskrit term ভাণ্ড by the process o metathysis (ভাজন=ভান্‌জ=ভাণ্‌ড ; *cf.* মূর্দ্ধণ=মুনঢা of Prākṛta=মুণ্ড, which is pseudo-Sanskrit.) হাঁড়ি as a variant of ভাঁড় is derived from ভাণ্ড.

In concluding this lecture I make this general remark, that to identify the Bengali language with any old time obsolete language, we have no doubt primarily to look to the Grammatical structure of the obsolete speech, but the examination of phrases and vocables is also necessary, for, pecial idiomatic expressions and peculiar formation of words bear peculiar marks of particular provincial origin ; as foreign words are naturalized according to the genius of every language, proper study of them cannot be also overlooked. Various are the sources from which we have derived material for our language, and there are languages which are allied to Bengali ; how very careful we should therefore be to determine the history of our words and in fine to determine the history of our language, should be duly appreciated.

LECTURE XIV

BENGALI AS DISTINGUISHED FROM ITS ALLIED VERNACULARS.

I propose to pursue in this lecture, a stratigraphical study of the Bengali language with the help of the facts set forth and discussed in the previous lectures. In the present state of our knowledge, we cannot make a definite pronouncement of the ethnic elements that came into the composition of our people; we are not in possession of a history which deals with the evolution of our social structure. It was therefore only possible for me, to state in a general manner, of some of the influences that have been at work in shaping our speech in its present form. I have however made it tolerably acceptable that philology can be employed as a good strata-metre, if this instrument be fitted into the handle of the history of the races speaking the language under investigation. We have seen, that in their old and archaic forms, the speeches of the Gauḍian group resemble one another so closely, that it becomes ordinarily difficult to distinguish them as separate speeches, by noticing those points of difference which determine their character as so many independent dialects. To recognise aright our early forms as differentiated Bengali forms, separate from the forms of allied languages or dialects, let us proceed first to examine the structure of our speech primarily with reference to declension in a comparative method, that is to say, by considering carefully the inflexions of nominal stems (both noun and pronoun) by means of such endings as represent the various cases. This involves the consideration of the nominal formations connected with the verbs as participles, infinitives, etc., and the finite verbs indicating different tenses and moods. Other important points of grammatical or structural changes or evolution will be next noticed to determine, or rather to confirm the proposition advanced before, regarding the origin and character of Bengali.

We may set down on the evidence of old literary records, the language of which must be accepted on all hands to be Bengali, that 'মই' and 'মুই' are the earliest forms of personal pronoun of the first person in singular number and 'আমি' or 'আম্হি' is the plural form of 'মই' and 'মুই.' The earliest Prākṛta form 'মি' from which 'মই' comes out, is in use in Mārhāṭi, but we do not meet with the form in old Bengali. 'মই' and 'মুই' occur indiscriminately in the "শ্রীকৃষ্ণকীর্ত্তন" noticed before; 'মই' is still current in the provincial Bengali dialect of Rangpur, and this is the form that obtains in Assamese. 'মুহি' was only the accented form of 'মুই' as 'আম্হি' was the accented or emphatic form of 'আমি.' In Oriya the singular form is 'মুহি' (though reduced very often to 'মুই' and 'মু' in colloquial speech) and the plural form is 'আম্ভে' which is a changed form of 'আম্হি.' 'আমি' the oldest singular form acquired the dignity of being treated as plural when 'মুই' came into use; it is still the plural form in Mārhāṭi and also in Assamese which is closely related to Bengali. As the ending 'এ' invariably occurred in old times to signify nominative case, 'আম্হি' became 'আম্হে' in Oriya and this 'আম্হে' when reduced to one word assumed the shape 'আম্ভে.' As we cannot be sure of the time of the 'বৌদ্ধ গান ও দোঁহা' edited by Pandit Hara Prasad Sastri, we must say (for want of literary evidence in support of any proposition to the contrary) that these differentiated forms cannot be shown to date from a time earlier than the 10th century A.D.; that the 10th century A.D. is the probable time when Oriya was formed as a distinct inde endent language, has been tried to be shown in the next preceding lecture by adducing some historical facts.

When the genuine singular forms were regarded non-honorific and vulgar, the plural forms were brought into use as singular and such plural-forming suffixes for nouns as রা (Beng.), মানে (Oriya), লোকে (Assamese), etc., were added to the real plural forms to make plural of them. The plural-forming suffixes 'রা' of Bengali, 'মানে' of Oriya and 'লোকে' (as well as 'বোরে,' 'হঁতে,' 'বিলাকে') of Assamese are of provincial growth of which মানে and লোকে can be traced to old Māgadhi source. It is interesting to note that though the original form of the Oriya speech flowed into Orissa, through Bengal, the Behari plural-forming suffix বন্ (which is only ন in two dialects) has been adopted as মান্ in Oriya; neither বন্ nor ন can be shown to have been in use in Bengali at any time. This confirms what has been stated before that two streams (one through Bengal and the other through the Kośala tract) flowed into Orissa to form the language of that country.

My remarks regarding the pronoun of the 1st person are applicable to the pronouns of the second person which are 'তু,' 'তুহি,' 'তুই' and 'তই' in singular and 'তুমি' (now singular in Bengali), 'তোমরা,'. 'তোমালোকে' (Assamese), 'তুম্ভে' and তুম্ভেমানে (Oriya) in plural. Regarding the form আমালোকে, it is to be remarked, that though আমালোকে is idiomatic in Assamese, and the very form আমালোকে is freely used in Naogaon and Tejpur, the form is considered incorrect to-day in the standard Assamese language.

The honorific form alike of 'তুই' and 'তুমি' is 'আপনি' in Bengali; the corresponding Assamese form is 'আপুনি' and the Oriya form is 'আপণ.' It comes from 'আত্মনঃ' in the possessive case; the oldest 'Apabhranśa' was 'অত্তন'

and the later form was 'অপ্পন'; the original possessive sense is retained by 'আপন' as adjective as in আপন ঘর (one's own house). 'আপনি' as pronoun, signifies literally 'your own self.' This form however is seldom met with in very old literary records to signify 'you'; its use was restricted mainly to indicate 'by one's own self' as adverb; 'I,' 'you' or 'he' did a thing, 'আপ্নি আপ্নি' (Bengali) or 'আপে or আপে' (Oriya) or 'আপুনি' (Assamese) means that the doer did not take the help of any other person in doing the act. At times it also signifies 'I myself,' 'you yourself' or 'he himself' as the case may be, as in যুগে যুগে আপনি হইব (first person) অবতার (Bengali) or in আপে আসি ভগবান দেলে দরশন (Oriya).

I need hardly point out, that the genuine Māgadhi form সে (the successor of the earlier form সো) is in use in Bengali and Oriya, and its slightly altered form 'সি' is in use in Assamese. The forms 'যে' and 'কে' may also be noticed along with it. Oriya wholly agrees with Bengali in the use of these forms; the use of কিএ for কে is wholly irregular being a new departure from the standard oriya use according to the Eastern Provincial peculiarity in pronunciation. I mention this fact, so that this provincial Oriya 'কিএ,' may not be mistaken for the Eastern মাগধী কি অ, of which the modern representative is কিবা.

The plural form of 'সে' is 'তে' in Māgadhi while যে and কে are found used both in the singular and plural. The plural form 'তে' is noticeable in old Bengali but not in old Oriya; 'তেঁহ' and 'তেঁই' as derived from it were in use in Bengali till the other day, and 'তে' itself is still in use (both as singular and plural) in the provincial speech of Chittagong, as a co-relative pronoun linked with 'যে,' which is introductory. That our 'তেঁহ' and 'তেঁই' are generally found in use in singular to indicate honour, need not be pointed out. 'তেঁই' (the honoured he) is not to be confounded with the identical form, which is an indeclinable to indicate 'for that reason': the pun on the word by Bharat Chandra in 'অনেকের পতি তেঁইপতি মোর বাম' may be referred to; the primary meaning is—He, who is the lord of many is my husband, and the other meaning suggested is—My husband is also the husband of others, and *for that reason* he is not favourably disposed towards me. They are identical in form but different in origin: তেঁই (for that reason) is derived from তহিঁ=তহি and our 'তাই' signifying the same meaning is a variant or a changed form of 'তেঁই'; this 'তাই' being wrongly spelt as 'তাহাই' is confounded with the provincial form 'তাহা+ই' of emphasis; the latter form is derived from তহ=তদ্. In our honorific তিনি, there is the pronoun 'ন' in an enclitic manner; in Pāli, we get this 'ন' in the accusative case only in the form of নং (=তাহাকে); 'that respected he' is the round about expression to indicate honour: তেনার and তেন্‌রা (his) are not unusual in the mouth of our vulgar people. The Bengalis who settled in Orissa, long ago, carried with them, as a matter of course many archaic forms, and their descendants now, not being in touch with the progress and change effected in Bengal, use তেনার (his), তান্‌রান (they), etc., very commonly. The forms, যিনি (occurs as জিনি in old Bengali), ইনি and উনি, as are peculiar to Bengali should also be taken note of here. I think, that the ন of direct pronominal origin, as has been noticed here, is not the ন which we get in কোন, signifying *certain* person or *certain* object. কোন appears to me to be the decayed portion of কেনচিৎ since কৌণসি almost representing কেনচিৎ obtains in Oriya as well as in Hindi. That the ন of কেন comes directly from ম of কিম্ need not be pointed out.

I may note here that both the earlier emphatic form of কে (who) as কেহ, and the later form কেউ, are in use in

Bengali; on reference to the modern Behari, we can see that কেউ (and not merely কেহ) grew in মাগধী on the very soil of Magadha, yet it is only কেহি (corresponding to our কেহ) which we get in Oriya.

Case declension—The sign for nominative.—The 'অ' sound of the non-হসন্ত finals of all nouns in the Nominative Singular was reduced to 'ও' sound in Pāli, to represent very likely the সংবৃত pronunciation of অ, as I have suggested before. This sound of 'অ' which is almost ও continues with us, as an inherent Bengali speciality but we do not write 'ধম্মো' for 'ধম্ম' to paint the special shade of our 'অ' sound. This form of the word in the nominative case did not become extinct in the মাগধী speech, when the ending এ for ও came into general use, for we get in the Jaina Prākṛta, that though all nouns in the nominative case took generally the এ final, the forms with ও final were also in use; along with the forms মহাবীরে, জালিয়ে, মেহে, etc., we meet with the older form with ও ending as occurs for instance in such a sentence as 'যহা মেহো তহা জালি.' As it is in the provincial Bengali of Rungpur, so it is in Assamese that the nouns in the nominative case take 'এ' final invariably. ই for এ in such cases in Assamese as গাধই (ass) লতাই (creeper), etc., is rightly explained in the Assamese Grammar as the euphonic mutation of 'এ.' This 'এ' was once much in use both in Bengali and Oriya, but now the use is limited to some special cases only. Almost all the nouns in the nominative case have 'এ' or 'ই' final in the শ্রীকৃষ্ণ কীর্ত্তন of a time not earlier than the 14th century A.D. The modern use of it in Bengali in such cases as লোকে বলে (so the people say), মানুষে করে (so men generally do), ছাগলে খায় (the goats usually eat) is sufficiently expressive to denote the idea of plurality in an indefinite way. In Oriya, however, when a particular Pandit for example is alluded to it will be correct to say পণ্ডিতে

কহিলে ; we cannot but notice that this Oriya idiomatic use indicates honour. As signification of honour is associated with the form of plurality, it may be noted here that when distinction between singular and plural was not being strictly observed, the nominative-forming suffix এ came to be used to signify singular and plural alike, and the older plural-forming suffix আ fell fully into disuse.

This supposition is not correct that the nominative-indicating এ originates from the sign-indicating instrumentality ; the reduction for instance of সো to সে may be sufficient to show the wrongness of the proposition ; the instances of the use of all sorts of words in the nominative case in the Jaina Prākṛta will clear up the situation. The nominative singular forms of pronouns are quite fixed ; in other cases the pronominal stems in the shape of আমা, তোমা, তাহা, etc., take those case-endings which are generally usual with the noun stems. It will also be seen, that some case-denoting suffixes though pronominal in origin, are applied equally to nouns and pronouns.

The sign for accusative.—It will not be less than 1400 years when the author of the Nātya Śāstra noted the predominance of এ sound in the speeches of the Eastern Gangetic valley extending from Behar to the Bay of Bengal ; perhaps the lines I cite below show this predominance of এ sound in modern Bengali, far in excess of what it could be in olden time. এ of different origins and of various significations may be noted in the lines :

গ্রামে লোকে এক-মনে পূজিয়ে দেবতাগণে
খড়্গে ছাগে কাটে লোক-হিতে

We see in the first place that এ as a case-denoting particle signifies many cases : লোকে is in the nominative case or has the প্রথমা বিভক্তি, দেবগণে and ছাগে are in the objective case, *i.e.*, in the দ্বিতীয়া বিভক্তি, খড়্গে is in the instrumental case, *i.e.*, in তৃতীয়া বিভক্তি, লোক হিতে (=লোক হিতায়) is technically in চতুর্থী বিভক্তি and গ্রামে indicating locative is in the সপ্তমী বিভক্তি. Then again the এ final of একমনে is adverb-forming, পূজিয়ে is in infinitive and কাটে is a finite verb; the last three cases will be dealt with in their proper places later on.

We have studied the history of the nominative-indicating এ; it is this এ which signifies accusative as well as dative at times; 'মো-এ,' (me) and 'আম্হা-এ' (us) have been in use, since long, and the modern form 'আমার' is but a slightly changed form of them. When অম্ or অন্ ceased to denote the accusative case in মাগধী, nominative sign of nouns came to be used to signify the accusative as well as dative in a large number of cases. When again, the noun stems ceased to take any nominative-indicating suffix, it was only at times that the accusative was marked with a suffix; this rule, I should say still holds good. The following sentence will be illustrative of the phenomenon, that *in the case of nouns*, it is with reference to syntax that we have to distinguish nominative from the accusative, and not by looking to the case-ending: মা-বাপ ছেলে শাসন না করিলে, ছেলে মা-বাপ মানে না; translated into old Bengali the sentence will stand as—জই (যদি) মাএ বাপে পো-এ শাসন ন করই পো-এ মা-বাপা (or মা বাপে) ন মানই.

The আ final of nouns to signify both nominative and accusative, as we meet with at times in the latest প্রাকৃত and in old Bengali, has not altogether fallen into disuse; this আ is more emphasis-indicating than case-denoting in such a sentence as ওগ্গর ভত্তা, (object)...দিজ্জই কন্তা, খা পুন বন্তা (nominative). It is at times diminutive-indicating, that is to say, indicative of affection or familiarity: in মা-এ বলেন পড় পুতা, the word পুতা is in diminutive form; in common conversation this আ is added to names to signify either familiarity or contempt.

As to the Dravidian origin of the suffix কে to signify dative as well as accusative, my remarks in the 5th lecture (pp. 59-60) should be referred to. The Dravidian কু remains unchanged in Oriya, and in old Bengali, we get it both in the shape of কে and ক; in the provinciality of Rungpur the form 'ক' is still in use, as may be noticed in the forms মোক্ (আমাকে) and তাক্ (তাহাকে).

To convert possessive form to objective, adding এ to the possessive form, we need not import any foreign influence; for, an idea, *relating to* an object may be expressed in the objective case, without drowning the sense of relation; the line—'যাদেরে চাহিয়া তোমারে ভুলেছি, তারাত চাহেনা আমারে,' will sufficiently illustrate the case, if the thought underlying the sentence is properly analysed. This form of the objective case is met with more in poetry than in prose, in our modern language; in Eastern Bengal, however, this form obtains in common conversation language; *cf.*, the Eastern Bengal sentences, মার-এ মারেনা= মাকে মারিতে নাই, and মোরে কও নাও ডুবাইবার? (How dare you suggest that the boat will be sunk by me?). We can easily trace this form of expression to a প্রাকৃত idiom : কস্স-এ বি পেক্খহ্ (whomsoever you may meet) is equivalent to যারেই (যাকেই) দেখতে পাও; 'কস্স' is in the possessive form being the অপভ্রংশ form of কস্স and এ is clearly object-indicating here.

Instrumental Case.—To signify the instrumental case we have in Bengali the suffixes এ, দিয়া, and হতে; their history may be briefly narrated here.

এ—The Pali Instrumental Plural suffix হি comes no doubt from ভিস্ or ভিঃ. It is well known that distinction between singular and plural was not much observed in the later Prākṛtas, and one well-formed suffix, no matter whether it was originally singular or plural-indicating, became the general case-denoting suffix. There are lots of instances of হি being used as suffix to denote instrumental singular; take for instance the line মানিনি, মানহি কাঁইফল (What does it avail, Oh Mānini, by becoming cross?). No doubt at first হি was reduced to ই as we meet with in the old literary Prākṛta works, but its reduction to এই is not also very recent. The instrumental ই ending in such cases as ইচ্ছাই (ইচ্ছয়া) বিদ্ধাই (বিদ্ধয়া), etc. as we meet with in the সেতুবন্ধ may be considered with some reasons to be derived from য়া, but the early history starting with হি is not in favour of this supposition. Be that as it may, we get the suffix ই, as well as এই, in old প্রাকৃত works of uncertain dates; ভমরেহি or লতাহি being reduced to ভমরেই or লতাই, the path for further reduction to ভমরে or লতা-এ (or লতায়) was paved. The history of the idiomatic use of the instrumental case forms, if studied in regular succession, it does not become easy to hold that 'এন' (say of দেবেন) generated the 'এ' in question by dropping the final ন. I have discussed in the previous lecture that in our proto-Bengali, 'এন' does not occur and that its occurrence in one passage in a বৌদ্ধ দোঁহা has been wrongly formulated because of incorrect reading of the text. The cases where 'এন' seems to occur in Oriya as instrumental suffix have not been in my opinion properly studied; it will be observed that the words with seeming এন suffix in Oriya have been used to denote locative case as well; I am inclined to hold, on reference to the use of ন as a particle of emphasis in Oriya, that the words with a suffix (denoting either instrumental or locative case) stand with additional ন to indicate emphasis. The half-nasal occurring in ইচ্ছেঁ (by the desire) or নেহাএঁ (by the affection) does not seem to represent the loss of ন, for the instrumental form with এন is not met with in the Prākṛta speeches which are later than Pali in date; corresponding to 'এ' we get 'এরে' in Assamese and রে in Oriya;

the growth of র here is but euphonic growth. In Bengali the noun-stems having ই or উ final take an additional ত which is but an euphonic growth to facilitate easy pronunciation; compare the forms হাতে ধর and ছুরিতে কাট. This euphonic transmutation is noticeable alike in Nominative and Locative, where এ is the case-denoting suffix. Where however difficulty does not occur in pronunciation, the euphonic ত does not occur; for instance ঘিয়ে ভাজ is commoner than ঘিতে ভাজ. Besides the ordinary examples of instrumental with এ final, I notice the instance where a peculiar Sanskrit idiom is expressed in Bengali: In আমায় তোমায় বোঝা পড়া আছে, আমায় and তোমায় correspond to ত্বয়া-ময়া as in অভূ যুদ্ধম্ ত্বয়া-ময়া.

দিয়া—We have noticed the instrumental case-ending 'তে' and its variant 'দে' in the Māgadhi Prākṛta which is usually designated as Jaina Prākṛta. It is surmised by some that this দে is but the changed form of earlier হি.

This দে can be clearly recognised in the instrumental case-ending 'দি' in use in the district of Rangpur and 'দেই' in use in Oriya. This archaic 'দি' of Rangpur is now used as 'দিয়া' in standard Bengali language; as such it has no connection with 'দা' to give; nor the upstart দ্বারা set up by the Pandits, can have any relationship with it.

হতে—I have traced the genesis of হতে in the previous lecture and have shown there, that in its origin as well as in its general use in our vernacular, হতে is purely the sign of the ablative case. In such a use as আমা হতে হেন কার্য্য না হবে সাধন, the word হতে signifies certainly instrumentality, but its ablative sense is also noticeable in the use; the action 'flowing out of me' can be construed to be the underlying idea.

Dative.—In Assamese we get 'লৈ' as a special dative case-ending, while in Bengali and Oriya, we have the same 'কু' or 'ক' or 'কে'-suffix both for accusative and dative.

This 'লৈ,' noticeable also in Nepalese and in a Behari dialect, is the reduced form of 'লাগি,' in use in Bengali as well as in Oriya; তোমার লাগি (for you) is rather a poetic use in Bengali.

Ablative.—হতে (not to be confounded with হইতে=to be) and থেকে are the two ablative suffixes in Bengali. How the ablative denoting অং generated the suffix হতে, has been discussed in Lecture XIII, p. 244. Both the প্রাকৃত forms হিন্তু and হিঁং are met with in old Hindi. হিঁং has been reduced to হতে in Bengali and to হুঁ in Hindi. It is the further reduced form of হুঁ in the shape of উঁ, that we meet with in Oriya as well as in Marathi. The Oriya form ঘরু, from house, is not the contracted form of ঘরহুঁ. Oriya ঠুঁ or corresponding Marathi থুন্ is quite another suffix as we shall presently notice. It has been stated that from অং we have got হতে (*cf.* বৃক্ষাৎ=রুক্খতে=রুকখ হতে) as a general ablative forming suffix; then again we have to notice that this very অং being joined to the demonstrative pronouns 'ই' or ইদ, and এ or এত (contraction of এতদ্) gave rise to the particular forms ইংথি and এংথি (from here) and this newly formed থি of এংথি and ইংথি, is the progenitor of the suffix থি or থে. We have to further note that it is থে and not থেকে which is in use in the speech of the Bengali-people all throughout the Northern and the Eastern districts and in the Districts of Jessore and Khulna. সেখান থে and not সেখান থেকে is what we hear in the tracts mentioned above. We can thus clearly see that থেকে of the standard language has acquired an otiose or euphonic ক.

In the district of Chittagong we get the form থুন্ for থে which by chance agrees with the Marathi form থুন্. Corresponding Oriya form is ঠু or ঠুঁ which is reducible to থু or থুঁ or থুন্. I have already suggested that the Marathi উন্ and Oriya উ are not contracted forms of

থুন্ and ঠুঁ respectively, but that they are derived from হু which comes out of ইং (the progenitor of হতে). থুন of Marathi and ঠুঁ of Oriya are additional suffixes; *cf.* the double Marathi forms এ থুন্ and আপল্যা পাশুন্ and the double Oriya forms এ ঠুঁ and ঘরুঁ. In ঠারু (Oriya), the suffix উ is added to ঠার.

Genitive—There have been various suggestions regarding the genesis of র, of which one or two will be noticed here. As such Sanskrit genitive forms as হরেঃ, গুরোঃ, etc evolve 'র' in their conjunction with vowels, semi-vowels, and consonants which are not surds, some suppose that the Vernacular র suffix has to be traced to this special phenomenon; in this supposition, it is lost sight of that বিসর্জ্জনীয় was never in use in the Prakṛtas, and the Sanskrit forms in question were never idiomatic in the Prākṛta speeches. What we have to really notice, is the Prākṛta idiomatic form to trace the history of র. We first notice that স্স took the place of স্য and then অ as the representative of স came into use. We have also noticed in earlier lectures that the suffix অ (indicating genitive) was not only liable to be mistaken for other suffixes but was incapable of expressing the idea of possession with some emphasis, on account of its fluid pronunciation or boneless character; that very often হ had to be substituted for the sake of forcible pronunciation, has been noticed in the course of examination of some Prākṛta forms. That the final boneless vowels have been at times either liable to be reduced to র, or require to be otherwise strengthened, may be noted over again: গ-উ has been reduced to গরু, and করিঅ has assumed the form করিয়া in Bengali. The tendency to put in র to ensure distinct pronunciation is observable in such a Sandhi conjunction in Pali, as পন্নরসে + ইব = পন্নরসেরিব, where according to Sanskrit Sandhi rule a র is not justified.

Most convincing proof of র coming out of স (or from a vowel sound representing স) is to be sought in the *phonetic peculiarity* which is almost *universal*: change of 's' into 'r' as a Dravidian peculiarity, has been elaborately noticed by Bishop Caldwell and others and this very peculiarity in all the Aryan languages of Europe has been well studied by the Philologists. How the 's' of the genitive-indicating স্ত of the Aryan speech has been reduced to 'r' in a very large number of cases in Italian, French, German and English, is too well known to scholars to require an illustrative statement. Thus in accordance with the universally prevalent phonetic law, and quite consistently with the actual idiomatic use of the old times, we get the history of the growth of our genitive-signifying suffix র. What is to be noted is that in tracing this history one is not forced to *create an imaginary condition of things*, disregarding the actual idiomatic use which has always been in force.

Having given the real history of র, I just refer to an untenable theory regarding it upheld by some learned scholars. On the flimsy basis of a form which cannot be shown to have been idiomatic in the Prākṛtas, 'কের' has been set up by some as the progenitor of র; only one solitary instance of very doubtful import is cited from the মৃচ্ছকটিক in support of the existence of the form কের, by wholly overlooking the clear cases of the use of genitive in the Prākṛtas. It is clear that the form কের has been specially favoured, by the scholars under review, as an explanation, regarding the form 'এর' has been needed; it should be seen, in the first place, that in Western Hindi and in Oriya, it is 'র' and not 'এর্' which is the suffix; in Oriya 'এর্' is wholly unknown and the Hindi forms হামারা, তোমারা, etc., point simply to a simple 'র' suffix. I proceed to show in the second place that এর্ is merely an euphonic mutation of 'র,' in Bengali; and কের্ as a suffix *has never been known* in our language.

That এর্ is but an euphonic mutation of র will be clearly seen on reference to the rules of idiomatic use of র and এর in Bengali: (1) এগার-র (where final is non-হসন্ত), আমার, দাদা-র, দিদি-র, রাণী-র, সাধু-র, বধূ-র, ছেলে-র, আলো-র are examples of words of various final sounds taking 'র' as the genitive-signifying suffix. (2) When the final is হসন্ত, which is never the case in Oriya, the simple suffix র cannot be assimilated with the word, and so এর is to be suffixed; *e.g.*, রাখাল্-র makes 'র' a separate or non-হসন্ত syllable unsuited to the genius of Bengali pronunciation, and so we have রাখাল-এর, এক-এর, দশ-এর, etc. (3) Non-হসন্ত words of one letter, *i.e.*, to say non-হসন্ত single consonants treated as words must take 'এর' to maintain their distinctness as words; *e.g.*, ক-এর আঁকড়ী, শ (contracted form of শব)-এর কড়ি, etc.; contrast with them কবিতায়, যত-র সঙ্গে এত-র ভাল মিল হয়না. (4) Words ending with compound letters always generate non-হসন্ত sounds (unlike what it is in Hindi) in Bengali and yet they take এর্ and not র as we may notice in কষ্টের, গন্ধের, চন্দ্রের, etc. In Eastern Bengal, however, simple র is affixed in such cases in spoken language following perhaps the general rule which is in the air. (5) When the final sound is ঐ (অই) or ঔ (অউ), the final ই or উ becomes separate syllable and as such the euphony requires the affixing of এর্; *e.g.*, দই-এর, বউ-এর, etc.

I have heard this example adduced by some to illustrate the use of কের as a suffix in Bengali, *viz.*, কতকের as in কতকের পর্য্যায় but it is overlooked that here ক is an otiose ক to which according to the previously illustrated rule এর has to be suffixed; if we refer to কতকে in such an expression as 'এ মাছটা কতকে কিন্‌লে' the situation will be clear. It will be invariably found, that where কের occurs, it does not occur as a suffix but only এর is added to a word which has an otiose ক as final.

ক *and* দিগের.—In Eastern Māgadhi and in proto-Bengali we meet ক as a sign for genetive; the history of it, as well as of দিগের is interesting. Sir R. G. Bhandarkar has rightly remarked that ক of say, অম্হাক (অস্মাকম্) once came to be used as a genitive-indicating suffix. Since difference between singular and plural has not been maintained in the Vernaculars, such forms as আমা-ক and 'গাইক ঘিত্তা' (noticed previously) may easily be explained; I need not state that this ক is now in use in Hindi. Sir R. G. Bhandarkar has also very rightly shown in his Wilson Lectures, that when মম or তব was not considered to be either very forcible or honorific, মদীয় and ত্বদীয়, etc., became highly fashionable in Sanskrit as well as in Prākṛta speeches; that the history of our plural দিগের is to be traced to this phenomenon is what I assert here. That the case-denoting suffixes for our nouns are generally pronominal in origin, and that a portion of an expression used as a post-position becomes a suffix, have also been ably illustrated by Sir R. G. Bhandarkar; দীয় or rather দিয় of মদীয়, ত্বদীয়, etc., being joined to the general suffix র to indicate honour, the plural-denoting দিগের has originated.*

The Locative sign 'এ' is as old as the hills, and so no remark regarding it is necessary. I have to notice that in old Bengali 'ত' (from তস্) was once in use, and this use is now noticeable in the provincial speech of Rangpur. It is on this account, that the unusual particle 'ত' comes now in such euphonic combinations as হাতিতে, গরুতে; this euphonic 'ত' though grown in locative formations appears

---

* For the history of the plural-forming রা and গুলি, *vide* Lecture V, pp. 676-8.

in other case formations also where এ is the suffix and ই, উ, etc., are the finals.

Verbs.—The history of the forms, which verbs assume in different tenses and moods, should next engage our attention. How the Vedic tense systems were gradually simplified in the Prākṛta speeches has been discussed at some length in Lectures X and XI; here our discussion will be directed more to the history of our current forms than to the history of the reduction of old systems into their present condition.

The Present system.—করোতি in the 3rd person singular gave rise to the form করই and from করই comes the modern form করে, which is common to Bengali, Oriya and Assamese. সে করে of Bengali as well as of Oriya has the corresponding Assamese form সি (as well as তেওঁ and আনে) করে. The older form করই—current in the Prākṛta speeches—is often met with in the old time literature of Bengal and Orissa. It is to be first noted, that unlike in Oriya, the Bengali verbs are alike in form in singular and plural. On reference to the archaic Bengali forms করন্তি, যান্তি, কহন্তি, etc., one may be led to suppose that once our verbs had plural forms; but it is not so. It should be first observed that the plural forms referred to here, were in use in the 3rd person only, and that use again was limited to present time; in the second place it is to be noted that a verb took the অন্তি ending when honour of the person agreeing with the verb was sought to be denoted. Of the অন্তি ending, now only ন remains and in the case of honorific mention, we say তিনি করেন, as well as আপনি করেন; it need be mentioned that though আপনি is treated as 2nd person, it is not strictly so from grammatical point of view. The সি of করোসি, in the 2nd person is not wholly obsolete; 'স' of করিস, as in তুই করিস, is the representative of it. Again, we may notice that the old সি has assumed the form সে and is treated as an indeclinable particle; when we say করসে, মরসে, etc., an emphasis is put upon the verb by the addition of সে; pure 'সি' to signify second person, occurs very much in the Srikṛṣna Kirtan.

It is wrongly urged by some, that the মি ending of the verb in the 1st person indefinite, so common in the প্রাকৃতs, is not met with in Bengali; the mistake is due to the fact that some provincial future-indicating forms which take the suffix ম or মি, are not recognized as forms of present indefinite. That in the following instances, the present indefinite has been reduced to future (as is done in all languages), may be easily noticed: (1) করিম্ as the contracted form of করিমি (*cf.* Oriya করিবি as well as করিমি where ব and ম are interchangeable) is in use as 1st person future in the provincial dialect of Rangpur; (2) the forms করিম্, খাম্, যাম্, etc., as well as করমু, খামু, যামু, etc., are current in the speech of the common people of Mymensing; (3) the 'ম' ending of the verb in the 1st person, present tense, as is traceable in the Singhalese speech, must be owing to the influence which the প্রাকৃত of old Bengal exerted there.

The Present Progressive.—presents a very interesting form. In করিতেছে, we get the infinitive form of the principal verb linked with the present indefinite form আছে (derived from অংথি=অস্+তি), in such a manner that the latter appears, not as an auxiliary but as a suffix. The formation of corresponding Oriya form করুঅছি has been exactly in the above manner. It is noteworthy, that a contracted form of Bengali করিতেছে, is in use in Assamese; it is therefore doubtless, that Assamese করিছে had its origin in Bengal; করিছে from করিতেছে is in use in Bengal and its further contracted form করছে is also in use in our common speech. As 'করিতে' (formed originally by the শতৃ suffix) is closes to the Prākṛta form করৎ, it is earlier in date than Oriya করু. Though the form করিতে is now unknown in the standard Oriya, it is in use in the Provincial dialect of Sambalpur, and was in use in old Oriya as noticeable in the writings of Balaram Das. As an example of its use in Sambalpur, I may cite this sentence, মু দেখতে আইলি (I was observing when I was coming). This 'করিতে' formed by শতৃ suffix should not be confounded with 'করিতে' (for doing) formed by the suffix তুম্. How words in English formed originally by the suffixes 'ing' and 'ung,' look now wholly alike, may be noticed as a parallel case.

Present Perfect and Past.—The Bengali present perfect has two forms such as করিল and করিয়াছে; to the archaic past forms of the verbs either the partic e ল signifying past participle or the verbal stem 'আছ' noticed above, is added or suffixed or agglutinated. That the introduction of past participle to denote present perfect, is of great antiquity has been shown in Lectures X and XI, but it is interesting to inquire how two distinct forms, to denote present perfect has been brought into use.

I have noticed before that the past form of অস্থি (অস্তি) is আসী (আসীৎ) in old Māgadhi; আসী as the past form assumed the shape আছী when আছ became the stem of the Bengali verb, derived from অস্. That in the analogy of আসী, the past forms করি, ধরি, হোই, etc. became the past forms in the Prākṛtas, has been shown before; it has also been shown that in the 3rd person singular, those past forms assumed the shape করে, ধরে, etc., in Proto-Bengali, when, করি, ধরি, etc., commenced to signify 1st person in the past tense; though the matter has been discussed before, I cite over again an example, to show that these archaic past forms are still in use in Bengali:—সে আমায় নিষেধ করে [*i.e.*, করিয়াছিল] তাই আমি 'করি' নাই [here করিয়াছিলাম না will be unidiomatic bad Bengali].

The agglutination of the present stem 'আছ' with the past form করি, to signify the present perfect, may very well be done in the formation of করিয়াছে করিয়াছ and করিয়াছি, but why in addition to the form with ল suffix, another form was introduced, has to be examined. We notice on examining the archaic paradigms, that when করি, ধরি, etc., became identical in form with the infinitives, and আছি (আসীৎ) could not clearly signify the past tense, being almost similar with the present form of the stem আছ, ল was given an extended use to signify the past, and the form আছি ল (Modern Bengali ছিল) was made to denote the past tense ; to distinguish then between the present perfect and the past, say of the verb কর, করিল আছে (contracted into করিলছে) was made the present perfect and করি-আছিল (করিয়াছিল) was made the past form. শ্রীকৃষ্ণকীর্ত্তন, which of all hitherto known old books abounds with archaic forms, furnishes us with the present perfect forms ফুটিলছে (ফুটিল+আছে), রহিলছে (রহিল+আছে) etc., Since করিল, ফুটিল, রহিল, etc., were in existence previous to the formation of করিলছে etc., we can clearly see, how the present forms with only ল-suffix could not be lost to the language.

Some special participle forms.—Though regarding the origin of ল no doubt exists now, I refer briefly to the history of it to notice some important grammatical forms. Professor Lassen has rightly suggested that কৃত underwent the changes কিদ and কিড and ল took the place of ড and became finally a sign for the past tense. Pointing out along with it the fact that the Slavonic preterites are formed by 'l,' Prof. Lassen has remarked that the characteristic 'l' of the Slavonic preterite, arises out of 'd' which in its original form again is 'l.' The analogy being complete, we have been rightly asked to compare in this connection such forms of our language as খাত, খাল,

দেখিলাম, দেখিনু, etc. It is very clear that ল of our past tense came out of either ত or ন of the past participle. The Prākṛta from which Bengali is directly derived, gives us অ as the অপভ্রংশ form of ত of the past participle; the অ of প্রাকৃত became আ in Bengali to give rise to special forms as করা কাজ, কওয়া কথা, গণা টাকা, ছাড়া কাপড়, ছেঁড়া কাগজ, মরা মানুষ, etc. The corresponding Oriya forms are however like these,—কলা কাম, গলা কথা, মলা লোক, etc. As to the ন forms of ত as we get in ভিন্ন (Sans.) and দিন্ন (প্রাকৃত), we may notice the Bengali past participle forms, such as আঁচড়ান চুল, কোঁচান কাপড়, সাজান বাগান, etc.

Special past form.—A special form in the past tense may be noted here. The particle 'ন' indicating negation coalesced with 'অত্থি' and gave rise to the form 'নত্থি' (does not exist) as a single word; 'নাই' in our vernacular being the decayed form of নৎথি is not a simple particle to signify negation but carries with it the verb 'to be' in enclitic form. 'নাই' is alone sufficient to express 'does not exist' and such a Hindi form as 'নেহি হায়' has no place in Bengali. I have already stated that if to indicate negation this word 'নাই' be joined to the archaic past form, the full-bodied modern past form will be dispensed with; 'করি নাই' fully signifies 'I did not do.'

The Imperative mood.—Before dealing with the future system, an examination of the Bengali Imperative mood is necessary. I had occasion to show in a previous lecture that such প্রাকৃত forms to denote the imperative mood in the 3rd person, as কর্-উ, জা-উ, খা-উ, etc., are in use in Oriya, and the Bengali forms করুক্, যাক্, খাক্, etc., are the very old forms with the addition of an otiose ক; that the forms in the 2nd person কর, যাও, খাও, etc., are almost universal, in the vernaculars, and that they come from the Prākṛta করহ, জাহ (as well as জাঅ), খাহ (খাঅ), etc., need hardly be pointed out. As in the Prākṛtas, so it is in the modern vernaculars, that the forms of the 1st person present indicative, signify the imperative mood in the 1st person. One special characteristic in Bengali is that to indicate stress or emphasis the particle 'গে' (which is the same in origin as 'গে' or 'গা' of Hindi, used almost as an auxiliary with the Hindi, verbs to indicate futurity) is used as a post-position after the forms in the imperative mood as illustrated above.

There is one special form of the imperative mood in the second person which is formed by the suffix 'ইও'; করিও, যাইও, খাইও, etc., signify অনুজ্ঞা or command in such a manner that the action indicated by the verbs, is asked to be done, not *immediately*; consequently the form with ইও in the imperative mood is akin to future tense. It is of much importance to note (though it is a very common fact of phonology) that ব and ও are very much interchangeable alike in Prākṛta and vernacular; it is certainly well known that করিও (contracted in ordinary speech into কোরো) is found at times in old Bengali in the shape of করিব (earlier করিহ). We shall presently see, that it has been quite organic with us, since dim past, to develop the sound of ই at the end of the verb stem, when even in a little degree the idea of futurity is sought to be conveyed. If on reference to the arguments to be adduced presently, this phonetic peculiarity be considered to be a genuine phenomenon, the 'ইও' suffix of the imperative mood may be held to tender a good explanation of the origin of the future indicating ইব. However, I proceed to consider the whole question in connection with the origin of our future system; I may only note here that in the imperative form discussed here, the idea conveyed by the Sanskrit suffix 'তব্য' is not present.

As the particle 'না' which is added to the words in the imperative form to give a stress, will be dealt with separately, I do not discuss here, such a form as করনা= rather do.

The future system.—Some general remarks regarding the evolution of tenses seem called for, to explain some phenomena connected with the formation of future tense. I do not state a new proposition, when I say that it is the *doing* of an act, or the *happening* of an event, that is to say, the present tense of a verb that arises first in the primitive grammar; it is also but a repetition of the recognised truth that an action in the past and an expectation of a thing to happen in the future, were at first expressed differently, only, by the change of accent, and not by changing the form of the verb in the present tense. I have discussed in a previous lecture, what the probable origin of 'তি,' 'সি' and 'মি' might be; it may be observed that the past-forming suffixes 'দ,' 'স' and 'অম্' are formed by clipping the final 'ই' sound of the present-indicating suffixes and thereby shortening the accent to indicate as it were the faded away past; this is also how 'তে,' 'সে' and 'এ' were reduced to 'ত,' 'থাস্' and 'ই.' The present creating অস্মি (derived from অস+মি) and the past creating 'স্ম' also disclose the same history. This analysis will help us to ascertain the character of the future-indicating suffixes.

The fact that the present indefinite which is the real present to start with, indicates futurity in all languages, proves that a special gesture or accent was only added to the present form to signify futurity. Some remnants of old forms justify us in supposing that the final vowel sound of the present-indicating suffixes was prominently intonated to indicate futurity; I bring up for comparison the Prākṛta present form 'হোই' which is changed into 'হোহি' to indicate future tense merely by the putting of an accent on the final 'ই' sound. As the 'ই' sound to denote futurity, was prominently intonated, the sound became a special characteristic of the future tense, and as such stuck to the root or stem of the verb, even when a special time differentiating suffix (স্যতি, স্যসি, etc.) was introduced.

It thus appears on examining the morphology of the future-forming suffixes, that the characteristic 'ই' to denote partly the future tense, became in a manner an inseparable part of the verbal stem as করি, গমি, ভবি, etc., and the present indefinite form of অস্ as স্বতি, স্বসি, স্বামি, etc., were made suffixes in the place of articulated gestures for signifying futurity. These newly formed suffixes assumed rather the character of auxiliary verbs like আছি, আছু, etc., of Bengali, which are joined to Bengali verbal stems to amplify the tenses. We notice this fact in the Māgadhi speech, that when the auxiliary portion was dropped, the simple ই remained with a special accent attached to it, to indicate futurity; at times হি was introduced to fully represent the future indicating stress, as may be noticed in such a form for example as জাই হি; in the subjunctive mood as well, we meet with 'জই (যদি) করিহি,' 'জই যা এ হি,' etc., for জই করই, জই যাএ (present forms indicating future sense), etc. Thus we clearly see, that in some প্রাকৃতs (specially in the মাগধী we are concerned with) ই or হি became sufficient to express the idea of futurity. As it is not simply ই but ইব, which is the future-forming suffix in Bengali, Oriya and Assamese, some scholars give us ইব from a source which is not connected with the future denoting form which obtained in the Prākṛtas. It has been formulated by some European scholars, that তব্য which forms the participle of the future passive, generated the complete form ইব as the future-forming suffix. I must fully admit that this theory explains the matter completely but as it implies *a break of continuity with the past*, I proceed to examine the claim which has been set up for তব্য.

The words formed by তব্য were adopted in the early Māgadhi speech in such forms as, কত্তব্বো, জ্ঞাতব্বো, পত্তব্বো, সোতব্বো, হোতব্বো or হোদব্বো,* etc. We see that there was no ই in these forms to begin with. I think that when the idea of futurity involved in those words had to be prominently brought out in the new infinitives with a shade of some difference in meaning, ই was inserted or rather grew up in the new forms করিব্ব, জানিব্ব, পাইব্ব, শুনিব্ব, হোইব্ব, etc. The forms ভবিতব্য, হোদব্বো, হোইব্ব, and হোইবার are arranged in a regular series or chronological order to show that হোইবার which comes directly out of হোইব্ব, does not fully express the meaning indicated by 'ভবিতব্য'; 'পত্তব্বং ঠানং' may be nicely translated by 'পাইবার স্থান,' but the full meaning of প্রাপ্তব্য is not obtained in the Bengali form and as such in addition to 'পাইবার' we have borrowd 'প্রাপ্তব্য' from Sanskrit in our modern Bengali. † ভবিতব্য has to be translated into Bengali by 'যাহা হইবার আছে তাহা.' This 'তব্য' which has given rise to such infinitive forms as দেখিবা, করিবা, etc., in Oriya and দেখিবার করিবার, etc., in Bengali, may very likely give us 'ইব' in question, but whether such an extraction was made out of তব্য to form future tense anew by *breaking with the past*, is a matter for much consideration. Purposeful coining of a new suffix to indicate a tense is not a natural phenomenon; that the old idiomatic forms are transmuted imperceptibly is what should be accepted to be the natural procedure.

It is difficult to imagine that the suffix which was not extracted from তব্য in the shape of ইব, even in the latest known প্রাকৃত to signify futurity, was given currency in

---

* Though 'ই' is attached to the verbal stem in 'ভবিতব্য,' its original Prākṛta form is without it.

† পাইবার আছে, করিবার আছে, etc., do not imply the idea of ঔচিত্য and যোগ্যতা.

that lost language which gave rise to the dialects (now languages) in which ইব is now used. How in a far-fetched way ইব has to be extracted from তব্য to make it a future-denoting suffix, and how in accepting the theory to be correct, we have to accept the situation that the idiomatic use of the past time was wholly ignored in some modern vernaculars, have been sufficiently discussed. We have seen, on the other hand, in our analysis of the forms of verbs in the imperative mood, that such a form as করহ্ (do immediately now) was naturally reduced to করিহ্ and then to করিঅ or করিও to denote a command relating to doing in future; that this naturally evolved suffix ইও, easily transmutable to ইব, could be taken up for use as a future-forming suffix, without violating the idiomatic use of the past time, is, in my opinion, sufficiently clear.

Auxiliary verbs.

It is not true, what is generally supposed to be the case, that most of the Bengali verbs require the help of the verbs of 'ভূ' and 'কৃ' origin to express their action. We can easily notice that the verbs in the old Māgadhi speech did not stand in need of any additional support from other verbs as auxiliaries; it is equally clear that our genuine Bengali verbs 'খাওয়া,' 'চলা,' 'শোওয়া,' etc., do not require the verbs of 'ভূ' or 'কৃ' origin to come to their help in expressing their own action. When in consequence of Sanskrit renaissance, our Bengali verbs were looked down upon as inelegant and vulgar, the Sanskrit verbal nouns were formed according to the rules of Sanskrit grammar, and a new method of expression being devised, the verbal nouns were made to be governed by the verbs of 'ভূ' or 'কৃ' origin. খাইতেছি, চলিবে, শুইল are the natural and genuine Bengali forms, while ভোজন করিতেছি, গমন করিবে, শয়ন করিল are unnatural Sanskritic forms. The influence of the Pandits became so very much dominating, that some verbs (denoting mental acts generally) were reduced wholly to noun forms; 'ইচ্ছ' to wish, 'চিন্ত' to think, 'পূজ' to worship, etc., are not allowed now to be declined as verbs and such forms as 'ইচ্ছিল' 'চিন্তিবে' and 'পূজিছ' are regarded as archaic or obsolete.

The peculiarity of the forms 'মেরে ফেল' (kill outright), 'ফেলে দাও' (throw away), 'জুটে পড়' or 'যোগ দাও' (join up), 'সরে পড়' (get away), সেরে নাও (finish up), etc., need be explained. That 'ফেল,' 'দাও' 'পড়,' etc., are mere stress-giving adjuncts and are not verbs in reality, cannot be easily noticed on account of the fact that these mere emphasis-indicating adjuncts take the tense-forming as well as other suffixes. It may be seen, that when emphasis is not put upon the verbal phrases of this class, the adjuncts naturally fall off; compare the sentences 'কাপড় ছেড়েছি' and 'কাজ সেরেছি' in contrast with 'কাপড় ছেড়ে ফেলেছি' and 'কাজ সেরে নিয়েছি.' It is amusing to note that the Pandits, considering the emphasis-indicating adjuncts to be the real verbs, sanskritise some of these verbal phrases in a highly ridiculous manner; not seeing that 'দেওয়া' in 'যোগ দেওয়া,' does not mean 'giving,' they use the hideous phrase 'যোগদান করা' for 'যোগ দেওয়া'; in their mania to sanskritise Bengali phrases and idioms, they forget also that the word 'দান' does not signify simple 'giving' in Bengali, but that it signifies 'giving away' or 'making a gift in charity.' The full absurdity of the situation will be realised, if in the analogy of 'যোগদান করা,' the phrases 'ছেড়ে ফেল' and 'সরে পড়' be sanskritised into 'ছেড়ে নিক্ষেপ কর' and 'সরে পতিত হও.'

Some verbs do not usually take suffixes in declension and exist as decayed forms of old verbs; when these verbs are used, additional verbs as auxiliaries are joined to them; as usual the added adjuncts are only changed in conjugation. The verb 'কাড়া' 'to snatch away is in use, but independently it cannot take verbal suffixes 'সে কাড়িল,'

'আমি কাড়িলাম' etc., are not in use; the forms in use are 'সে কেড়ে নিল,' 'আমি কেড়ে নিলাম,' etc.

The infinitives called 'অসমাপিকা' verbs formed by আ (= Pr. অ=S. য় and ত্বা), as করিয়া, ধরিয়া, ছাড়িয়া, etc., are identical with Prākṛta করিঅ, ধরিঅ, ছড্ডিঅ, etc.; as their later contracted forms করি, ধরি, ছাড়ি, etc., are only met with in Oriya literature, and the fuller early forms cannot be proved to have existed at any time in Oriya, we may presume that the forms as contracted on the soil of Bengal flowed into Orissa. In addition to the forms 'করি,' 'ধরি,' etc., we meet with 'করিণ,' 'ধরিণ,' etc., in use in the literature of Orissa and not in the common speech of the people; this exclusively literary ণ suffix of Oriya, is in existence in Marathi, but it is not from Marathi that Oriya borrowed it, since from the earliest known time, the use of this suffix is noticeable in Oriya literature. We do not exactly know, who those Marhattas are, who have been named in the Purāṇas, along with the wild hordes of the frontier of Bengal.

The adverbial use of the অসমাপিকা verbs in Eastern Vernaculars, including Bengali, is interesting. হেঁটে (*i.e.*, হাঁটিয়া) is অসমাপিকা verb in such a sentence as 'আমি হেঁটে যাচ্ছি,' but it is adverb, having the meaning "quickly" in the sentence "বেলা যাচ্ছে হেঁটে চল"; in some cases, 'করিয়া' being compounded with some adjectives or nouns, adverbs are formed, such as, 'ভাল করে পড়,' 'যত্ন করে রাখ,' 'বুদ্ধি করে কাজ কর,' etc.; করিয়া or করে referred to here, is identical with করিয়া which indicates instrumental case, as in হাতে করে ধর. A class of compounds similar in form is in use in the Burdwan Division, but the compounds of this class are adjectives and their final component 'করে' conveys the meaning 'মত' or like, as may be noticed in such phrases as 'রোগা করে লোকটি,' 'কালকরে মেয়েটি,' etc. It may also be noted here, that in the idiom of some Eastern Districts, for such a phrase as 'রাম নামে' (as in রাম নামে এক লোক ছিল) 'রাম করে' is used.

It is necessary to point out, that the adverb-forming এ suffix, as noticeable in 'জোরে,' 'ধীরে,' etc., is identical with the এ which signifies the instrumental case ; as such the forms 'ধীরে,' 'জোরে,' etc., should not be confounded with the contracted forms of 'হাঁটিয়া,' 'করিয়া,' etc., which are used as adverbs.

Voice.—Our Bengali idiom does not admit such an expression as 'ইহা আমা-দ্বারা' (or তোমা-, or তাঁহা-) কৃত; only our Pandits at times write such horrid things in close imitation of ময়া (or ত্বয়া or তেন) কৃতমিদম্. It is a peculiarity with our Māgadhi vernaculars that even when the voice is not active, the finite verbs retain their usual form; *e.g.*, 'গাছ কাটা হইয়াছে, মন্দির গড়া হইবে, ভাত রাঁধা হয় নাই' etc.; in these cases what is called the অনুক্ত nominative cannot be introduced anywhere in the sentence by putting দিয়া, দ্বারা or কর্ত্তৃক after the অনুক্ত nominative. In those cases where there is a distinct reference to the person doing an act, the অনুক্ত nominative takes the form of genitive case, *e.g.*, আমার ভাত খাওয়া হইবে না, তাঁহার নাওয়া হইয়াছে, etc. It is noticeable in all the above illustrations, that verbal nouns, কাটা, গড়া, রাঁধা, খাওয়া, and নাওয়া have been made objects of the finite verbs. In the following examples, আমায় যাইতে হইবে, তোমায় করিতে হইয়াছিল, etc., আমায় and তোমায় are certainly in the instrumental case, but the verbs are unchanged in their form, and the infinitive forms যাইতে, করিতে, etc., have been used with the finite verbs. It is also noticeable, that আমায় and তোমায় of the above sentences, may be optionally reduced to আমাকে and তোমাকে, indicating perhaps thereby, that the ক final of আমা and তোমা is wholly otiose, and is not a sign of the accusative case. The following impersonal form এটা ভাল দেখায় (or শোনায়) না=it does not look (or hear) well, shows that the causative forms of the verbs to see and to hear, have been idiomatic in such a case in Bengali; in Oriya in such cases we get স্বুব্ and দিশ্ for ordinary শুনা and দেখা respectively, but they are not causative forms; in some ordinary cases too দিশ্ and স্বুব্ occur optionally in Oriya, *e.g.*, গোটিএ শব্দ স্বুবুছি or শুনা যাউ অছি (একটা শব্দ শুনা যাচ্চে) and, খণ্ডিএ নৌকা দিশুছি or দেখা যাউ অছি (এক খানা নৌকা দেখা যাচ্চে). According to special Bengali idiom, such honorific expressions as আপনার আসা হলো, and তাঁহার যাওয়া হবে, are very common. As for special peculiarities of Bengali voice, the above examples will quite do.

Some particles and indeclinables.—The scope of these lectures does not allow me to deal with all the parts of speech and with all primary and secondary suffixes; it is not to write a regular grammar, but to trace the history of our language, that these lectures are intended. I proceed now to deal with those particles and indeclinables, which being peculiar to the Bengali language, differentiate Bengali from the allied Vernaculars, and which have to disclose to us the interesting history of their origin.

(1) আই. This peculiarly Bengali interjection is no longer in use; we get it, for example in the অন্নদামঙ্গল, "আই আই আই! অই বুড়া কি এই গৌরীর বর লো?"; in some Eastern districts however, it survives in the form of আউ as an interjection expressing disgust, and is often heard with ছি at the end of it, as আউ ছি?

(2) আজ্ঞা in respectful response to a call, is not much in use in the sea-board districts of Orissa, where the Hindi word জি is much in vogue, but this Bengali form is fully in use in the Sambalpur tract.

(3) আবার, আর, আর-উ and ও—from অপর we got অবর and this অবর is আবর in Hindi and Oriya and is আবার in Bengali; in Hindi the pronunciation is আউ-অর, but in Oriya it is pronounced with 'b' and not with 'v.' We

should remember that আবার has no connection with আরবার, for আর has a different history. আ as a variant of অ (derived from চ) was once compounded with another particle উ to form the compound conjunction আউ, which is still in use in Oriya; this আউ reduced to the form আরু is in use in Bengali, but আরু is now generally confounded with আর-ও; 'আর' is a changed form of আউ or rather আরু, and its signification is 'and' as well as 'also.' To denote 'also,' the particle বি, a broken part of অপি or অবি, has been in use in Hindi and Oriya, and never in Bengali, so far as literary records show. 'অবি' was very likely pronounced in Bengal, as ওবি, as our phonetic peculiarity warrants us to hold; and thus perhaps we got ও which signifies 'even' as in আমি ও; this ও is different in meaning and origin from ও which signifies 'and' which comes from অ (=চ) by virtue of the peculiarity of our Bengali pronunciation. It is significant, that ও (=and) is also in use in Oriya, though the full সংবৃত sound of অ does not prevail in Oriya. [For another ও see (5) below.]

(4) উঁ—a particle, uttered in response to a call; though a variant of হুঁ (=yes), it has a different signification; the corresponding Oriya form is অঁ which is different from হুঁ (Bengali হাঁ) as signifies assent.

(5) ও—which is uttered in response to a call as well as in addressing a man, is in use in Oriya as well. Vedic হয়ে was reduced to অহে and then to ওহে; ওহে is used in Bengali in addressing, following the traditional meaning, but its decayed form ও is generally uttered in response to a call.

(6) কতি and ততি.—These two Vedic indeclinables, signifying 'how much' and 'that much' respectively, are not met with in Sanskrit. We have added পয় (from পদ to signify many steps perhaps) to কতি and the compound form কতিপয় is in use in high-flown Bengali; 'তভি' being compounded

with ক্ষণ, once came into use in Bengali as তত্তিক্ষণ; this form is wholly different from তক্‌খন (Prākṛta as well as old Bengali) which is derived from তৎক্ষণ.

(7) গে—Its use with verbs in the imperative mood has already been commented upon. Its another use as a resting ground for thought, like 'ওর নাম কি' (*cf.* Sanskrit and Prākṛta, নাম of singular use) or অর্থাৎ or কিনা, etc., may be noticed, in such phrases as আর হচ্চেগে (further more), কথা হচ্চেগে (the thing is), etc.

(8) চাই—in such a sentence as চাইকি তিনি যদি নাই যান, is but the representative of চেৎ which was reduced to simple চে in Prākṛta.

(৮) ছি—It is curious that some scholars have missed its real derivation which is from ধিক্ (ধি=ছি).

(10) টি and গোটা.—The fact that the derivation of the particle has been a puzzle to many scholars, is partly in support of its origin from the Dravidian source. A very definite and distinct root of this particle is found deeply planted in the Dravidian speech or speeches; all the branches of the Dravidian language possess it in one form or another, and the very form টি is in the speech of the Andhras, who once established intimate relation with all parts of Northern India. This টি of Telegu which corresponds to other forms in other Dravidian languages, is a characteristic inflectional increment at the end of neuter nouns. That in our use of টি, as definite article in Bengali and Oriya, we agree with Telegu, will be convincing on reference to the history of this particle as given in Caldwell's Comparative Grammar of the Dravidian Languages (*vide ibid*, p. 264). It seems that to begin with, টি used to be affixed to neuter nouns only, and its variant 'ড়ি' was being used with other nouns, for in old time idiom, we meet with গাছটি, পাহাড়টি, মাটিটি, etc., on one side and বহুড়ি, ঝিউড়ি, শাশুড়ি, etc., on the other side;

we may notice that in Eastern Bengal, such forms as ভাইডি, বোনডি, etc., are still in use. We may compare with the above forms, the Hindi particle ঠৌ used with adjectives and neuter nouns, as in Telegu and so also the Hindi use of ডি as agreeing with বহুড়ি, ঝিউড়ি, etc. I may further remark, that the pseudo-Sanskrit form বধুটি, of a very late time Sanskrit, points to the extensive use of the particle in question in past time.

The supposition, that the definite article টি comes from গোটা (=entire in Bengali), is doubly faulty. We have no doubt seen that টি in its form and function as agreeing with our usage, is in its natural position in the Dravidian language, but we have to further notice that গোটা has never been in use in Hindi, and yet we meet with ঠৌ and ডি in that language ; I should note that I exclude purposely Nepalese from the list, as owing to a special Dravidian influence the word গোটা has gone over to that country to signify exactly 'one' as in Oriya. In the next place we have to take note of the fact that গোটা signifying either 'entire' or 'one,' comes from the Telegu cardinal numeral okaṭi ; that okaṭi is not an adaptation of Sanskrit এক, but is connected radically with the original Dravidian term for 'one,' cannot be discussed here and the students may refer for it to Caldwell's work as named above. I only notice that গোটা in the form of গোতান্ is a suffix in the speech of our Dravidian neighbours the Orāons.

(11) তরে (*for the purpose of*).—It is specially to be noted that to indicate the meaning 'for the purpose of' the particle হি was in use in the Chhāndasa or Vedic language, and this হি was not adopted by the Sanskrit language ; it is well known that we meet with 'তরে' in Pali, exactly to serve the purpose of the Vedic হি, and so we may rightly presume that this তরে is a genuine দেশী particle ; we then notice that in Sanskrit the corresponding form is তর্হি,

which is nothing but an amalgamation of the Prākṛta তর and old-time হি.

From তর্হি of Sanskrit again, came the Prākṛta তহি (for that reason), which should not be confounded with তহিং and its later form তহিঁ as derived from তস্মিন্. From তহিঁ of প্রাকৃত, there came out another form তেহিঁ or তেঁই of which তেঁ became the contracted form. In my opinion তেঁ does not come direct from 'তেন' to indicate তেন কারণেন. That our old Bengali তেঁই and modern তাই have to be derived from প্রাকৃত তহি of তর্হি origin, has been already discussed. We have to note that 'তরে' of old-time প্রাকৃত or পালি, is itself in use in the Bengali language.

(12) না, নি, *and* নেন্—It is well known that the particle নু of Vedic times (as in কৃণবাবহৈ নু—*ante*, p. 109) has always been in use in Sanskrit, and 'ন' has been its form in the Prākṛtas. I am strongly inclined to hold by differing from the time-honoured opinion of the grammarians of old days, that ন as occurs for instance with 'তে' and 'সমযে' in such Pali sentence as তেন খো পন সমযেন, has the force of হি and is the ন of নু-origin, and not the sign of instrumental case, for, the regular locative forms are in plenty in পালি. This suggestion of mine, however, has no concern with what I am going to illustrate. I have no doubt that our emphasis-indicating না as in এসনা (please do come) is identical with প্রাকৃত 'ন' of নু origin. In Oriya we meet with the particle both in the shape of 'ন' and 'নি'; the latter is in literary use (as in হেলা নি—it is done) and the former is in the mouth of all people, along with নি in the Sambalpur tract; দশ বাজিলা-ন and দশ বাজিলা-নি are used alike in common parlance. In some parts of the District of Jessore, in the Eastern parts of the District of Nadiya, and in Northern Bengal, নে and নি are of general use as articles of emphasis; আমি যাবনে (Eastern parts of

Jessore and Nadiya) and সে যাবি নি (Eastern Nadiya and Northern Bengal) are examples. I think these examples from various quarters, show, that না, নে, নি, and ন itself, are identical with প্রাকৃত 'ন' of ancient স্নু origin.

We have noticed in the 13th Lecture, that 'হি' performing the function of ন or স্নু, was reduced to সি (as in সে-সি of শ্রীকৃষ্ণকীর্ত্তন=modern সে-ত); it is pretty clear that this সি with the appendage of aforesaid ন or না, appears in Oriya, as সিনা (*e.g.*, সে সিনা কহিথিলা=সে ত করেছিল) and in the Eastern Districts of Bengal, as সেন্ (*e.g.*, সে সেন্ বলেছিল=সেত বলেছিল). It may be supposed that সিনা or সেন্ comes from Sanskrit স্বিৎ; but as স্বিৎ in any form does not occur in the প্রাকৃতs, the derivation, I have suggested, seems to be the right one.

(13) বই, as in তোমা বই আর জানিনি is certainly the decayed form of ব্যতীত; it will be very wrong to identify it with Sanskrit particle বই of the series, চ, বই, তু, হি. I need hardly point out that ত comes from তু of the above series.

(14) যদি *and* যাই.—I notice যদি, as re-sanskritised from প্রাকৃত and old Bengali জই, for this reason that it has been mostly in use in Bengali, and the introduction of it in Oriya has been at a very recent date. In Oriya যেবে (Bengali যবে, Hindi যব্) has been always the form in use. The প্রাকৃত form of যদা as জাই has been in use in Bengali only, in the form of যাই (*e.g.*, সে যাই এল, অম্‌নি আমি গেলাম).

(15) স—This particle which is used as a prefix is of much interest. Formation of adverbs with this prefix in strict accordance with the Sanskrit usage, is no doubt in vague in Bengali, as may be noticed in such expressions as সদর্পে, সস্নেহে, etc., but it is the non-Sanskritic use of this prefix, which we have to note here. 'স' as opposite of privative 'অ' in such an expression, for instance as সকিঞ্চন (opposite of অকিঞ্চন) has been in use in Pali as well as in

other Prākṛtas of later days; it is this use which is now idiomatic in our Vernacular. Such instances as সকর্ম্মা, সপারগ, সক্ষম, etc. (opposite of অকর্ম্মা, অপারগ, অক্ষম, etc.), are often met with in Bengali; here the form সক্ষম for instance may be bad according to Sanskrit Grammar, but it is not so according to Bengali idiom, as may be noticed on reference to the following Bengali idiomatic expressions. ঠিক is an adjective and it takes the prefix স, signifying very much, to express intensity of meaning; সঠিক (very much accurate) does not change its character and remains an adjective; সকাতর, সচকিত, etc., are similar expressions. Neither the adjective form সজাগ (very wakeful) nor the adverb form সজোরে (with force), should be referred to any rule of Sanskrit Grammar.

Some Secondary Suffixes.—I proceed now to notice a few secondary suffixes of Bengali, as disclose some special characteristics of our language.

Feminine-forming suffixes.—It has to be noted that the ছান্দস rules for reducing masculine to feminine were not always strictly followed in Pāli; the feminine form of 'চোর' is চোরী in Pāli, and it will be seen that our modern rules are fully in harmony and accordance with the spirit of the Māgadhi usages. The suffix আ of the Sanskrit Grammar, did not come into use in the Prākṛta from which Bengali originates. In the প্রাকৃতs ঈ and নী were the two suffixes which have been inherited by Bengali; our Pandits only at times violate our idiomatic use by importing the Sanskrit suffix আ.

It is rather a simple rule in Bengali, that all masculine nouns having অ or আ final, take ঈ (occasionally ই in feminine), and all other words (*i.e.*, having ই, উ, এ and ও finals) take ইনী (at times reduced to আনী in euphonic mutation) to indicate feminine forms; the only important proviso is, that the words having অ or আ final do also take ইনী, when they signify a class or a trade-guild. The examples are:

(1) *From words having* অ *final.*—নির্লজ্জী (শ্রীকৃষ্ণকীর্ত্তন) রামী (চণ্ডীদাস), বাঁদরী, শয়তানী, etc. Here we notice two exceptions, *viz.*, সাপিনী from সাপ (ভারতচন্দ্র) and বাঘিনী from বাঘ, which is usual in our speech; in respect of these two exceptions, I should say, that they are due to euphonic reasons. In বোনাই from বোন, and নন্দাই from ননদ perhaps we get the ই to denote masculine from the ending of জামাই by false analogy. It may also be supposed that the words were compounded with পতি which was reduced first to পই and then to অই.

(2) *From words having* আ *final.*—কাকী, খুকী, ছুঁড়ী, বেঙ্গমী (from বেঙ্গমা), বুড়ী, চন্দ্রমুহী or -মুখী (from Prākṛta চন্দমুহা), পোড়ারমুখী (mas. is not-মুখো but virtually-মুহা or মুখা), আহুরী (really from আহুরিআ, which is only reduced to আহুরে; আদরিনী is a pseudo-Bengali form coined by Jatrawalas to make the word dignified). Like আদরিনী, পাগলিনী is a pseudo-Bengali term, for in our speech the word পাগ্‌লী (be it from পাগল or পাগ্‌লা) is in universal use.

N.B.—As the feminine forms of words of আ final have the suffix ঈ, the masculine words, formed grammatically from feminine words, with ঈ final, have been made words with আ final; for example, from মাসি and পিসি (orig. মাউসি, and পিউসি), we have got মাউসিআ (মেসো) and পিউসিআ (পিসে). Similarly when from ব্যক্তি the অপভ্রংশ form বেটি was formed, a new regular masculine word was coined as বেটা.

(3) The words signifying class or trade-guild must take ইনী (or its variant আনী or নী), no matter whether the final is হসন্ত or has অ or আ or any other vowel. The examples are: বৈদ্য—বইগ্যানী, নাপিৎ—নাপ্তিনী or নাপিতানী, কামারনী, গোয়ালা—গোয়াল্‌নী, ময়রানী, ধোবানী, বাগ্‌দি—বাগ্‌দিনী তেলিনী, কলু—কলুনী মালো—মালুনী etc. We have also

to notice, when new words are formed by our villagers they follow the unwritten law of our grammar and coin such feminines from words denoting occupation as মাষ্টারনী, ডাক্তারনী and পণ্ডিতানী.

N.B.—When the feminine forms themselves have come to us having already been formed in Sanskrit, as a matter of course, we do not Bengalicize them, even when we make অপভ্রংশ of them; thus it is, that though the word ব্রাহ্মণ signifies a class, the অপভ্রংশ of ব্রাহ্মণী, as বাম্‌নী remains unchanged in Bengali. It may also be said in respect of this particular example that as ন happens to be the final of the word in question, ন of the suffix ইনী is bound to be dropped for euphonic reasons.

I notice also here the words having ওয়ালা suffix which seemingly appear as exceptions; the words having been borrowed from Hindi, the Hindi forms are used in feminine, and the suffix ইনী appropriate to trade-signifying class, is not used.

I make this general statement that all masculine forms as do not come under (1) and (2) above take ইনী for feminine forming suffix. What I have stated in commenting on আদরিনী and পাগলিনী may be said in respect of the following words; some words which are never used in Bengali as মাতঙ্গ, কুরঙ্গ, etc., present the forms মাতঙ্গিনী, কুরঙ্গিনী, etc.; we clearly see that these forms could never be coined in a natural way in Bengali, and certainly our Jatrawalas coined them to make a show of pedantry. Our genuine Bengali words conform to the rules I have enunciated.

Suffix আ *of various significations.*—The diminutive-forming আ is rather universal in Northern India, and as such special examples need not be cited in using such a form as হরিয়া (হরে), for হরি to signify non-honorifix address; we agree with other Indian Vernaculars, but we may note that to signify affection, we use the suffix উ where euphonic combination becomes possible; কানু, হরু, খুকু, etc., are examples. It is supposed that the উ suffix mentioned above is virtually the contracted form of উ আ which is a variant of ই আ or rather the euphonic mutation of আ. For examples of আ as signifying diminutive, and as not connected with or derived from the final ক which is diminutive-indicating in Sanskrit, I may just mention two words namely বাসা (temporary lodging or nest) from বাস, and ঘরা (a little hole, say, a button-hole) from ঘর. That পুতা for পুত্তা (*e.g.*, মায়ে বলেন পড় পুতা) from পুত্রক is entirely different from either ঘরা or বাসা, is clear and so we may hold that there is a pure and independent আ which signifies diminutive.

The adjective-forming কা is generally considered to be a combination of ক and আ; this appears doubtful to me, on reference to the signification of the following forms, *viz.*, (1) পল্‌কা=liable to break easily (from পড় to fall +কা), (2) হাল্‌কা=light (লঘু=লহু=হলু+কা), (3) খট্‌কা, that which causes a খট্‌ or doubt in the mind (here old agency-signifying ক in the form of কা may be the suffix) (4) বলকা as in বলকা দুধ (which is slightly বৰ্ত্তিত or rather আবর্ত্তিত or boiled).

As to the adjective-forming আ, derived from past-participle-forming ক্ত=ত=অ, remarks have already been made in a previous lecture.

The adjective-forming ইয়া as in বৰ্দ্ধমানিয়া or বৰ্দ্ধমেনে has no connection with general আ suffix; it is Sanskrit ই (as in মদীয়) which is our adjective-forming ইয়া; this ইয়, we clearly see, indicates relation.

I have omitted to take notice of the Sanskrit suffixes and forms in use in Bengali, as no special remarks regarding them may be considered needed in these lectures, though it is interesting to know when and under what circumstances Sanskrit language was made to contribute to the stock of our language. I should not omit to mention, however, that a real necessity impelled our writers to import Sanskrit words and Sanskritic forms. It has already been mentioned that as our proud ancestors did not care to express their high thoughts in the vernaculars of the people, the living speeches dragged on a miserable existence. We needed suitable expressions and new serviceable suffixes to express ourselves properly. Sonorous Sanskrit words were also laid under contribution, to maintain an elegance of style. I may remind you that classical words and old flexions are for the very reason employed in modern European languages to give vent to æsthetic ideas in an effective manner. Some fine sentiments and associations may only be best expressed, if, as in English, classical forms are resorted to. The remarks of the English philologists, that while the old forms are useful and effective in an elegant composition to express æsthetic ideas, the modern simple forms are very much necessary to make very accurate and lucid statements of facts, are wholly applicable to Bengali. I mention these facts, not so much to justify the procedure in question, as to show how changes are effected and have been effected.